The Corporate State

Corporatism and the State Tradition
in Western Europe

Edited by
Andrew Cox and Noel O'Sullivan
Hull University

EDWARD ELGAR

Published by
Edward Elgar Publishing Limited
Gower House
Croft Road
Aldershot
Hants GU11 3HR
England

Gower Publishing Company
Old Post Road
Brookfield
Vermont 05036
USA

British Library Cataloguing in Publication Data

The corporate state: corporatism and the
   state tradition in western Europe.
   1. Europe. Corporatism
   I. Cox, Andrew   II. O'Sullivan, Noel
   321.9

ISBN 1 85278 009 6

Printed in Great Britain at the University Press, Cambridge

Contents

List of contributors

V. R. Berghahn, Professor, Warwick University.

Patrick Birkinshaw, Lecturer and Barrister-at-Law, Hull University.

Martin Bull, Tutor at St. Anne's & Balliol, Oxford University.

Andrew Cox, Reader, Hull University.

Neil Elder, Reader, Hull University.

J. Martinez-Alier, Professor, Barcelona University.

Noel O'Sullivan, Reader, Hull University.

Jordi Roca, Assistant Professor, Girona University.

Michael Smith, Lecturer, Hull University.

Preface

The interest in corporatism which characterised the previous two decades shows surprisingly few signs of waning, despite the advent of the New Right during the present decade. The more critical note struck in recent literature on the subject, however, suggests that the present time provides an opportune moment for a general stock-taking. It is with this aim in mind that contributors from the related disciplines of political theory, political science, jurisprudence and history combined together in order to construct a balance-sheet which will clarify the existing situation.

On the credit side, the study of corporatism has yielded at least four valuable results. In political theory, it has produced an extensive (and long overdue) reappraisal of the pluralist theory of democracy, as well as adding further ingenious dimensions to the Marxist endeavour to explain why capitalism has still not collapsed. In political science, it has produced empirical research on aspects of the decision-making process which had hitherto been relatively neglected. In contemporary history, it has produced such notable reinterpretations of the challenges faced by the parliamentary system during the present century as Keith Middlemas' study of 'corporatist bias' in British politics since the First World War.[1] Finally, in jurisprudence it has encouraged a process of radical reconsideration, not only of legal and political procedures for ensuring accountability, but of the traditional western conception of law itself. Since the last area of research is likely to be somewhat less familiar than the previous three, Patrick Birkinshaw's review of the case for replacing the traditional concept of law by a 'reflexive' system is of particular interest. Reflexive law is intended to deal with a situation made acute by corporatist arrangements, and one with which the traditional system of law is widely felt to be unable to cope; a situation, that is, where accepted modes of bargaining between the state and organised interests regularly by-pass rights and responsibilities previously protected by established legal and political channels.

Although the credit side of the account is not in doubt, the debit side must also be considered. Foremost amongst the problematic items on that side is the controversy which still persists about the theoretical coherence of the 'liberal' or 'societal' form of corporatism with which much of neo-corporatist theory has been concerned. This form of

corporatism has three characteristics. It is marked, firstly, by the use of
voluntary methods for securing social integration. Secondly, it is
marked by the privileged position in the political process which is
conferred by government upon élite representatives of relatively small
numbers of broadly-based and well-organised economic interest groups.
And it is marked, thirdly, by the belief that corporatist arrangements
are uniquely appropriate to advanced industrial societies in which ideological changes no longer appear to be a major threat to stability. In the
broadest perspective, the importance of this liberal version of corporatist theory lies in the novel dimension it gives to the quest, which
extends back to the interwar era, for a middle way between capitalism
and socialism.[2]

The first chapter in the book (by Noel O'Sullivan) examines the
neo-corporatist version of the middle way, and finds it unsatisfactory. It
is unsatisfactory, because it conceals a tension which lies at the heart of
the European state tradition, and is especially acute at the present day.
This tension is created by the conflict between two different styles of
politics. On the one hand, there is a limited style of politics, which is
marked primarily by hostility to arbitrary power, concern for the rule of
law, and preservation of responsible government. On the other hand,
there is what may be termed a managerial style, in which the primary
aim of the state is not to promote the rule of law but is, rather, to
achieve social integration by implementing a particular end (such as
economic growth). Viewed from the standpoint of this tension, the
claim that 'societal' or 'liberal' corporatism opens up a novel middle way
to the industrial democracies is dismissed as implausible. Far from
uniting limited and managerial politics within a harmoniously integrated
society, the neo-corporatist ideal inevitably favours the managerial style
at the expense of the limited one. It inevitably does so, O'Sullivan
suggests, because the neo-corporatist perspective is a functionalist one,
within which the non-instrumental values and concerns of limited politics can have, at best, only an incidental place. In principle, therefore,
there is nothing to prevent the supposedly 'liberal' or 'societal' ideal of
neo-corporatism from sliding over into the unconstitutional (or
'authoritarian') practices to which its supporters profess to be opposed.

Since the neo-corporatist middle way inclines so heavily towards
managerial politics, it is worth noting that the editor of an otherwise
admirable recent anthology on the subject was somewhat wide of the
mark when he announced that it was now time for the 'internal contradictions' of the 'hybrid' neo-corporatist ideal to be clearly recognized.[3] In fact, if follows from what has just been said that this ideal is
far too unequivocally managerial for it to contain any significant

'contradictions.' As Andrew Cox maintains in the second essay, the real weakness of the concept arises not so much from its contradictions, as from the progressive disintegration which it has suffered as its proponents have retreated from an initially ambitious vision of a novel kind of socio-economic system, at one extreme, to a minimalist view, at the other. On the minimalist view, towards which recent usage has tended, Cox writes that corporatism becomes merely 'a convenient label for any form of specialised bargaining between the state and social interests.' As such, Cox argues, it does not offer 'any significantly new insights into how policy is made or implemented', and is indeed not even 'in any way unique to modern advanced industrial states or the contemporary historical period.' (p.35).

The theoretical coherence of the neo-corporatist ideal is not, however, the only problem presented by the literature on the subject. A further problem has been the assumption that social and economic factors are the ultimate determinants of interest representation. In this respect, Suzanne Berger's introduction to her substantial anthology on pluralism and neo-corporatism reflects a growing tendency to jettision even the more muted forms of economic materialism. Interests, Berger remarks, can no longer be regarded as independent givens. In this respect, the case studies included here fully support her contention that 'the impact of national historical experience, the weight of intraorganizational factors in defining interests, and the role of the state in structuring relations among interests are so significant for group formation that we cannot analytically define the "real" interest of a group which would be given by socio-economic structures, and distinguish it from the "forms" of these interests, which would be determined by national specificities and politics.'[4] A similar critical attitude is now evident in relation to the almost *a priori* assumption often hitherto made, that neo-corporatism offers a peculiarly flexible way of representing key economic interests. The very success of corporatist arrangements, Ilja Scholten has acknowledged, 'may also be the worst enemy of their own benefits', in so far as success breeds a process of beaucratisation which inevitably destroys the original flexibility.[5] All such problems, however, may be subsumed under the main problem which has been posed by neo-corporatism. This concerns the 'fit' between neo-corporatist theory and the concrete historical experience of the various nations to which it has been applied. It was with this fundamental problem in mind that the case-studies which comprise the second part of the book were selected.

So far as attempts to apply the corporatist model to the recent history of European states are concerned, the case studies suggest that serious oversimplification has often been involved. Oversimplification occurs because the process of 'interest intermediation' between equal and independent partners which is postulated by the corporatist model does not correspond to the variety of complex conditions that surround policy-making in the states to which the model has been applied. At one extreme, the kind of oversimplification in questions emerges with especial clarity in Martin Bull's analysis of the conditions which have been either ignored or misrepresented by those who have tried to use the corporatist model to interpret the course of change within the postwar Italian political system. Permeated as that system is by 'client-ela' and 'parentela' relationships, the state has never been sufficiently distinct from civil society for it to have embarked upon the incorpor-ation of sectional interests; indeed, Bull notes, the tendency has been in the reverse direction, with civil society constantly threatening to absorb the state. Within this system, it is not only the state, but labour and capital as well, which have lacked any distinct organisational identity. In Italy, then, the equal and antonomous partners postulated by neo-corporatism are not to be found. What holds this intensely par-ticularised system together, Bull argues, is the network of political parties within which the play of pressure-group politics occurs, and above all, the DC party.

At the opposite extreme, the state may be so much more powerful than civil society, and be confronted by such a weak or precarious parliamentary tradition, that the most pronounced tendency is for an authoritarian pattern of integration to emerge. This pattern is especially likely to assume a corporatist character when a government deliberately fosters direct bargaining relationships with a few powerful groups, either in order to by-pass the parliamentary system or because it finds it difficult to pursue its objectives by any other method. West German politics under the Prusso-German monarchy, and again in the Nazi era, illustrate the former tendency, whilst Spanish politics under the dictatorships of Primo de Rivera and Franco illustrate the latter. In both cases, recent history has been hailed as providing evidence of a shift towards a more liberal system of corporatist integration.

In the West German case, particular attention has been focused upon the programme of 'Concerted Action' which was inaugurated in January, 1967. Whilst granting that it is fruitful to examine develop-ments of the 1960s and 1970s with the help of the liberal-corporatist paradigm, Volker Berghahn notes that there has been a tendency to oversimplify past history by reading it backwards, in the light of contem-porary developments. In reality, Berghahn maintains, the attitudinal preconditions necesssary for corporatist concertation did not exist on the part of any of the partners to Concerted Action – the unions, industrial élites and ministerial bureaucracy – until the 1950s. Even during the decade of Concerted Action, interests remained 'too divergent for stable compromises to be achieved'. (p. 119) The formal abandonment of concerted action in 1977 did not, however, mean the end of informal trilateral contacts. These have continued, indicating acquiescence in the 'unspoken assumption that the problems of the advanced industrial societies of Western Europe had become so complex as to require the consensual cooperation of the government with the main power blocks of the economy'.

In the Spanish case, Martinez-Alier and Roca lend cautious support to the idea that the post-Franco era has also seen a movement away from state corporatism to a more liberal kind. More precisely, they argue that the authoritarian practices of the Franco regime cannot properly be called corporatist at all, whilst suggesting that the series of wage pacts initiated by the Moncloa Pact (in 1977) may be interpreted in neo-corporatist terms. Wheather the pacts will lead to a stable, full-fledged neo-corporatist system is, however, a matter about which the authors have doubts, in view of a further weakening of the position of the unions due to economic recession, the low rate of affiliation which makes them dependent on state support, and the presence of strong regional pressures which undermine the feasibility of centralised neo-corporatist agreements.

In between the two types of state-society relationships just considered lies a variegated middle-ground which has frequently been regarded as providing the most fertile soil for neo-corporatism. The literature of the past decade has focused, in particular, upon a group of states which includes, on the one hand, so-called 'consensual democracies' such as the Netherlands and Belgium and, on the other hand, states like the post-war British polity. What members of the group allegedly have in common (or had until recently, in the British case) is a firm commitment to a middle way consensus based upon the cooperation of a strong socialist party. The case studies contained here suggest, however, that even when applied to this group of states the neo-corporatist model is at best a somewhat problematic fit.

In the Swedish case, Neil Elder questions the propriety of using the corporatist model to describe the three decades of peaceful 'concertation' which followed the Saltsjöbaden Agreement of 1938, on the ground that the state played almost no part in the running of the economy. When hard times finally came during the 1970s, the state became increasingly active, and something which seems on the surface to be more like the corporate model of interest intermediation emerged. In reality, however, it is impossible to regard the élites involved as representing wholly independent groups. In particular, the Social Democratic Party continued to enjoy the ascendancy which began in 1932, despite six years out of office (1976–82), and this makes it impossible to treat government and labour as completely independent, even though tensions between the party and the unions became pronounced after 1970. Provided that such qualifications are borne in mind, however, Elder concludes that Swedish dependence on foreign operations places 'a premium on corporatist power-sharing mechanisms which tend to lower the level of distributive conflict'. In this restricted sense, he observes, 'to talk of a "partnership" between capital and labour in Sweden is not political naivety, nor on present evidence does the the partnership appear to be dissolving'.

The Netherlands provides a case study of especial interest, constituting as it does a point of convergence for corporatist theory and the 'consociational' critique of pluralism which developed independently but contemporaneously during the late 1960s and 1970s.[6] Michael Smith's essay offers a direct challenge to the assumption at the heart of consociational analysis, which is that a corporatist pattern of negotiation between summit organisations had been the key to the stability of democracy, providing a method of containing cultural, political, social and economic cleavages which would otherwise have destroyed the 'pillarised' society of the Netherlands. Although it is now generally allowed that the forces which made the concept of liberal corporatism relevant are no longer applicable, Smith insists that the real problem is that they *never* were applicable, at least in the form in which consociational analysis took them to be.

Finally, Andrew Cox explores the reasons which led nascent neo-corporatist tendencies to be rapidly discredited in Britain, and finds that these reasons extend far beyond the sphere of economic considerations. Cox concludes that, although there may still be 'pockets of tripartite bargaining and intermediation in specific policy areas in contemporary Britain,' any significant departure from the trend towards a neo-liberal state is more likely to veer towards pluralistic Keynesianism, rather than towards the discredited and derided corporatism of the 1960s and 1970s.

What then is the overall conclusion suggested by the essays? It may best be described as one of qualified scepticism. At the theoretical level, the scepticism is reflected in the suspicion with which both editors, from their different perspectives, view the neo-corporatist claim to offer a novel kind of liberal middle way. At the empirical level, it is reflected in the sensitivity displayed by contributors to the complexities of different national political traditions, a sensitivity which effectively eliminates every remaining vestige of the dream of constructing a generic model of neo-corporatism, applicable to all advanced industrial societies. In the informal and extended sense in which corporatism merely refers to a wide variety of cooperative relationships that may exist between government and industry, however, a number of contributors are nevertheless willing to assign a continuing position of significance to it in the vocabulary of contemporary political science. But the most important conclusion to emerge, the editors believe, is one which may also be regarded as the least controversial aspect of the whole debate over neo-corporatism. This is the extent of the confusion it has revealed about the meaning of, and preconditions for, the limited style of politics with which the liberal democratic state was once associated.

Notes

1. *Politics and Industrial Society: The Experience of the British System Since 1911*, London 1979.
2. We prefer the idea of a middle way when referring to neo-corporatism despite the rejection of this concept by Schmitter (see in particular his article: 'Interest intermediation and regime governability in contemporary Western Europe and North America' in Suzanne Berger, *Organizing Interests in Western Europe* (Cambridge University Press, 1981), pp. 287–330). It is somewhat disingenuous to argue that a form of political rule which allows the state a determining role in allocating participation rights within a political system is not likely to have a significant modifying effect on the control of industrial decision-making and the distribution of the material benefits within that system. While such a system might still allow for private property rights, in so far as it curtails the enjoyment of those rights and shapes outcomes, it may properly be seen as distinct from capitalism or socialism in ideal typical terms.
3. *Political Stability and Neo-Corporatism*, ed. Ilja Scholten (Sage Publications, London 1987), p. 142.
4. Suzanne Berger, ed., *Organizing Interests in Western Europe* (C.U.P. 1981), pp. 9–10.
5. Ilja Scholten, ed., *Political Stability and Neo-Corporatism*, (London, 1987), p. 30.
6. The 'consociational' critique drew attention to what its proponents considered to be the economic influence of the Anglo-German consensual model of democracy, which stressed cultural homogeneity. By contrast, the consociational model drew attention to the cultural heterogeneity which characterised states like Belgium and the Netherlands without, however, destroying democratic stability. See, for example, A. Lipjhart, 'Typologies of Democratic Regions', in *Comparative Political Studies*, 1986, Vol. I, 3–44. See also his essay 'Consociational Democracy', in *World Politics*, 1969, 21(2), pp. 207–25.

PART I:
Neo-Corporatism: Theory

1 The political theory of neo-corporatism

Noel O'Sullivan

The most remarkable feature of western political thought during the past two decades has been the reintroduction of the concept of corporatism into the vocabulary of contemporary political science. It is remarkable not only because the interwar association of the concept with fascism seemed for long to have put paid to any prospect of rehabilitation, but also because interest in it has even survived the rise to prominence of New Right ideology during the present decade. In the eyes of theorists of neo-corporatism indeed the New Right episode is no more than a temporary deviation – more apparent than real – from corporatist trends which are likely to reassert themselves even more strongly should the current recession deepen. In this situation three questions deserve careful consideration. The first is why this revival of interest has occurred. The second concerns what neo-corporatist theory actually maintains. The third involves assessing what contribution neo-corporatism makes to an understanding of contemporary social and political trends.

Consider, first, the question of why there has been such a revival of interest in the corporatist concept. The main reason was growing dissatisfaction with the two great models of society which have dominated western political thought since the Second World War. These are the Marxist model on the one hand, and the liberal-democratic one on the other. Neo-corporatism is mainly intelligible, in the first instance, as a critique of these two models. Both are unsatisfactory, neo-corporatist theory holds because both either exaggerate or else ignore certain vital aspects of western political experience in the period since 1945. In the case of Marxism, neo-corporatism rejects class conflict as the ultimate reality of social existence, although it must immediately be added that a number of writers sympathetic to Marxism have attempted to reformulate the theory of class conflict in ways which turn neo-corporatist theories to their own purposes. Further consideration of the Marxist interpretation of neo-corporatism must be postponed for the moment, however, in order to concentrate on what has been the principal object of the neo-corporatist critique. This is the pluralist version of liberal

3

doctrine which has dominated democratic theory for the past half-century or more.

In order to appreciate fully the nature and impact of the neo-corporatist critique of liberal pluralism it is necessary to recall briefly the principal defect of postwar democratic theory at large. This was an endemic complacency, induced initially by relief at the defeat of totalitarianism, and subsequently fostered by the prosperity and stability of the 1950s. The most influential expression of this complacency in political theory was pluralism.[1] Although originally an American creation, the pluralist stress on the primary reality of a multitude of interdependent and relatively harmonious groups found sympathetic echoes in postwar European political theory. There a traditional concern with constitutions, parliamentary institutions and, more recently, political parties had come to seem excessively formal and legalistic, with the result that professional academic interest was directed increasingly towards empirical research on the part played by interest groups in policy formation. What made pluralism especially welcome in every western democracy, however, was not so much its empirical pretensions as its reassuring declaration that all was well with the democratic world.

Most wonderful of all, pluralism announced that the century-old liberal fear of the tyranny of the majority was a mere phantom, excluded from the reality of life in the democracies by a system of polyarchy which is, in turn, embedded in a framework of consensus on fundamental values. So profound is that consensus, Robert Dahl wrote, that politics itself is merely the all but dispensable froth on the surface of democratic life: 'It is the surface manifestation, representing superficial conflicts. Prior to politics, beneath it, enveloping it, restricting it and conditioning it, is the underlying consensus on policy that usually exists in the society among a predominant portion of the politically active members ... With such a consensus, the disputes over policy alternatives are nearly always disputes over a set of alternatives that have already been winnowed down to those within the broad area of basic agreement.'[2] So benign and efficient is the polyarchic consensus that it almost entirely replaces all the old liberal devices – such as natural rights, constitutional restraints, an independent judiciary and the separation of powers – as the guarantor of liberty: 'the more fully the social prerequisites of polyarchy exist, the less probable it is that any given minority will have its most valued freedoms curtailed through governmental action', so Dahl wrote.[3]

There were of course always critics of pluralist optimism. Among them, Talmon's stress on the totalitarian strand within the democratic tradition itself, Kornhauser's stress on the atomising effect of democracy and C. Wright Mills's work on power elites were the most notable non-Marxist examples. None of this sceptical literature, however, did more than dent the pluralist orthodoxy. Only in the 1960s, with the advent of neo-corporatist theory, did that orthodoxy finally encounter a challenge which secured widespread intellectual sympathy. It is illuminating to remember in this connection that while pluralism was an American creation, neo-corporatism was primarily a European one. Originally inspired by reflection upon the different relationship between the state and subgroups which distinguished the European world from the USA, interest in it was subsequently intensified by the economic problems of the 1970s, which made pluralist faith in the almost self-regulating character of the social order appear the height of naïvety. What, it must now be asked, are the features of the neo-corporatist critique of pluralist theory?

The critique consists of a three-pronged attack upon the three corresponding components of the pluralist model. The first of these components is the assumed existence of a multiplicity of voluntary interest groups, all competing with one another on equal terms for members, resources and influence over government policy. In reality, corporatist theory insists, competition is effectively confined to a very small number of very large interest groups in which membership cannot properly be regarded as voluntary, since to be excluded from their ranks is, *ipso facto*, to be excluded from key aspects of the policy process, and thus to be condemned to a kind of second-class citizenship. The second component of the model is the assumption that the state plays a fundamentally passive or reactive role in relation to the various interest groups, merely responding to their independent aims and objectives. In reality, corporatist theory holds, the modern state plays a highly active part in the formation of both the groups and their interests, through its ability to license their existence and either include them in the policy-making process or exclude them from it. Finally, the pluralist model assumes the existence of a clear division between a public and a private realm, or between state and society. Once again, corporatist theory maintains that this emphasis is wholly at odds with the reality of modern life, within which the public–private division is constantly blurred. On the one hand, governments continually step beyond the public into the private realm in order to participate in interest politics; while on the the other hand, interest groups acquire a quasi-public role, partly by virtue of the privileged position they hold in policy formation and partly by virtue of the delegated powers they enjoy.

Although the neo-corporatist critique of pluralism is a comprehensive one, it by no means entails the wholesale rejection of liberal principles. On the contrary, the essence of neo-corporatist theory is the claim that it provides a liberal – or 'societal', as it is also called – version of corporatism which is better placed than the free market to cope with the economic problems of advanced industrial societies, while simultaneously avoiding the bureaucratic and coercive measures associated with authoritarian regimes. In this sense, the recent literature on neo-corporatism harks back to the earlier quest for a 'middle way' which began in the interwar era. The neo-corporatist version of the middle way, however, claims to differ from three other familiar versions of that ideal, all of which had been either wholly discredited or at least considerably tarnished by the beginning of the present decade. The first of these is the fascist version; the second is the postwar Keynesian version; and the third is the étatiste ideal of direct intervention in the economic order.

Neo-corporatist theory claims to differ from fascism not only in pointing to a largely unplanned, non-ideological series of trends in western life, but also in its rejection of the techniques of integration entailed by the fascist ideal of a 'third way'. Unlike the neo-corporatist middle way, the fascist 'third way' entailed outright rejection of all constitutional restraints, open advocacy of coercive methods and the submersion of all forms of pluralism in a dynamic mass movement. By contrast, the neo-corporatist middle way claims to be a fundamentally benign system of integration which scrupulously eschews coercion and accepts diversity, provided that the latter does not conflict with the primary goods of economic growth and political stability. It is this benign, anti-authoritarian character which the term 'liberal' or 'societal' corporatism is intended to denote.

The neo-corporatist version of the middle way also claims to differ, moreover, from the two postwar versions. On the one hand, it offers an alternative to the fiscal control of Keynesianism, while on the other hand, it also claims to be independent of direct state controls. It relies instead upon a high degree of self-regulation by the various powerful interest groups involved. In order to decide whether neo-corporatist theory succeeds in establishing this claim to offer a novel version of the middle way idea, we must turn to the second problem, which is that of determining more precisely what the neo-corporatist thesis actually asserts.

In outline at least, an answer to this question can be discerned in what has already been said. To the pluralism of liberal-democratic theory corporatism opposes the vision of an emergent social order which is, in important respects, neither competitive nor wholly voluntary, in which the role of government is highly active and not merely passive or reactive, and in which the division between state and society is systematically contravened. The degree to which these corporatist tendencies are displayed in different countries varies, as does the manner in which they reveal themselves in different societies. However, the problem is that none of these characteristics suffices to establish precisely what the corporatist thesis is, since even in combination, they are difficult to distinguish both from étatisme and from a modified form of pluralism. In either case, any distinctively 'corporatist' conceptual identity as yet remains to be specified. If the request for a clearer definition of neo-corporatism is now pressed, then no single, homogeneous concept emerges from the literature; instead two partially overlapping, but ultimately divergent, schools of thought must be distinguished within it. The first school presents what may be termed a strong version of the neo-corporatist theory, while the second offers what is, by contrast, a weak version.

Consider, first, the strong version. According to the best-known representative of this version, J. T. Winkler, contemporary corporatism is a wholly novel type of political economy, quite distinct both from capitalism and socialism. In an off-quoted formulation Winkler described this novel economic system as one 'in which the state directs and controls predominantly privately-owned business according to four principles; unity, order, nationalism and success'.[4] Political scientists have failed to notice the emergence of this new type of economy they have concentrated their attention on the extent and quantity of state intervention, thereby obscuring the main point; this is, 'some increase in intervention involves the state taking on a new and different economic function, a *qualitative* change in its role. Stripped to its essentials, corporatism is principally defined by one particularly important qualitative change, the shift from a supportive to a directive role for the state in the economy.'[5] The nature of this new 'directive' role, Winkler insists, must be precisely specified. It does not mean that the state merely influences, facilitates or supports private firms, but that it actively controls their internal decisions.[6] Corporatist control differs from other types of intervention, in that it is not intended merely as a corrective device, but is considered to be the best and most positive means of achieving collective success. The idea of 'collective success' is perhaps the best clue to the novelty of the corporatist type of economy. The collectivism in question is far more than a kind of economic organisation. It is indeed nothing less than

a mobilisation system. It operates from the belief that goals are better achieved through the progressive organisation of collective effort than through spontaneous individual response to perceived opportunities. Concretely, this means a corporatist regime would attempt to establish control over the investment process . . . and asssume some degree of responsibility for economic planning . . . This is more than conventional state intervention, more than Keynesian demand management, indicative planning, technocracy or socially responsible capitalism. It is a planned, organised and corporatist economic system, justified by its ability to achieve collective ends.[7]

The second, or weak, version of neo-corporatism has been much more influential than the first, precisely because it is much more modest in scope. The original formulation of this version is generally credited to Philippe Schmitter, but for present purposes we may concentrate on the more recent formulation provided by Alan Cawson in the authoritative *Blackwell Encyclopedia of Political Thought*. Cawson writes:

> Corporatism is a specific socio-political process in which a limited number of monopolistic organizations representing fundamental interests engage in bargaining with state agencies over public policy outputs. In exchange for favourable policies, the leaders of the interest organizations agree to undertake the implementation of policy through determining the co-operation of their members.[8]

Cawson's definition is modest in the sense that, in line with the work of Schmitter, it confines corporatism to a particular kind of bargaining process which is believed to be a distinctive feature of the modern industrial state.

Descriptions of the precise nature of this bargaining process vary, but the central idea is clear enough. What we are confronted by, it is suggested, is the dissolution of the sovereign state as it has existed in the west since the seventeenth century. This dissolution is occurring because sovereignty, which has hitherto been concentrated in the state itself, is now flowing away from the state to society, where it is increasingly being shared with private groups. Established pluralist theory, it is maintained, is wholly unable to conceptualise this major change in the character of the modern state because it assumes that the various groups involved in the policy-making process play only an intermittent, discontinuous part which is limited to single issues. The difference between the classical pluralist theory of pressure group activity and the emergent pattern of neo-corporatist policy-making has been aptly summarised by Leonardo Parri. In classical pluralism, Parri observes, 'the associations have no political status: they are considered by the state as external partners, with chiefly an economic field of action'.[9] As Parri stresses, it is important to notice that 'the number and the nature of the intermediate organizations involved do not affect the neo-corporatist characteristics of the arrangement', since the 'essential feature is the presence of concertation and of the connected stable political exchanges between public and private actors'.[10] The neo-corporatist state, in a word, must not be narrowly identified with the kind of tripartite 'social contract' that seemed to be emerging in, for example, the England of the later 1960s and 1970s. On the contrary, the corporatist system 'can be bi-, tri- or quadrilateral, with or without unions and so on'.[11]

According to this interpretation of the neo-corporatist thesis, then, what has emerged in the postwar industrial democracies is a new 'politics of concertation' which is marked – so Ionescu has argued – not merely by the decentralisation of state sovereignty, but also by a novel pattern of horizontal 'consultation-commitment', in place of the traditional vertical pattern of 'command-obedience'.[12]

These observations, however, offer only an abstract, unhistorical characterisation of neo-corporatism. In concrete terms the strengths and weaknesses of neo-corporatist theory can best be appreciated by considering a work which was hailed by one reviewer as 'the most challenging book so far attempted on the political history of twentieth century Britain'.[13] This is Keith Middlemas's study of *Politics in Industrial Society*, which examines a major change that Middlemas believes occurred in the whole character of British politics between 1911 and 1945.[14]

Searching for a term to describe the change in British politics, which is his subject, Middlemas rejects any reference to the corporate state, or even to corporatism; instead he chooses the term 'corporate bias'[15] on the ground that it conveys the absence of any conscious design or theoretical underpinning. What this refers to can best be understood in terms of the departure it involves from the version of the working of the constitution which is still generally accepted. This is the Victorian system of parliamentary democracy, suitably modified to take account of the emergence of mass parties and ideological competition between them for electoral support.

In the twentieth century, Middlemas argues, the established constitutional theory has gradually become irrelevant since the party system has proved increasingly unable to act as a means for generating popular consent and conveying popular wishes to governments. The failure of the system in this respect, he maintains, originally became apparent during the First World War. From that time onwards new methods of creating consensus and social integration were gradually adopted, among which the unplanned emergence of a tripartite system of government is the most striking. The result is that the nineteenth-century concept of the state as a neutral arbiter, standing above all the various groups in society, 'has now become wholly outdated, even when the

modifications of early pluralist theory are taken into account'.[16] In its
place there has arisen the modern state, which includes not only the
government and the state apparatus, but also various politically privileged producer groups, to which Middlemas gives the name 'governing
institutions'. When the triangular system broke down during the 1960s
and 1970s, Middlemas maintains that most observers failed to recognise
that what really occurred was in fact less a breakdown than an evolution
of corporate bias into new forms. The precise shape which these forms
are likely to assume is still difficult to foresee since the truly modern or
'post-industrial' phase of our existence which produces them is itself
only now beginning. In general terms, however, what characterised this
phase of social and political 'incorporation' – which has not yet been
reached by countries such as France, Italy and Spain, Middlemas
remarks – is the disappearance of the last vestige of the old hierarchical
or pyramidic social order, and the emergence of a wholly horizontal
pattern of relationships.

Unfortunately, this suggestive thesis is marred by a series of unresol-
ved ambiguities. In the first place, Middlemas assumes that the growth
of the new system of corporate bias was the main reason why England
enjoyed social and political stability during the interwar period. This
argument, however, can immediately be overturned by the contention
that the system of corporate bias only worked because of the prior
existence of the very consensus which Middlemas believes it created.
But even if we pass over the chicken and egg objection, there is a second
source of confusion, which is the gross oversimplification entailed by the
corporate bias theory of the factors which have contributed to consensus
and stability in British politics since 1945. Above all, the theory unduly
minimises the contribution made by the party system. Here, the root of
the problem is that in order to dramatise the theory of corporate bias,
Middlemas relies upon a corresponding exaggeration of the extent to
which the primacy of the party system has been superseded by the new
system. This makes it impossible to explain, for example, the creation of
the welfare state. The corporate bias theory cannot explain this, because
the overriding significance it attaches to the power of producer groups
could at best only account for selective welfare benefits, and not for the
universal ones which the welfare state in fact provides. More generally,
a theory which postulates *a priori* the decline of party makes it impossible to explain, not only the welfare state, but many other events in the
postwar decades. On this view, indeed, every event in which party plays
a key role has to be dismissed by Middlemas as a desperate and
reactionary attempt to thwart the new system of corporate bias by
restoring the out-moded party system.

The historical detail of Middlemas's analysis, however, is less relevant for present purposes than the overall picture which emerges from it. In its essentials, this picture has long been familiar from the writings of scholars like Samuel Beer, who has also charted the rise of producer groups to the position once held by the medieval estates of the realm.[17] Middlemas's treatment of the corporatist theme differs from that of his predecessors and his successors in two respects, however. On the one hand, his approach is more sceptical and cautious than that of Beer, for example. For Beer, writing in the prosperity and relative tranquility of the mid-1960s, postwar Britian was the period when 'the new group politics . . . came to maturity'.[18] Amid the disenchantment of the 1970s, Middlemas was the most impressive of the scholars who stood this interpretation on its head, by identifying the 1960s as the very period in which the postwar corporate consensus had begun to disintegrate. On the other hand, Middlemas differs from the majority of neo-corporatist theorists in adopting a political emphasis. In this respect, his own historical interpretation of the evolution of corporate bias may be contrasted, for example, with the work of Nigel Harris.[19] For Harris, writing from a Marxist standpoint, corporatist tendencies are naturally seen as primarily induced by economic change. For Middlemas, the political requirements of consensus politics are the crucial factor. Nevertheless, his analysis of the breakdown of consensus shows the influence of continental neo-Marxist theory. Drawing on the work of Habermas, Middlemas ends with a chapter tentatively suggesting that the modern British state now faces a 'legitimation crisis'. The meaning of this concept will be examined more closely later. The immediate task is to assess the merits of the two principal versions of neo-corporatist theory which are now before us.

Unfortunately both the strong and the weak versions of the theory present major problems, and neither can be regarded as offering a satisfactory answer to the request for a coherent definition of neo-corporatism. We must now consider the difficulties they present. Anticipating what follows, it may be said the difficulty with the strong definition is exaggeration, while that with the weak one is vagueness.

According to the first view, neo-corporatism marks a novel form of political economy, distinct from both capitalism and socialism. However, this comes very close to resurrecting the claims made by Italian fascism in the interwar period, with the qualification that the postwar 'neo'-form of corporatism is fascism with a human face.[20] Even if the obvious objections to totalitarianism are ignored, the model hardly seems a convincing one since it is only in Japan that anything can be found which fits it. As two scholars recently observed of Japan in this connection, both the pre-Second World War period, and the first two decades after the end of that war, displayed 'strong pressure towards the corporatist version of a political economy written of by Pahl and Winkler – state direction and private ownership, plus pressures on all sectors towards order, unity, nationalism and success.'[21] But even in the Japanese case, the authors note, the late 1970s began to reveal cracks in the corporatist structure.[22] The relevant point in the present context, however, is the fact that Japanese social and political traditions are so different from western ones that they do not provide a viable basis for any generalisation at all about western experience.

The exaggeration inherent in the first concept of neo-corporatism is easy to discern. In the case of the weak concept, however, the problems which arise are more elusive. They appear in the form of three crucial areas of vagueness.

The first of these areas relates to the key concept of 'interest inter-mediation', which is the term frequently used to distinguish the new corporatist phenomenon from the old and familiar one of étatisme. One scholar, Wyn Grant, explains that the basis of the distinction is that, while corporatism is certainly interventionist, 'it is indirectly rather than directly interventionist; its character is, of course, action by the state in conjunction with the organizations that are based on the division of labour in society'.[23] Unfortunately, the difference between 'direct' and 'indirect' state action is often too vague for this to be a very helpful observation. This vagueness about the meaning of interest intermedi-ation has meant, in practice, that it has proved difficult to distinguish neo-corporatism from what is, at best, only a new species of the very pluralism which it set out to reject. This is acknowledged by Cawson, for example, when he writes that 'as empirical evidence feeds into success-ive refinements of the theory, it is becoming clear that corporatism and pluralism should not be seen as exclusive alternatives, but as end-points in a continuum according to the extent to which monopolistic and interdependent relationships between interest organisations and the state have become established'.[24] Cawson is judicious, but the 'con-tinuum' to which he refers does nothing to stabilise the concept of corporatism. At one extreme, the corporatist end of the continuum remains vague since there is nothing in it to exclude the state-imposed corporatism of both totalitarian and authoritarian regimes, while the pluralist end, at the other extreme, shades over into a complacent vision of spontaneous social harmony. The more recent work of Schmitter amounts to a further admission of ultimate failure to give the concept precision. The true novelty of corporatism, Schmitter now maintains, consists neither in its being a new phase of capitalist organisation, nor in its being an unprecedented extension of bureaucratic government. Rather it is to be found only at what he terms 'the meso-level', where the (plural) interests of classes and societal organisations mesh with the interests of the state.[25] Switching the level of analysis, however, merely relocates the core of intellectual vagueness, without thereby reducing it at all. This core is especially evident when Schmitter proposes a model of what he terms 'associative order' as the key to neo-corporatism. According to this model, 'modern social order is composed of a mix of institutions with different actors, motives, media of exchange, resources, decision rules, cleavage patterns and normative foundations'. The great defect of the 'traditional trio of community, market and state', he continues, is that it 'fails to explore all the possible bases and combinations'.[26] To 'explore all the possible bases and combinations', however, is only to dissolve the quest for a new synthesis into an endless series of classifications – and that is mere taxonomy, not theory of any kind.

If we now return for a moment to Cawson's sophisticated definition of neo-corporatism in terms of a 'continuum' with pluralism, then a second crucial area of vagueness becomes apparent. This is that neo-corporatist theory systematically blurs the central ethical problem of politics, which is the problem of coercion. In other words, it is not clear whether 'interest intermediation' (or 'concertation') is to be achieved solely by consensus, or whether it permits various kinds of authoritarian pressure 'from above'. Unfortunately neo-corporatist theory side-steps the whole issue of coercion, largely because it perpetuates the great weakness of traditional corporatism, which was the assumption of a basic harmony of interests in society at large. This evasion is disastrous because it leaves it unclear whether the model of 'liberal' or 'societal' corporatism is really as distinct from, say, the fascist kind as theories of neo-corporatism assume it to be.

The problem of coercion points, in turn, to a third difficulty, which is that neo-corporatist techniques of social integration appear to leave the more powerful interest groups free to use the new corporatist 'intermediation' procedures as a means of turning the state to their own purpose at the expense of weaker, or less well-organised, groups. Although theorists differ about the precise lines along which the new neo-corporatist élite is differentiated from the new class of have-nots, Cawson adopts one of the most influential schemes when he argues that, in the British case, contemporary politics 'exhibits a dualism between a politics of production and a politics of consumption which are embedded in different state agencies and are associated with different modes of interest politics and policy-making'.[27] Cawson recognises that, in practice, this 'dualist' order means that those outside the charmed process of concertation are left to fall back on the established political order, thereby downgrading the state into a device for offering such meagre protection as it can to the outcasts of the neo-corporatist system. He argues, however, that corporatist tendencies are not in principle incompatible with democracy, although no institutions have as yet been devised adequately to counteract their malign influence. The task facing modern democracies is, at any rate, clear: it is 'to preserve what little protection democratic institutions offer for the "victims" of dualism. It is not that corporatism is incompatible with democracy, but rather that exclusion is incompatible with democracy.'[28]

This position – best described, perhaps, as an élitist form of social democracy – is characteristic of most theorists of neo-corporatism, although any overt ideological commitment is usually avoided. However, the neo-corporatist position is vulnerable to a much more extreme interpretation than the social-democratic one. Such an interpretation is to be found in neo-Marxism, for which corporatism is merely the latest strategy deployed by capitalist society in order to maintain profitability in a time of recession. The most influential theorising has come from two leading members of the Frankfurt school, Jürgen Habermas and Claus Offe. The latter, in particular, has developed an interesting but elusive type of systemic structuralism in order to elaborate the implications of neo-corporatism for Marxist theory.

Offe acknowledges that the traditional Marxist view is unable to explain the fact that the modern welfare state simply does not appear to act in the way in which an oppressor of the proletarian masses might be expected to do so. In order to take account of this, he rejects the old Marxist theory, according to which the state is an intrument for promoting the common interests of the ruling class. Instead of being a direct oppressor of the masses, he maintains, the state is now an essentially indirect one, working not so much as the instrument of an oppressive capitalist class, as the sustainor of an oppressive social system. As Offe himself put it, 'What the state protects and sanctions is a set of institutions and social *relationships* necessary for the domination of the capitalist class'. Thus, 'While it does not depend on the specific interests of a single class, the state nevertheless seeks to implement and guarantee the *collective* interests of all members of a class society dominated by capital'.[29] It is against this background of overall systemic (rather than class) oppression that corporatist techniques of 'intermediation' emerge as a contemporary device for welding state and society into a seamless web of exploitation. As Offe points out, the seamlessness of the systemic web arises because 'the centres of political power have more and more visibly moved away from the official institutions of the state (such as parties, Parliament, the Presidency or bureaucratic policy-making) and rather have assumed, within the boundaries of a corporatist politics of group accommodation, an increasingly social character.'[30] The crucial point, however, is that the type of system integration made possible by the 'politics of group accommodation' can only endure so long as there is sufficient economic growth for all the different political and social groups to prosper. Once growth slackens or disappears, the neo-corporatist consensus is threatened, with the result that the legitimacy of the state is increasingly undermined by disaffected groups who no longer have anything to gain. The result is the prospect of 'legitimation crisis', a concept which has already been mentioned in connection with the work of Middlemas.

The Marxist interpretation of neo-corporatism is unconvincing mainly because too high a price has to be paid for the increased flexibility achieved through the systemic analysis of the social order. This type of analysis does indeed enable thinkers like Offe to explain, for example, one of the most striking facts about neo-corporatist development, which is that support for them cannot be correlated with class. Opposition to corporatist measures has frequently been associated, for instance, with the very groups, namely capitalist ones such as the banks, the CBI, the pension funds and insurance companies, the City and large multi-national companies – that might have been expected to support them, on traditional Marxist premises; and the working class, likewise, cannot be cast in the simple role of victim of corporatist measures, which have often been supported by the trade unions. For neo-Marxism of the systemic kind, however, these unpalatable facts present no insuperable difficulty since class is no longer a decisive consideration. The price paid for this revision of Marxism is a retreat from empirical reality, and the absorption of everything into a world of disembodied systemic relationships. Within this wholly abstract world the distinction between what is functional and dysfunctional is left entirely to the discretion of the neo-Marxist theorist. Within this kind of Marxism it is of course possible to 'explain' neo-corporatism as a subtle device for perpetuating capitalist exploitation, but only – as was just indicated – by completely detaching Marxism itself from any connection with empirical reality. There is consequently no solid theoretical basis for the neo-Marxist claim that systemic collapse is likely to be triggered by a 'legitimation crisis' brought about by economic recession. Indeed the very notion of a legitimation crisis is itself hopelessly confused. It is confused because legitimacy is treated by neo-Marxism as a function of government policies; that is, it is treated as an attribute of governments which is created and maintained solely by desirable policies and successful substantive performance. But legitimacy is not a function of the desirability and success of what governments do; rather it attaches to compliance with formal constitutional conditions which governments must observe in order for them to possess authority. In other words, legitimacy relates not to what is done, but to the observation of procedures which distinguish authority from power. For neo-Marxism, however, no clear distinction between authority and power can be made since a concern with forms and procedures is merely a way of concealing the structural sources of capitalist oppression.

This inability to distinguish between authority and power must be dwelt upon since it is not a peculiarity of neo-Marxism. Indeed it is shared by neo-corporatist theory as well. In the latter case, blindness to the distinction occurs mainly because neo-corporatism is imbued with a managerial perspective. Within this perspective no objection of principle is raised to the control of policy by semi-public interest groups; the only important consideration is whether unity is achieved efficiently, and on the basis of consensus. The managerial perspective means in consequence that neo-corporatist élitism remains unchecked by any concern for constitutional restraints.

Neo-corporatist theory, then, is too vague about various crucial issues for its version of the middle way to be considered as a satisfactory compromise between liberty and authority. However, in spite of this conceptual vagueness, it may still be felt that neo-corporatist theory nevertheless gives at least some degree of intelligibility to important social and political developments that have become increasingly apparent in the industrial democracies during the past few decades. We must therefore turn at this point to the last of the three questions which were to be considered, and ask to what extent neo-corporatist literature illuminates the facts of contemporary life. Unfortunately it may be said immediately that the very nature of neo-corporatism serves to obscure, rather than to illuminate, the course of recent history. This is because the neo-corporatist perspective is essentially a functionalist one which suffers – precisely because it is functionalist – from three kinds of blindness, each of which results in oversimplification (and therefore misrepresentation) of the contemporary social and political world. In the first place, functionalism oversimplifies the recent history which it purports to illuminate. In the second place, it oversimplified the nature of the state itself, by ignoring the constitutional foundations of western political experience and treating the state in wholly managerial terms. And in the third place, it results in an oversimplified, and therefore distorted, framework for comparative analysis. However, before illustrating these various types of oversimplifications, it is necessary to explain the meaning of <u>functionalism itself, in the neo-corporatist context.</u>

Neo-corporatist functionalism assumes two forms, political and economic. The political version is exemplified by Middlemas's version of modern European history as a process of modernisation in which the industrial democracies at large tend to follow a common trajectory that passes through three stages. Since Middlemas believes that each of these is clearly illustrated in the British case, British political history is tentatively endowed with paradigmatic significance for the study of neo-corporatist trends.[31] On this view, the first stage is illustrated by British <u>history before 1911</u>, when the greatest problem was how to assimilate working-class political demands into the British state structure. The second was the <u>interwar years</u>, when the great task became that of incorporating the <u>institutions</u> of working-class industrial life into the state structure. The third stage, which corresponds to our present situation, is the 'post-industrial' one, in which 'there are no more organizations or classes to incorporate (unless the concept of class is strained to include categories such as the unemployed, women or youths) and the problem is to satisfy individual, multiple aspirations, and remedy the structural rigidities of traditional parties and of traditional trade unions'.[32] Within this schematisation functionalism consists, as has been observed, in assuming that the problem of the state in the twentieth century can be adequately analysed primarily in terms of a conflict between two rival modes of integration, namely the parliamentary one and the corporate bias one.

However, Middlemas's political brand of functionalism is much less common in neo-corporatist theory than economic functionalism. This latter kind takes the form of the assumption that there is some kind of causal or 'systemic' connection between corporatist trends and what are regarded as the functional requirements of advanced capitalism. The widespread prevalence of an assumed connection between corporatism and capitalism is evident from even the most cursory survey of the literature on the subject. Schmitter's article, 'Still the century of corporatism?' (1974), for example, hinges upon the assertion that corporatism in all its forms seems to be 'related to certain basic impetuses of capitalism to reproduce the conditions for its existence and continually to accumulate further resources'.[33] In a similar vein, Lehmbruch asked rhetorically, 'How can one explain the apparently growing importance of liberal corporatism in a number of Western European countries?', and replied that: 'To arrive at a probabilistic theory . . . we obviously have to consider certain functional exigencies of the economic system.'[34] 'More specifically', Lehmbruch added, 'corporatism appears to serve such [exigencies] by regulating the conflict of social classes in the distribution of national income and in the structure of industrial relations'.[35] For Jessop, a fully corporatist state would be 'the best possible shell' for modern capitalism.[36] Cawson, too, has written in the past of corporatism as the political form most suited to the requirements of modern capitalism.[37] For Wyn Grant, 'corporatist analysis focuses on the groups that arise out of the divisions of labour in society, whereas pluralism is concerned with the analysis of any organized (or latent) interest'.[38] It need hardly be added that the consensus of neo-corporatist theorists about the primacy of economic factors does not entail any uniformity of opinion about the precise relationship between capitalism and corporatism. As has been seen, for thinkers like Pahl and Winkler, for example, corporatism is not a development within capitalism, but is 'a distinct form of economic structure', constituting an alternative or sequel to it.[39] For others, like Westergaard, such a view is unacceptable because it attributes to the state a degree of independence from the economic order incompatible with the Marxist theory of social reality.[40] Still others, like Panitch, hedge their bets on the relationship between corporatism and capitalism, rejecting economic determinism, but nevertheless insisting that there must be *some* connection with the capitalist order. Thus Panitch, for example, asserts that corporatism 'is a *political structure* that attends, if it is not actually produced by, the emergence of the *advanced capitalist economy*'.[41]

The first defect of this ubiquitious functionalism consists, as we have said, in the oversimplification of the recent history of advanced industrial democracies in order to detect significant corporatist tendencies at almost any cost, no matter what violence is done to the relevant data. In a trenchant critique of corporatist theory as it has been applied to Britain in particular, Andrew Cox has traced in detail the misinterpretation which it entailed, for example, of the nature and significance of the increased state intervention which occurred during the 1960s and 1970s.[42] Cox notes, in particular, a misleading tendency in corporatist theory in general to attribute undue significance to measures such as the formation of the National Economic Development Council (NEDC) in 1961, Labour's attempts to develop indicative national policy in 1964 and the Industry Act of the Conservative government in 1975. It is true, as Cox notes, that at first sight these measures partially correspond to the kind of corporatist programme which both Labour and Conservative supporters have advocated while in opposition. On the Labour side, for example, both Stuart Holland[43] and more recently, Bryan Gould[44] have supported a form of 'étatiste' corporatism, while Conservative support for corporatism goes back to the 1930s, when a version of the corporatist state was defended by MacMillan, Stanley and Boothby. In office, however, policy was shaped by many conflicting considerations, and in face of these no government has either wanted, or been able to, adopt programmes of the kind considered in opposition. What the 1960s and 1970s indicated, indeed, was that no government stood any chance of 'incorporating' either business or unions into the state, even if it wished to do so. There was indeed occasional willingness on the part of both sections to cooperate with government; but the brief success of the incomes policy of 1975–7 represented an exception and not the norm, Cox observes, in a story of which 'history may well conclude that business and labour in Britain were able to win concessions from government at very little cost to their respective and traditional roles'.[45]

It cannot even be shown, Cox continues, that governments in office have created anything resembling the new kind of activist state which, according to corporatist theory, is to supersede the neutral pluralist one. For example, the creation of bodies such as the National Economic Development Office (NEDO) and NEDC in 1961–2, which is usually taken to inaugurate the new state, did not in fact introduce an era of planning at all. In the face of the Treasury's and other opposition to any planning role, such bodies were quickly reduced to tripartite talking-shops.[46] The same absence of any sustained government attempt to play an active directing role in the economic order is evident at the micro/level. Once again, the evidence cited – e.g. the creation of the Industrial Reorganization corporation (IRC) in 1966, the Industrial Expansion Act 1968 and the Industry Acts of 1972 and 1975 – does not bear analysis. On closer inspection, 'it is clear that far from a continuing effort by governments to control and direct micro-economic practices these measures indicate an ad hoc, supportive and subventionary, reactive role for the state'.[45]

The first defect of neo-corporatist functionalism, then, is historical oversimplification. The second defect, which is gradually being recognised as the weakest link in the chain of neo-corporatist theory, is closely connected with the first, and consists of the inability to develop a coherent theory of the state. As P. J. Williamson recently acknowledged in the course of concluding a thoughtful defence of neo-corporatism:

> Probably the most significant topic on the contest [between pluralist and corporatist theory] was the state. Having thrown the state into the spotlight, the [corporatist] act is taking a long time to get together.

Indeed, the Act is still in such appalling shape that 'the development of state theory is now more than ever an imperative factor in the future of corporatist analysis'.[48] Unfortunately, Williamson's own conception of 'contract corporatism' does not carry the analysis of the state any further. Although it distinguishes his preferred type of corporatism from the state-imposed type implemented by authoritarian regimes, the concept of contract corporatism does not clearly distinguish his position from pluralism. The relationship between the state and the corporatist order is not greatly clarified by the vague assertion that 'corporatism should not be regarded in terms of the existence of certain prominent national institutions, but has to be seen in a more dynamic evolutionary manner, reflecting the changing role of the state in advanced capitalist economies'.[49] It is precisely the 'changing role of the state in advanced capitalist economies' which needs to be explained. Instead of explanation, however, there is once again only the dogmatic assumption that the modern industrial state is inevitably impelled in a corporatist direction by 'its imperative need' to cope with its dependence upon producer groups.[50]

Is there any way, it may be asked, by which this deficiency in the neo-corporatist theory of the state can be remedied? Not, as Pierre Birnbaum has recently argued, unless the abstract, universalistic methodology upon which much neo-corporatist theory relies is abandoned. The analysis of corporatism has suffered because this abstract methodology mistakenly assumes that the state 'must always be the same in all western capitalist societies.'[51] To this ahistorical, universalistic concept of the state, Birnbaum opposes the method of historical sociology, for which the state is to be defined in a restrictive maner. Specifically its existence is to be confined to western societies which have experienced 'a particular crisis – the crisis of feudalism'[52] From this vantage-point, Birnbaum reaches a simple but important conclusion, which significantly modifies the neo-corporatist interpretation of recent history. This is that the development of corporatism should be related to the political history of a country, instead of to its economic or social structure, or to the forms of interest intermediation it displays. When seen in this way – i.e. in the light of historical sociology – Birnbaum concludes that corporatism is a 'quasi-impossibility'[53] in both the British and the French cases. In Britain it is excluded by the 'relatively unstructured' character of the state tradition.[54] By contrast, in France the state is highly structured, but in the French tradition, 'antagonistic social actors would rather turn towards the state and its counts, and preserve their own autonomy, than negotiate'. Hence the strength of the French state

> shows itself through a three sided game, in which management and the working class remain on the outside. The state, as a product of differentiation, cannot

promote the integration of particular social interests in its centre without jeopardizing its own institutionalization and its own autonomy – hence, the impossibility of corporatism.[55]

Birnbaum's demand for greater sensitivity to different historical traditions, as well as his stress upon the autonomy of the state, is a potentially valuable antidote to the functionalist oversimplifications of neo-corporatist theory. Unfortunately, however, the theoretical perspective which he himself wishes to put in its place is ultimately unsatisfactory, mainly because the ideal type in terms of which he defines the state is extremely restricted. It is restricted, because it inexplicably omits the most important ethical characteristic of the western state tradition. This is the concept of the state as an embodiment of the rule of law. In other words, the ironic outcome of Birnbaum's position is that it neglects the very characteristic of the state which neo-corporatist functionalism itself omits. In fairness, it must be added that Birnbaum does in fact include law among the various characteristics which he attributes to the ideal state;[56] but the law he refers to is *administrative* law, and not the non-instrumental kind of law which is the essence of the constitutional ideal.

The third defect inherent in neo-corporatist functionalism concerns the comparative method. Neo-corporatist theory has produced a very considerable body of comparative literature, but comparison between different states in terms of functional similarities frequently serves (as Birnbaum's remarks may already have suggested) only to conceal more fundamental dissimilarities. This problem has become increasingly acute over the past two decades as a theory which was originally developed by Schmitter in the light of Portuguese developments has been extended to advanced industrial societies. Perhaps the best illustration of the problem which have arisen is provided by Austria, which has been held up as the ideal type of a liberal or 'societal' corporatist order, in the period since 1945. The details of the neo-corporatist interpretation of Austrian experience are not relevant here;[57] what is mainly of interest is that the interpretation takes hardly any account of what might be thought to be the most important thing about the Austrian political tradition. This is that Austria was the supreme example of the European system of government known as enlightened despotism. In the light of this tradition, it is hardly surprising to find that Austrian 'economizing politics' subordinates everything to 'system necessities' (*Sachzwange*).[58] What is surprising in this perspective is how little has changed. History, however, is at best only peripherally relevant to the functionalist approach, which mainly relies on an abstract conception of the supposed requirements of the economic and political order.

What, then, is to be concluded from this examination of neo-corporatist theory? The main impression is that its terms have been so loosely defined that it has been able to mean all things to all men. Nevertheless, if we try to steer a straight path through the mists which surround the theory and once more directly pose the question of what is neo-corporatism, then it has been suggested that the unifying element is the vision of a middle way which combines certain features of democracy with full employment and economic growth, within what is believed to be a more flexible and stable framework of consensus than any that has hitherto been achieved. The difficulty is to decide whether this quest for a middle ground between the old model of liberal pluralism on the one hand, and the authoritarian and totalitarian corporatist alternatives on the other, is anything more than the pursuit of an illusion. Drawing on what has been said above, a sceptical conclusion seems proper for three reasons.

The first relates to the difficulties created by the neo-corporatist interpretation of the facts themselves. As we have seen, critics have not been slow to point out that the various tendencies upon which neo-corporatist theory relies are oversimplified and misrepresented when they are described in terms of a process of 'incorporation'. The second relates to the terms of the theory which have never been fully clarified since central concepts, such as that of interest intermediation, have been left vague. The implied contrast is of course with the imposed forms of corporatism associated with totalitarian and authoritarian systems of rule, but this contrast is difficult to sustain since the version of a wholly voluntary corporatist system is a familiar utopia.

The third reason for scepticism is that neo-corporatism is vitiated by a functionalist perspective which systematically obscures the main dilemma faced by modern European states. This dilemma is the existence of a basic tension between two conflicting styles of politics. These two styles may be termed 'managerial politics' on the one hand, and 'limited politics' on the other. In this perspective, neo-corporatist theory merely perpetuates what has been the principal vice of all versions of the middle way: it fudges the issue. What this issue is can best be made clear by a brief clarification of the concepts of 'managerial' and 'limited' politics.

For a limited style of politics, government is a matter of making and implementing law within a constitutional framework consisting of checks and balance, a system of representative institutions to secure political accountability and an independent judiciary. For managerial politics, by contrast, government becomes instead a means of promoting certain ends. It must be stressed that these ends need not be economic ones: the managerial style of politics antedates industrialisation, originating in a pre-modern era when the managerial enterprise was more likely to be the religious one of salvation, or the military one of territorial aggrandizement. However, what is important at present is not the precise purpose of managerial politics, but the fact that the mere existence of any purpose always imposes on the managerial style a common structure. Within that structure the primary bond of the state is not the rule of law, but common commitment to a shared purpose; and for implementing that purpose, controls and decrees are more appropriate than laws, while administrative bodies, inspectors and tribunals, planning agreements and various types of interest group 'intermediation' are preferable to an independent judiciary and police force. It follows that the distinction between public and private life, or between state and society, which is crucial in a limited style of politics, has no secure place in managerial politics. It also follows that managerial politics tends to attach great significance to government by specialists since the managerial definition of politics in terms of a specific purpose naturally tends to endow an appropriately qualified élite with special authority. Finally it follows that the traditional function of parliamentary institutions within limited politics, which was to ensure political accountability, has no place within the managerial style for which any interference by such institutions is prone to be treated as a form of inefficiency and an obstacle to 'integration'.

However, it is not the case that managerial and limited politics are totally incompatible. They may coexist, provided that the managerial purpose does not acquire overriding significance. Nevertheless, there is always a tension between the two styles, for managerialism, while it may not offer outright opposition to the rule of law, is in principle indifferent to its requirements. When one leading theorist of neo-corporatism asserts that: 'pluralism and corporatism should not be seen as rival contenders for a general theory of politics in capitalist democracies',[59] he is right, in so far as corporatism need not launch an overt attack upon limited politics. He is wrong, however, in so far as he fails to acknowledge the inescapable tension between the two styles of politics. If the tension is not acute in practice, this is more a matter of good fortune than of political lucidity.

But what of the future of neo-corporatism, or rather of the kind of 'politics of concertation' which have been identified as neo-corporatist? The postwar consensus which nurtured these trends turned out to be far more fragile and evanescent than neo-corporatist theory had foreseen. In particular, after 1979 a falling trade union membership, and the ascendancy of the New Right, took neo-corporatism completely by surprise. Whether the current free market ideology represents more than a brief interruption of the underlying long-term trends stressed by neo-corporatist theory is difficult to say, but what is clear is that the broader managerial style of politics to which neo-corporatism belongs has definitely not been rejected by the New Right; all that has been changed is the type of economic strategy favoured, and not the managerial mentality itself. Consequently it is a mistake to regard New Right politics as marking a complete break with the world of neo-corporatist theory. It would be a mistake, therefore, to become so deeply involved in the minutiae of either neo-corporatist or New Right theories that the most important problem of our age escaped notice. This is that we no longer have a way of clearly distinguishing between economic man, with his problems of economic growth and interest justification on the one hand, and political man, with his constitutional concerns on the other. From this point of view, the 'liberal' ideal of neo-corporatism is but one more symptom of the foolish desire to ignore the constant tension which exists between economic man and political man. At the most general level, neo-corporatist theory may indeed be seen as the prime exemplar of what Sheldon Wolin has suggested is the most fundamental feature of modern political thought. In an apt phrase he described this as 'the chopping-up of political man' into a collection of fragmented identities.[60] This is a theme which, in varying forms, has found sympathetic echoes in such works as Richard Sennett's *The Fall of Public Man* (1977), Judith Shklar's *After Utopia* (1957) and Hannah Arendt's *The Human Condition* (1958), all of which present the main tendency of the past century of western political life as a flight from politics. In this broadest of persectives, then, the interest of neo-corporatism lies not so much in any new political theory it may claim to offer as in the eclipse of politics of which it is symptomatic.

Notes

I am grateful to Volker Berghahn, Andrew Cox, David George, Stephen Ingle and Christophe de Landtsheer for commenting in detail on a draft of this paper.
1. The term is vague. A brief but useful attempt to clarify its ambiguities, while simultaneously retaining some overall coherence, was recently made by William E. Connolly, in *Blackwell Encyclopaedia of Political Thought* (ed. David Miller) (Oxford, Blackwell, 1987), pp. 376–8. In the present context it is used in the unsophisticated sense in which it refers to a theory of democracy which rejects both the absolutism of Lockian individualism and the collectivism of the Rousseauian doctrine of popular sovereignty, in favour of the 'polyarchical' model of society associated in particular with Dahl. In a broader perspective pluralist theory is not of course novel. In one form it was fundamental to de Tocqueville's thought, for example.

2. Robert A. Dahl, *A Preface to Democratic Theory* (Chicago, University of Chicago Press, 1951), p. 132.
3. *Ibid.*, p. 135.
4. J. T. Winkler, 'Corporatism', *Archives Européenes Sociologiques*, XVIII (1) (1976), p. 103.
5. *Ibid.*, p. 105; emphasis in original.
6. See *Loc. cit.*
7. *Ibid.*, p. 107.
8. A. Cawson, *Blackwell Encyclopaedia of Political Thought, op. cit.*, p. 105.
9. L. Parri, in *Political Stability and Neo-Corporatism* (ed. Ilja Scholten) (London, Sage Publications, 1987), p. 71.
10. *Loc. cit.*
11. *Ibid.*
12. G. Ionescu, *Centripetal Politics* (London, Hart-Davies, 1975), p. 1–2.
13. Paul Addison, in *Times Literary Supplement*, 2 May 1980, p. 504.
14. See K. Middlemas, *Politics in Industrial Society: The Experience of the British System since 1911* (London, André Deutsch, 1979).
15. *Ibid.*, p. 20.
16. *Ibid.*, p. 460.
17. See 'Samuel Beer, *Modern British Politics* (London, Faber and Faber, 1965).
18. *Ibid.*, p. 386.
19. Nigel Harris, *Competition and the Corporate Society: British Conservatives, the State and Industry, 1945–64* (London, Methuen, 1972).
20. For a subtle analysis of the difficulties of developing a coherent theory of the state appropriate to this model form, see P. C. Schmitter, 'Neo-corporatism and the state', in Wyn Grant, ed. *The Political Economy of Corporatism,* (London, Mac-Millan, 1985), p. 32–62.
21. See R. E. Pahl and J. T. Winkler, 'The Coming Corporatism' in *New Society*, 10 October, 1974, pp. 72–76.
22. T. J. Pempel and Keiichi Tsunekawa, 'Corporatism without coercion? The Japanese anomaly' in P. C. Schmitter and G. Lehmbruch (eds.), *Trends towards Corporatist Intermediation* (London, Sage, 1971), p. 257.
23. W. Grant, *The Political Economy of Corporatism, op. cit.*, p. 8.
24. See Cawson, in *Blackwell Encyclopaedia of Political Thought*, p. 106.
25. P. C. Schmitter, *Neo-Corporatism and the State* (Florence, EUI, 1984).
26. Quoted in Grant, *op. cit.*, p. 29.
27. A. Cawson,*Corporatism and Political Theory* (Oxford, Blackwell, 1986), p. 148.
28. *Ibid.*, p. 147.
29. Claus Offe, in J. Keane (ed.), *Contradictions of the Welfare State* (London, Hutchinson, 1984), p. 120, emphasis original; see also 'Political authority and class structure', *Internat. Jour. of Soc.*, 11 (Spring 1972), pp. 95–6.
30. Offe, *Contradictions of the Welfare State, op. cit.*, p. 250.
31. Middlemas, *op. cit.*, p. 23.
32. *Ibid.*, p. 461.
33. Schmitter, in *The Review of Politics* (January 1974), p. 107.
34. G. Lehmbruch, 'Liberal corporatism and party government' in P. C. Schmitter and G. Lehmbruch (eds), *Trends towards Corporatist Intermediation* (London, Sage, 1979), p. 151.
35. *Loc. cit.*
36. Bob Jessop, 'Capitalism and democracy: the best political shell?' in Gary Littlejohn *et al*, (eds), *Power and the State* (London, Croom Helm, 1978), pp. 10–51.
37. A. Cawson, 'Pluralism, corporatism and the role of the state, *Government and Opposition*, 13 (Spring 1978), pp. 178–98.
38. Grant, *The Political Economy of Corporatism, op. cit.*, p. 21.
39. R. E. Pahl and J. T. Winkler, 'The coming corporatism', *Challenge* (March – April 1975), p. 31.

40. John Westergaard, 'Class, inequality and corporatism' in A. Hunt (ed.), *Class and Class Structure* (London, Lawrence Wishart, 1977), p. 174.
41. In *Trends towards Corporatist Intermediation*, *op. cit.*, p. 123; emphasis in original.
42. Andrew Cox, 'Corporatism as reductionism: the analytic limits of the corporatist thesis', *Government and Opposition*, 16 (1981), pp. 78–95.
43. See Stuart Holland, *The Socialist Challenge* (London, Quartet Books, 1975), and *Strategy for Socialism* (Nottingham: Bertrand Russell Peace Foundation for Spokesman Books, 1975).
44. See *Daily Telegraph*, 20 February 1988.
45. Cox, *op. cit.*, p. 86.
46. *Ibid.*, p. 88; see also M. Shanks, *Planning and Politics: The British Experience, 1960–1975* (London, Allen and Unwin, 1977).
47. Cox, *op. cit.*, p. 88.
48. P. J. Williamson, *Varieties of Corporatism* (Cambridge, Cambridge University Press, 1985), p. 186.
49. *Ibid.*, p. 201.
50. *Loc. cit.*
51. Pierre Birnbaum, 'The state versus corporatism', *Politics and Society*, 11 (4) (1982), p. 477.
52. *Ibid.*, p. 478.
53. *Ibid.*, p. 487.
54. *Ibid.*, p. 495.
55. *Ibid.*, p. 500.
56. *Ibid.*, p. 477.
57. See Bernd Marin's essay on Austria in Ilja Scholten (ed.), *Politics Stability and Neo-Corporatism* (London, Sage Publications, 1987), chapter 2; see also Marin's essay, 'Austria –the paradigm case of liberal corporatism?' in Grant (ed.), *The Political Economy of Corporatism*, *op. cit.*, p. 123.
58. Marin, 'Austria – the paradigm case of liberal corporatism?', *op. cit.*, p. 116.
59. See Cawson, *Corporatism and Political Theory*, *op. cit.*, p. 148.
60. Sheldon Wolin, *Politics and Vision* (London, Allen and Unwin, 1961), p. 430 *et seq.*

2 Neo-corporatism versus the corporate state

Andrew Cox

This chapter makes a distinction between the concepts of neo-corporatism and the corporate state. Neo-corporatism refers to those writers who have argued that corporatism is a new explanation of the way in which the modern state makes and implements policy.[1] The corporate state refers to the idealised vision of an organic, hierarchical society, with a state bargaining between various functional interests, which would be the antithesis of both liberal-democratic and socialist ideal-typical political forms, and which is not tied to any particular historical period.[2] The basic question posed in this chapter is whether model 1 (neo-corporatism) is preferable to model 2 (the corporate state) conceptually and analytically.

The broad conclusion of this chapter is that, despite the claims made for it, neo-corporatism has not led to any significantly new insights into how policy is made or implemented. Furthermore, it is not clear that the policy process it is said to describe is in any way unique to modern advanced industrial states or contemporary historical periods. Finally, using corporatism in this way has contributed to the systematic confusion which now surrounds the concept, and which threatens to render the concept not only essentially contested, but meaningless as an aid to academic research and understanding. Having said this, however, if neo-corporatism has little analytic or conceptual utility, the idea of a corporate state – an ideal-typical political form of the state – does have some merit. It can be used as a guide to the development of a typology of political forms and act as a point of comparison with other political forms, like pluralism or monism.

The chapter concludes, therefore, that Schmitter's original formulation of corporatism can serve a useful purpose, but only when it is shorn of its state and societal variants, and be allowed to stand merely as one of many ideal-typical political forms of the state. This may be far less ambitious a goal than Schmitter intended – he clearly saw himself as the theorist of a new state-society relationship and soothsayer[3] – but it seems the only logical approach if we are to save corporatism from the eclectic and multifarious hybridity which has descended upon it. The

debate about the concept has, however, had one benefit: it has assisted
in the re-clarification of pluralist theories of the state by defenders and
detractors alike.[4] It is argued here that the same re-appraisal is now
necessary for corporatism. Only in this way can it be saved from the
recent tendency to use it as a convenient label for any form of
specialised bargaining between the state and societal interests.

Why a Growth Industry?

Before developing these arguments more fully, it is important to place
the development of the corporatist debate in context. In this way, we
can understand perhaps why there is so little agreement about what the
concept means. There is no question that something spontaneous happened in the early 1970s. A number of academics from different backgrounds and countries came together to argue that something new was
happening to the traditional pluralist state–society relationships of
advanced industrial societies.[5] What they were pointing to was the
growth of a relatively institutionalised and permanent relationship
between government, business and labour interests at the policy-making
level of the state. This incorporation of key functional groups into the
executive branch of government was seen to lead to bargaining over
policy outcomes, often resulting in the leadership of these groups inter-
mediating (on behalf of the bargained agreements entered into with
their copartners) and disciplining their own membership behind the
deals arrived at.

Clearly this was very different in practice to the idealised model of
policy-making characterised by pluralist theories of advanced industrial
societies. Instead of groups representing their members' interests
upwards to government and, thereby, pursuing group interests, here
was evidence that leaders of key groups were acting in an élitist manner
and entering into agreements which often necessitated them in disciplining their own membership. Similarly, the leadership by compromising
with other functional groups was, in a sense, diminishing its commitment to the pursuit of unalloyed group self-interest. But the government's role was also changing. By giving a relatively permanent and
preferential treatment to key functional groups in the formulation of
policy in return for assistance with policy implementation, the state was
giving up some of its political authority to groups. This tendency directly
challenged the sovereignty of legislative and territorial forms of
decision-making on which liberal-democratic regimes are supposed to
be based. Individual parliamentary representation through the vote was

becoming less important than functional and group representation.

The first point to make is that there was certainly evidence at the time that a number of countries, which had been presumed to most closely approximate the pluralist model, were in fact moving in this direction. Britain and West Germany were certainly cases in point, and even Nixon had flirted with prices and incomes policy deals in the USA.[6] Indeed, given the conjunctural economic crisis which developed after 1974 – with a revolution of rising expectations, increasing international competition, declining profit levels and growth rates, rising unemployment, rapid technological change and the stagflationary impact of the oil crisis – it is hardly surprising that social democratically inclined governments should move from the relatively hands-off Keynesian demand management policies utilised before the 1970s to a more incorporationist and interventionist approach. The problem for soothsayers, however, has been that while incorporation and intervention may well have been the knee-jerk response of social democratic governments after 1974, the failure of these policies to sustain rising expectations and material living standards in the short term led to the discrediting of this approach and its replacement by a neo-liberal or New Right policy framework characterised by Thatcherism, Reaganomics and privatisation. In this policy network tripartite bargaining, incorporation and intermediation at the macro level of the state no longer have much resonance or institutional manifestation.

If this is so, one might wonder why it is that corporatism persists and appears to draw ever more eager converts to its ranks from a variety of academic disciplines. Surely the evidence shows that Schmitter and Pahl and Winkler were wrong? Neo-liberalism belies the claim that this is the century of corporatism. In order to understand why the corporatism debate still rages we need to know more about the development of ideas within a profession than the fit between conceptual theorisation and empirical reality; we also need to know something about the psychology and politics of the social science profession itself. Perhaps the best way to approach this is by way of an analogy.

Social scientists are like architects. Architects spend a considerable amount of time during their training studying past architectural theory and practice, but they rarely design buildings exactly the same as those built by architects in the past. On the contrary, modern architects have a vested interest in tearing down what was built in the past and replacing it with something new. If they did not design new buildings, they would clearly have no livelihood. This is bad enough, but architects must also justify what they are doing. So although they may often pull down buildings which were functional and desirable (terraced houses with gardens) and replace them with buildings using the latest technologies and designs (high-rise tower blocks) which are less desirable as living space, they will always rationalise the pursuit of their own pecuniary and career self-interest by declaring that such housing forms are superior in all respects to that which they have demolished. The problem is further compounded when those living in the tower blocks, or a minority of architects who are not convinced by the new technological solution to living space, raise their voices in opposition and call for a return to earlier designs. The new school of architects will reject all opposition, and in order to preserve their dysfunctional designs, blame the people living in their buildings for not conforming to what was expected of them, and resort to every more esoteric arguments and novel designs to reaffirm their commitment to the original approach which has made their name. At this point, we have two entrenched camps who talk past one another and refuse to accept the basic premises of the other side. Empirical reality – the fact that people, by and large, do not like living in high-rise flats and prefer houses with gardens – gets lost in the ensuing conflict.

It seems to me that academic debates are similar in most respects to this. For Le Corbusier and the Modern movement read Schmitter and the Coming Corporatism. The idea of corporatism, which Schmitter brilliantly and forcefully summarised in his 1974 article, was an idea which struck a chord, but not just with empirical reality. There clearly was evidence to support his and Pahl and Winkler's claims in 1974; but what enabled the corporatist movement to blossom was the state of the social science profession itself in the early and mid-1970s. Like the modern movement in architecture, corporatism came at a time when a younger generation was looking for something to make a name with. At the same time, the profession was fertile ground for a new attempt to hypothesise a novel theory of the state. Marxists were engaged in an increasingly arid, incomprehensible and internecine debate about the nature of the captalist state and the ruling class; while the majority of the political science profession was weighed down with the torpor of élitist and Marxist critiques of pluralist explanations of power. Furthermore, a debate which seemed only to be resolvable if one ventured further into the esoteric world of Marxist theory.[7] But corporatism offered a theory of the state which was not Marxist, but was clearly anti-pluralist. It was the 'middle way' by which a largely non-Marxist profession could take on and defeat the inherent pluralist bias of the profession. It offered a convenient panacea and stimulus for the profession. It offered for ready converts a brilliant future, led by their Florentine *podestà*, towards a new renaissance of social scientific explanation and insight.

Unfortunately, as I have argued elsewhere, the corporatism preferred left a great deal to be desired analytically.[8] It was the equivalent of architecture's New Brutalist high-rise, glass and concrete living-space – it was not always what it appeared to be once you ventured in to the glamorous and glossy high-tech veneer. And yet, even though Schmitter and Lehmbruch and Pahl and Winkler were by 1980 no longer as sure that they had found a new approach to the analysis of the state, the converts to the concept seem to be never ending. It would appear that there is now a second generation of believers who are prepared to resist all analytic or theoretical attacks on the sanctity of the concept by creating successive refinements of it such that the definitions now offered bear little meaningful relationship to those originally proferred by the founders of the genre; and serve to do nothing other than discredit an otherwise useful concept by exposing it to multiple theoretical specification.

Given this problem, why should anyone wish to contribute to this debate and compound the problem? It seemed to the writer that there was something useful about the concept when it first appeared in the 1970s. Indeed it proved extremely useful in helping me to order my own thoughts about the state and its various political forms, even though it was not as analytically useful in explaining state behaviour as the original theorists had first thought. However, since then, even while the early proponents have largely left the field, the disciples appear to have decided to write the new testament of corporatism. In doing so they appear to have lost sight of the conceptual and empirical reality which originally informed the writings of Schmitter, Lehmbruch and Pahl and Winkler. This new version of corporatism – referred to here as neo-corporatism – appears to have been redefined, so that it is now limited to a process of policy-making and implementation which is no longer tripartite, no longer related to the basis of political representation in the state and no longer distinct as a concept from the policy-making process normally associated with pluralist theories of state forms. In other words, neo-corporatism is neither a theory of state forms nor a novel approach to the analysis of policy processes. By applying the neo-corporatist label to bipartite negotiations between interests and government the new generation of corporatists have hopelessly confused the analytic clarity of the concept. It is to rectifying this mistake that the rest of this chapter is addressed.

Drift from a Theory of the Political form of the State to Neo-Corporatism

What seems to have happened to the corporatist concept is that it started life historically as an idealised or normative vision of how state–society relationships might be ordered politically. Historically it harks back to the idea of a hierarchical or organic structure of society associated with the political pre-eminence of the Catholic Church and the Estates and guild systems of the Middle Ages and feudalism. It was perhaps given its greatest boost during the nineteenth and twentieth century by continental European writers such as Durkheim, La Tour du Pin, Walter Rathenau, Othmar Spann and Manoilescou.[9] Writers within this tradition were opposed to the disruptive effects of industrialisation and the ideas of liberal democracy or socialism. They appear to have been concerned about the economic and political consequences of the pursuit of individual self-interest and mass democracy. They saw these as a threat to national economic self-reliance, political order and existing status and property rights. Only a corporate state – a state based on functional rather than class or individual forms of representation – could ensure order, stability and national self-reliance.

Whether or not any such political form of the state was ever created is open to question. Simply because writers lay down blueprints does not mean that any society will construct this political design. Nevertheless, as Schmitter argued in 1974, there is empirical evidence which shows, historically, that there have been states which have closely approximated the corporatist model. Schmitter named Brazil, Spain, Portugal, Greece, Austria, Italy and Germany as countries where these trends towards state licensed and controlled systems of interest representation had developed in different historical periods.[10] One might go further and include in this list Vichy France and wartime Britain as well. However, the important point to make is that when Schmitter drew our attention to this phenomenon and hypothesised that there might be trends towards a downgrading of liberal democratic and pluralist forms of political representation in advanced industrial societies, he – along with Pahl and Winkler – was making a statement about the political form of the state. This involved not only a discussion of the key actors in the process of making public policy and its implementation, but also involved a discussion of the way in which the forms of political representation were changing. This involved – according to both Schmitter and Pahl and Winkler – a downgrading of liberal, parliamentary forms of representation in favour of a tripartite incorporation of key functional groups and their relatively permanent involvement as bargaining partners with government over the direction of public policy. Ultimately it was argued that this would lead to a situation in which the social partners would assist the government in policy implementation by inter-mediating on behalf of the policy bargains arrived at with their own members. Lehmbruch also concurred with this view, concentrating as he did on trends within incomes policy formulation in western societies.[11]

It is worth stressing, however, that Schmitter's original definition of corporatism was primarily concerned with the political form of the state and was *not* concerned primarily with the process of policy-making, who benefited from this or how policy was implemented. It was a statement about how interests were represented politically rather than a statement about policy-making.[12] However, the problem for Schmitter was that this broad definition of corporatism offered no real distinction between advanced industrial and underdeveloped countries. It is at this point that we see the beginning of the shift from a description of a non-value-laden political form of the state (which can be clearly differentiated from other forms like pluralism and monism) and the drift into corporatism as a definition of policy-making. To resolve the problem of calling both formally liberal-democratic, advanced industrial and undeveloped countries, with anti-liberal regimes of an authoritarian type, corporatist Schmitter made a distinction between state and societal corporatism. State corporatism involved the state imposing corporatist forms, while the societal variant was not imposed but somehow developed voluntarily by a process of natural osmosis from liberal or pluralist democracy.

This seemed to resolve the dilemma. Unfortunately, as we shall see, this ingenious solution merely served to confuse and complicate matters. With hindsight, the main difficulty appears to have been that Schmitter and Lehmbruch did not want to accept that corporatism was anti-democratic or authoritarian if it developed as a political form of the state in the west. Implicit in their analysis was the view that when it occurred in the west, it did so voluntarily. Yet, as Cohen and Pavoncello have argued, implicit in Schmitter's definition of corporatism was a key phrase that implied that the state 'recognized or licensed (if not created)' the units of interest representation. This means that even under Schmitter's defintion of societal corporatism, the state ultimately must dominate, through its ability to grant a monopoly of representation rights to certain interests, even if it chooses to bargain rather than dictate its policy goals.[13] This is an important point to which we shall return later. For the moment, it is only necessary to recognise that this was a crucial oversight by Schmitter which invalidates the distinction between societal and state variants of the concept. The distinction was important, however, because it provided an avenue by which the concept could be sustained and developed by neo-corporatists when Schmitter's original formulation was attacked empirically and theoretically.

The main lines of attack on the corporatist concept were threefold:

the first came from Marxists who ridiculed the lack of class analysis in the concept; they were followed by empiricists who doubted that the evidence in the west supported the predictions made for the concept; and finally came the defenders of pluralist analysis who denied that what corporatists were saying was in any way novel to what pluralists had always been saying. As each of these attacks was pressed home the response of corporatists was not to go back to their original formulation, rather they shifted ground. Instead of accepting that the concept might not be as widely applicable as first thought, to save its integrity they redefined it, so that its meaning subtley shifted from being a descriptive concept about an ideal-typical political form of the state to become a catch-all phrase for special interests bargaining with the state. This is the shift to neo-corporatism which we can now trace in more detail.

Interestingly, the first major series of studies of societal (bargained or liberal) corporatism were largely confined to discussing the concept as a political form of the state.[14] Most of the critical pieces were from the Marxist perspective and correctly criticised corporatists for failing to specify whose interests were served by the development of incorporation, tripartism and intermediation.[15] Indeed the most severe criticism was meted out to Winkler by Westergaard, who displayed all the strengths and weaknesses of Marxist critique. He showed convincingly that a corporatist state must serve some interests; but then insisted that these must be the interests of capital, even though the empirical evidence reveals that it is often capital which demonstrated the greatest hostility to corporatist forms of the state.[16] Marxist critiques demonstrated quite clearly that Schmitter and Pahl and Winkler might well have theorised a form of the state, but had not gone very far in specifying how or why it should come about or whose interests it would serve. But in arguing that there was empirical evidence of the capitalist state becoming corporatist, even the Marxists seemed to confirm that a new political form was developing as Schmitter was predicting. It was left to the empiricist critique to pose a more fundamental question for this perspective.

Even in the first edited volume by Lehmbruch and Schmitter, two articles had appeared explaining that Japan and the USA were not corporatist, and that there was little chance of them becoming so in the future, whatever the predictions by corporatists.[17] Soon afterwards, a whole series of articles appeared explaining why it was that the corporatist label could not be applied to Britain, France, Italy and Switzerland. Others even went so far as to imply that apart from aberrant cases like Austria, it was highly unlikely that corporatist structures could be sustained within advanced capitalist societies with international markets and liberal democratic state forms.[18] There was no effective reply to this empirical critique. Indeed, Lehmbruch and Schmitter recognised these criticisms of their hypothesised state form by publishing many of them in their 1982 edited collection.[19] But given the time and effort put in to the concept, it was not surprising that they and, in particular, their disciples, should seek to defend the concept. It was at this point that we begin to see explicitly the shift from a concept dealing at the macro level with a particular form of the state and its slippage into a concept concerned with a process of policy-making. Lehmbruch himself signposted this shift in 1982 when he recognised implicitly that the concept may have been overly ambitious and that, on reflection, one should look for it only in particular policy areas or at particular levels (meso, micro) of state policy-making.[20] Schmitter concurred with this when he began to differentiate between corporatism 1 (a political form of the state) and corporatism 2 (a distinctive mode for making and implementing public policy).[21]

But if this resolved the problem of having to recognise that the concept did not have such predictive utility at the macro level of the state, it achieved this only by making the concept totally confused and, one may argue, of little analytic difference to the pluralist paradigm which it was supposed to challenge. As soon as Lehmbruch and Schimitter started to use the concept to refer to a distinctive mode of policy-making and implementation, they laid themselves open to the charges levelled at them by the third wave of critics – the defenders of pluralism. This attack was led by Heisler and further developed by Almond, Martin and Jordan.[22] While we cannot do full justice to their individual critiques here, we can at least pin point the major charges they have levelled at neo-corporatists – i.e. those who define corporatism in terms of a distinctive mode of policy-making and implementation.

The first point to make is that if corporatism is to be taken as an ideal typical form of the state to be used as a heuristic device for comparison of regime types at the macro level, there is no disagreement over this. The real debate arises over whether or not neo-corporatists are telling us anything new about the way policy is made and implemented in advanced industrial societies at the meso and micro levels. The crux of the matter seems to be with Schmitter's claims that the corporatist paradigm has highlighted significant insights in to policy-making that pluralist theory did not and could not achieve. The main claims of Schmitter and his primary defenders – Crouch, Cawson and Grant – are that neo-corporatism has revealed that monopolies of interest representation exist; that hierarchies develop in associations; membership of associations is not always voluntary; interest associations shape members' views and coerce and discipline them; the state is not just a neutral referee or arena of group conflicts; and interest associations intermediate and become incorporated and deliver the compliance of their members to government policy goals by delegated self-enforcement[23]

There is no disagreement that the empirical evidence presented to substantiate these claims is valid, the crux of the issue is whether or not one requires the concept of neo-corporatism to explain this phenomenon. Heisler, Almond, Martin and Jordan doubt that the concept is necessary or that it is saying anything which is superior to the long-held pluralist paradigm in the profession. It would appear from a review of the literature that they may well have a case. The bedrock of their critique is that neo-corporatists can only argue that their concept is superior to pluralism by first defining pluralist theory incorrectly, and then ignoring the empirical details that pluralists have historically unearthed in their research. Jordan argues that pluralist theory has had two traditions: one which emphasised open competition between groups with a relatively neutral state; and one which emphasised closed group–departmental relationships and sectorised policy-making. The latter he (along with Heisler and Rokkan) refers to as corporate pluralism and argues that it encompasses all that the neo-corporatists claim is new in their analysis.[24] Indeed he goes further and provides evidence to demonstrate that Herring (1936), Truman (1951) and Dahl (1956) – the arch enemies of the neo-corporatists – were in fact sensitive to most of the insights neo-corporatists are claiming for their concept.[25] Although Jordan accepts that pluralist writers did not always emphasise sufficiently the degree of regularised and structured participation in policy-making, nevertheless he also shows that writers like Beer, Rokkan, McConnell and Lowi (and one might add Lindblom) had begun to take cognizance of this pheno-menon.[26] In other words, the neo-corporatists are in danger of re-inventing the wheel so far as analysing policy-making is concerned.

But there is a further criticism one may make of this approach, and it relates to the original conception of corporatism and its relationship with pluralist theory. It is important to stress that the original novelty of the concept lay not so much in its demonstration of closed policy networks, but rather in its conceptualisation of a tripartite state form based on incorporation and intermediation. Such a state form, if it did exist, would be very different from the pluralist political form. It would be different because the whole nature of political representation, policy-making and implementation would have changed. It would be a consis-tently élitist system of political rule in which voluntary participation would be precluded. This is implicit *and* explicit in Schmitter's original formulation of the state licensing and/or creating representational monopolies (even if he himself failed to grasp the point). In this sense, there is a logical inconsistency in Schmitter's claim that there is a societal variant of corporatism. If the state decides who should have a monopoly of representational influence, how does an interest not participate and hope to achieve its intended effects? If refusing to participate is of no consequence to the achievement of a group's goals, why participate in the first place and discipline your own members? Clearly this is illogical. What was novel about Schmitter's original formulation was the very fact that there would be no pluralist freedom to associate or participate voluntarily if corporatism came to pass. Indeed, as Pahl and Winkler (two writers strangely ignored by neo-corporatists) showed with surgical logicality, a corporatist state would involve the key functional groups negotiating on any and all major policy problems within a tripartist structure of incorporation stretching down from macro, through meso to micro levels of policy-making. The point, which critics have been quick to point out, is that such a political form of the state, in societies based on capitalist market relationships and with a history of liberal-democratic freedoms, is inherently contradictory and difficult to sustain.

Nevertheless, one cannot deny that interest groups and governments do have a vested interest in using tripartite or closed policy networks in specific policy areas. Indeed, as pluralist and neo-corporatist research reveals, governments and interest groups regularly do close access; and economically and socially powerful interests do seem to have more political clout than the poor. However, the point here is that even if we did discover – as Lehmbruch implied might be the case – that in incomes policy there was a drift to tripartite policy deals and intermediation across all countries, this would still not justify us in using a new concept to characterise the political form of the state.[27] What we would have is an example of a particular method of policy-making in one particular issue area. It would be corporatist in style but the political form of the state would still be pluralist.

This would be so because pluralist theory is not as neo-corporatists seem to believe predicated on there being open access, equal participation and a neutral state in each particular policy area; rather it is a theory based on the notion that there is a lack of similarity of interests and styles shaping policies across the whole range of public policy-making. In other words, we might find policy areas with corporatist, licenced and closed structures, but the political system would still be characterised as pluralist so long as the majority of policy areas were not shaped by similar interests. The indeed was the original basis for Dahl's pluralist formulation as he responded to the charge that local decisions were always dominated by an élite. To show that there are special interests shaping policy in housing, welfare, defence and agriculture is not a refutation of the pluralist framework. To refute the pluralist framework one would have to demonstrate that the vast majority of policies made by the state were shaped by the same interests most or all of the time. This is clearly something that Marxists understand, even though they have grave difficulties in demonstrating their theories in practice at the policy level. It was also implicit in what Schmitter implied in his original formulation of corporatism; and it was certainly explicit in Pahl and Winkler's definition. Corporatism as originally defined would have been a complete refutation of a pluralist state form. Unfortunately the fact that some countries may have corporatist-style deals over incomes policies can be evidence of a trend to a corporatist style of policy-making; but it is not on its own a refutation of the pluralist theory of the state.

But the problem goes further than this. Recently there has been a spate of publications from the disciples of neo-corporatism which demonstrates that the concept is now being redefined once more. The gist of this reorientation is the desire to move away from the discredited macro level of analysis, which is no longer a fertile ground for corporatist theorising, for the reasons set out above. Clearly, Lehmbruch and Schmitter precipitated this shift of emphasis, which was signposted in 1982.[28] But what seems to have happened, if one now reads Cawson and Grant,[29] is that the drift from macro to meso and micro levels has also resulted in a significant redefinition of the concept. The most significant change is that these writers no longer use the concept to refer to tripartism – arguably one of the most interesting ideas behind the original theory. On the contrary, for Cawson and Grant – and indeed for Crouch[30] – neo-corporatism is said to exist whenever the state is involved in bargaining with any single special interests and uses this interest to discipline its own membership.

This idea of bipartite deals between government and interest groups is interesting; but it would appear we are now a long way from the corporatist state that Schmitter and Winkler were talking about in 1974. Indeed, for Cawson, corporatism exists if the government gives a special contract to a firm and lets it implement it! On reading this, one can be excused for throwing one's hands up in horror. When a colleague is forced to redefine large firms as interest groups, in order to accommodate their bipartite deals with government within the corporatist schema, then one knows that there is something radically wrong with that concept.[31] Interestingly enough – and one can at least applaud them

for this), Schmitter and Streeck, who have been studying the relationship between government and business associations, seem to have seen
the light and refer to these bipartite and special interest relationships as
private interest government, not neo-corporatism.[32] Perhaps the
disciples should follow their leader more closely?

One is not making cheap points here. The research that Schmitter,
Streeck, Crouch, Cawson and Grant have been engaged in is extremely
important. We do need to know more about the detailed relationships
between the government and special interests. Furthermore, the study
of business associations and firms has been significantly underdeveloped
within political and social science. The point that has to be made,
however, is that there is no logical reason why we need the neo-
corporatist label to define this behaviour. This type of issue was already
well developed within pluralist research in the 1960s and early 1970s.
The work of Rokkan is a case in point, but there was already a considerable body of literature on the public use of the private sector and
quangos as well.[33] What this literature demonstrates conclusively is that
bilateral deals with special interests is not new. One might argue that it
has been going on as long as there have been governments and interests.
Indeed the formation of the East India and the Hudson Bay Companies
in the Mercantilist era demonstates the historic ability of governments
to achieve foreign and economic policy goals, without direct government participation, through the granting of monopoly trading rights.[34] It
is probable that historians could provide copious examples of this type
of behaviour throughout the ages. There seems no logical reason to use
the concept of neo-corporatism to refer to this behaviour since,
ironically enough, such a relationship between the state and societal
interests might well be wholly compatible with a pluralist form of the
state; but it is *not at all* compatible with the corporatist state form
originally developed by nineteenth- and twentieth-century theorists –
including Schmitter, Pahl and Winkler.

The Corporate State: Towards a Conceptually and Analytically Useful Definition

The task facing us, then, is not that which Schmitter set himself in 1974.
He saw his task as saving corporatism from its association with fascism
and rendering it into a useful concept for social scientific research. Our
task is to save the concept from the neo-corporatists in order that it can
become a usable concept again. But in so doing we do not want to make
the same error that Schmitter fell into namely seeking to develop a

theoretical definition which could replace pluralism. On the contrary, the only useful way in which corporatism can be saved is if we recognise that it is a concept which is not in competition with pluralism in so far as explanation is concerned.

This is so because pluralism as a concept is not an *explanation* of anything; on the contrary, pluralism is a *description* of a political form of the state in which the question of which interests dominate is an open empirical question. Since policy-making under a pluralist state form is, by definition, open and competitive, one cannot say who, or which, interests will dominate in advance of research. All one can say is that in a pluralist system we can expect there to be no continuous and pervasive influence by any single or combined interests over time across all, or significant majority of policy areas. If we did find such a development, we would then not have a pluralist form of the state, but something else which we would have to describe by using another concept, like for instance corporatism or monism. In this light, pluralism and corporatism are not competing explanatory perspectives, but alternative concepts for describing real differences in the political form of the state in terms of the scope, range and openness of political representation and participation. To find tripartite or bipartite forms of policy-making and implementation, with groups or firms discipling their members, in specific one-off policy areas does not warrant the utilisation of a new political concept as neo-corporatists contend.

How, then, are we to define and use the concept of corporatism? It is not the case as some of the arch-opponents of corporatism seem to imply that we do not need the concept at all. Clearly the concept would not have aroused so much professional interest if it had not resonated with reality in some way. It can be argued that the two key factors which the early theorists touched on were the moves towards tripartism, incorporation and intermediation at the macro level of the state in advanced industrial economies in the early 1970s and the fact that many in the profession were unhappy with the hegemony of an undifferentiated pluralist description of advanced industrial societies. One can go further and argue that if the tendencies or experiments introduced at that time in Britain, Germany and elsewhere, had been sustained and institutionalised, then Pahl, Winkler, Schmitter and Lehmbruch would have been correct – this would have been the century of corporatism in many advanced industrial societies. As we have seen, this was not the case.

But having said that, it is not the case – and European social scientists like Rokkan and Heisler, in particular, have stressed this for years – that the simple competitive pluralist model is a useful description of political representation and participation in the policy process of countries like Austria, Sweden, Norway, Denmark or the Netherlands. This is why they have used the concept 'corporate pluralism' to refer to the *tendency* to closed and sectorised policy-making in these countries, which they see as a distinct from pluralism. On the other hand, these theorists reject the concept of corporatism because their empirical research demonstates that, if we take Schmitter's original definition of state licensing and monopoly of representation at the macro level, only Austria comes anywhere close to this model. Thus while some countries are, or have been, closest to the corporatist ideal type – i.e. Austria, Portugal, Brazil and Franco's Spain – others may have some of the characteristics, but not all of them – i.e. Sweden, Norway, Denmark, West Germany and the Netherlands. However, some countries may have little existing resemblance to a corporatist political form – i.e. the USA, France, Britain and Italy – but in the past may well have experimented with such forms.[35]

What stands out from this discussion are two important conclusions. First, it is nonsensical to attempt to define the political form of states in all countries of a particular economic stage of development under one heading as pluralists and corporatists have done. The empirical evidence indicates that advanced industrial countries have, for example, very different political forms – for instance, compare South Africa with Britain and Austria. Furthermore, the empirical evidence demonstrates that the political form of the state can change at different historical periods and under changing socio-economic circumstances in particular countries. Secondly, if corporatism as a political form can be applied to countries as distinct as Mussolini's Italy, Salazar's Portugal, wartime Britain and present-day Austria, then clearly there is a need to differentiate political forms of the state not just in terms of the institutionalised structures of interest representation and participation, but also in terms of the interests who benefit from those types of political form. However, the point here is that the creation of a particular form of the state does not tell us directly who will benefit from its institutionalisation. Thus the creation of a corporatist form of the state tells us nothing about whose interests are served; it is an empirical question, just as it is under a pluralist form of the state.

Where does this leave us? First, we are arguing that there should be no real disagreement about what a corporatist political form of the state looks like. Indeed we can happily use Schmitter's original definition which implies the state bargaining with, licensing and/or creating monopoly representatives of functional interests at the level of the state. Such a state form would be very different from a pluralist state form which has no monopoly representatives and open competitive bargaining over policy outcomes. The problem, however, is that if the pluralist model avoids controversy because it does not, by definition, have to specify whose interests are served by this state form – it is an empirical question – corporatism suffers because theorists have in the past, as Schmitter demonstrated, associated it with fascism. This led Schmitter to make a distinction between societal and state corporatism in order to save the concept for present-day use. This was a major mistake because in so doing he created, as we have seen, the confusion which led to neo-corporatism. But it led to perhaps an even greater problem: it created a false and misleading dichotomy.

If one follows closely the logic of the distinction between state and societal corporatism, one appears to have arrived at a useful distinction which accords with empirical reality. Historically some states did have corporatist-style political forms which were used by backward-looking, conservative and anti-democratic leaders to resist the advance of liberalism, capitalism, socialism and democracy. On the other hand, if corporatism is developing in the advanced industrial economies, then it must be through the relatively free acquiescence of formally free interests in a liberal-democratic society. But if one dwells on this for a moment, one sees that Schmitter has made a serious blunder, in that his definition of corporatism as an ideal type implies that the state licenses and controls the monopoly functional groups. If it were not the dominant partner, then the key groups in society would be under no compulsion to discipline their members or to take part in corporatist compromises and bargains.[36] Thus on closer inspection of corporatism, we discover that in fact the state must dominate the relationship, by definition, and that Schmitter's distinction between societal and state corporatism is invalid and a *non sequitur*.

Having said this, we run immediately into a further problem and one which Marxist critics have always highlighted. If it is the case that under corporatism the state always dominates, then in whose interests does the state act? This was the problem with which Schmitter was trying to grapple and which led him to make his false distinction between state and societal types of corporatism. Neither of these types, it can be seen, tells us anything directly about whose interests the policies of the corporate state serve. State corporatism is about imposition by the state – a tautology on reflection. Societal corporatism is about societal interests agreeing to the state imposing decisions – which is hardly distinct from pluralism. Unfortunately, if Marxist theorists have pinpointed this weakness in the analysis, they have not gone very far in resolving it. This arises because, being Marxists, they have to explain any and all changes in the form of the state in terms of the needs and requirements of capitalism.

Thus Westergaard, Panitch and Jessop, who first pinpointed this weakness, fail to provide an empirically valid analysis of whose interests are served by the development of the corporatist state, even when the form is institutionalised within capitalist societies.[37] The problem for Marxists is that they want to argue that the empirical development of corporatist forms is in some way congruent with the development of oligopoly and concentration within postwar capitalism. The problem with this perspective is clear, once we begin to view corporatism as an ideal-typical political form which has no particular congruence with any historical period or economic system. The corporatist form has been institutionalised and experimented with in advanced capitalist and backward economies in many different historical periods, thus it is almost impossible to argue logically that it must somehow be associated with the needs of advanced capitalism. Indeed it may well be that the most potent and persistent corporatist forms persist in backward economies – for example. Salazar's Portugal.

The fact of the matter must surely be that Marxist analysis of corporatist forms have already decided on the causal factors behind the development of the phenomenon before they undertake empirical research. Because the base ultimately determines the superstructure, then corporatism must be the best shell for capitalism. Through a priori reasoning the state must serve the interests of the dominant fraction of capital and, *ipso facto*, corporatism must be the best shell for capitalism to sustain itself. Unfortunately the empirical evidence of corporatist political forms in advanced industrial economies seems to repudiate this simplistic logic. All too often, it has been the leading sectors of capitalism – the banks and financial institutions, large oligopoly multinationals, as well as small and medium-sized businessmen – who have opposed corporatist developments. Indeed private and profitable industry has been in the vanguard of attempts to roll back the state and outlaw incorporation, tripartism and intermediation.[38] Of course, Marxists can always argue that this is only because capitalists do no understand their own best interests, but as Mandy Rice Davies once said so perceptively, 'they would wouldn't they'. When the evidence does not fit the theory, we can always argue that the evidence is wrong and that empiricism is a pseudo-science.[39]

If we want to save corporatism as a useful concept for analysis, it would appear that we ought not therefore to rely too heavily on Marxist specifications of whose interests are served by the state under corporatist forms. Having said this, however, this does not mean that corporatist forms are never used by the representatives of business to favour their interests. Whether or not corporatist forms are biased towards business or labour, or any other interest for that matter, is an empirical question. It is therefore not something that can be determined in advance of research as Schmitter and the Marxists have assumed, rather, like pluralism, corporatism only can be seen as an empty shell into which anything can be poured, depending upon the balance of political forces shaping the policies of the state. Therefore, it may be possible to conceptualise a social democratic form of corporatism, in which the political deals undertaken mitigate the worst aspects of the pursuit of individual and group self-interest while, at the same time, defending private property rights and inequality in social and economic allocation. On the other hand, one could also conceptualise a corporatist form which favoured a sector of the economy, say, agriculture and landowners, at the expense of the majority, by incorporating and buying off the representatives of the people. The political form would still be the same (corporatist) but the social and economic consequences would be different – indicating that the state serves different interests under the same political form.

This is a crucial point, and one which is important in our understanding of all political forms of the state, including pluralism. To define a political system as corporatist or pluralist is actually to say nothing specifically about those interests who will benefit from this state form. For pluralist forms, this is fairly easy to understand because the concept implies that no one interest dominates the state. But the point is also crucial for the analysis of a corporatist or monist political system. To use either designation tells us nothing about who gets what, or how or when, from this political form. It is merely a description of the form of the state. Who benefits is always an empirical question. This is a point that Aristotle understood only too well in his own description of political forms. For Aristotle, the three classic forms of the state were monarchy, aristocracy and democracy; but each had its perversion, tyranny, oligarchy and ideology. Furthermore, Aristotle was sensitive to the fact that within each type of state there were variants of the basic type. Thus he describes four variants of democracy.[40] The point to draw from this is clear. First, the form of the state does not tell us how the state will be used, and secondly, we need to develop a more sophisticated typology of state forms to take account of both the institutionalised forms that states take and the uses to which these forms are put and by whom.

What are the lessons, then, for corporatism as a concept? First, we need to define corporatism as an ideal type. Having achieved this, we need then to discover if there are any actual countries in which this ideal type has been approximated historically; and then having achieved this, we need to ask the fundamental questions about who benefits from this political form and whether this characteristic form of the state has a tendency to serve any interests at the expense of others. If this is the case, we may conclude that corporatism as a concept does also tell us about who benefits. On the other hand, it may well be the case that we discover that the corporatist form has different outcomes at different times and in different countries. Therefore, we cannot see corporatism as a single type, but rather we have to begin to create a more sophisticated differentiation of types of corporatism. Whatever shape this takes, it is likely that it would be very different from the stark choice of state and societal variants.

But the lessons for theory-building and concept specification do not end here. For what is true of corporatism is also true of pluralism as a concept. If pluralism is nothing more than a description of a particular form of the state which meshes individual with functional forms of representation in open competition, what we need to know is whether the pluralist form has a totally random consequence in terms of policy outcomes, or whether in certain times and in particular countries some interests dominate more than others. This is of course additional to discovering whether or not any country does in fact at all approximate to the pluralist form in the real world. Indeed one could argue that the reawakening of interest in corporatism has served one extremely important function: it has reawakened interest among pluralists, like Lindblom and Dahl, in specifying more closely what a pluralist state form might look like and who benefits from it.[41]

While this work is only just beginning, one might suspect that Lindblom's realisation that business may benefit more than other interests under pluralist state forms in capitalist societies is a major advance towards a more sophisticated analysis of the consequences of pluralist systems and a more complex typology of this form of the state. Having said this, however, the most pressing task for the future must surely not be in debating the vagaries of corporatism and neo-corporatism, but in agreeing on what we mean by ideal-typical state forms and trying to discover if they exist in the real world and what the consequence of their implementation may be. Only by doing this can we move on to the even more urgent task of developing a typology of political forms of the state that is differentiated descriptively and analytically. Simply reworking the same old debates between pluralists and corporatists will not allow us to move on to a world where social scientists can specify more concretely the institutional forms and policy outcomes of particular state forms. After all corporatism is only one state form and we do not even know yet the range of possible outcomes that this form alone can sustain.

Notes

1. In particular, see the work of Alan Cawson, *Corporatism and Political Theory* (Oxford, Blackwell, 1986); Alan Cawson (ed.), *Organised Interests and the State: Studies in Meso-Corporatism* (London, Sage, 1985); C. Crouch, 'Pluralism and the new corporatism; a rejoinder', *Political Studies 31,* **3** (1983), 452–60; Wyn Grant (ed.), *The Political Economy of Corporatism* (London, Macmillan, 1985).
2. This interpretation is outlined rather simplistically in Otto Newman, *The Challenge of Corporatism* (London, Macmillan, 1981), pp. 3–39, and in more detail in Peter J. Williamson, *Varieties of Corporatism* (Cambridge, Cambridge University Press, 1985), pp. 19–80. P. C. Schmitter, 'Still the century of corporatism', *Review of Politics*, 36 (1974), 85–131, also provides a brief historical overview.
3. Schmitter, *op. cit.*, 85–8.
4. On this see: C. E. Lindblom, 'Another state of mind', *American Political Science Review*, 76 (1982), 9–21; J. Manley, 'Neo-pluralism: a class analysis of pluralism 1 and 2', *American Political Science Review*, 77 (1983), 368–83; and the replies by Lindblom, p. 384; and Dahl pp. 386–9.
5. The main papers were: Gerhard Lehmbruch, 'Consociational democracy, class conflict and the new corporatism', *IPSA Round Table on Political Integration, 9–13 September 1974*; P. C. Schmitter, 'Still the century of corporatism', *op. cit.*; and Ray Pahl and Jack Winkler, 'The coming corporatism', *New Society*, (10 October 1974).
6. On Nixon, see: D. R. Fusfeld, 'The rise of the corporate state in America', *Journal of Economic Issues*, 6 (March 1972), p. 1–20.
7. On the debate about power, see: Steven Lukes, *Power: A Radical View* (London, Macmillan, 1974); and Andrew Cox *et al.*, *Power in Capitalist Society* (Brighton, Wheatsheaf, 1985). On the Marxist debate the best introductions are: Bob Jessop, *The Capitalist State* (Oxford, Martin Robertson, 1982), and Martin Carnoy, *The State and Political Theory* (Princeton, NJ, Princeton University Press, 1984).
8. Andrew Cox, 'Corporatism as reductionism: the analytic limits of the corporatist thesis', *Government and Opposition*, 16 (1980), 78–95.
9. For details, see Williamson, *op. cit.*, pp. 16–74.
10. See Philippe C. Schmitter and Gerhard Lehmbruch, *Trends towards Corporatist Intermediation* (London, Sage, 1979), p. 38.
11. See *ibid.*, pp. 28–30, 302–3; and Pahl and Winkler, *op. cit.* 72–6. The influence of Andrew Shonfield is particularly marked in these passages.
12. Schmitter and Lehmbruch, *Trends towards Corporatist Intermediation*, *op. cit.*, p. 13.
13. Youssef Cohen and Franco Pavoncello, 'Corporatism and pluralism: a critique of Schmitter's typology', *British Journal of Political Studies* (January 1987), 117–22.
14. Schmitter and Lehmbruch, *Trends towards Corporatist Intermediation*, *op. cit.*, *passim.*
15. See the articles by Leo Panitch, 'The development of corporatism in liberal democracies', and Bob Jessop, 'Corporatism, parliamentarianism and social democracy', in Schmitter and Lehmbruch, *Trends towards corporatist intermediation*, *ibid.*, pp. 119–46, 185–212.
16. See J. Westergaard, 'Class, inequality and corporatism' in A,. Hunt (ed.), *Class and class Structure* (London, Lawrence and Wishart, 1977), and the implied criticism of this perspective in Cox, *op. cit.*
17. See articles by Salisbury, Pempel and Tsunekawa in Schmitter and Lehmbruch, *Trends towards Corporatist Intermediation*, *op. cit.*, pp. 213–70.
18. See Cox, *op. cit.*; Andrew Cox and Jack Hayward, 'The inapplicability of the

corporatist model in Britain and France: the case of labour', *International Political Science Review*, 4 (2) (1983), 217–40; and also see Arthur, F. P. Wassenberg, 'Neo-corporatism and the quest for control: the cuckoo game', Marino Regini, 'Changing relationships between labour and the state in Italy', Hanspeter Kreisi, 'The structure of the Swiss political system' and Graham K. Wilson, 'Why is there no corporatism in the United States?' in Gerhard Lemhbruch and Philippe C. Schmitter (eds), *Patterns of Corporatist Policy-Making* (London, Sage, 1982).

19. *Ibid.*
20. Gerhard Lehmbruch, 'Introduction: neo-corporatism in comparative perspective' in Lehmbruch and Schmitter, *op. cit.*, pp. 26–7.
21. Philippe C., Schmitter, 'Reflections on where the theory of neo-corporatism has gone and where the praxis of neo-corporatism may be going' in Lehmbruch and Schmitter, *ibid.*, pp. 262–4.
22. M. Heisler, 'Corporate pluralism revisited; where is the theory?', *Scandinavian Political Studies*, 2 (1979) 278–98; G. A. Jordan, 'Iron triangles, woolly corporatism and elastic nets', *Journal of Public Policy*, 1 (1981) 95–123; G. A. Jordan, 'Pluralistic corporatism and corporate pluralism', *Scandinavian Political Studies*, 7 (1984) 148–53; Rose Martin, 'Pluralism and the new corporatism', *Political Studies*, 31 (1983), 86–102; G. A. Almond, 'Corporatism, pluralism and professional memory', *World Politics*, 35 (1983), pp. 245–60.
23. In particular, see Schmitter, 'Reflections on where the theory of neo-corporatism . . .', *op. cit.* 260–1.
24. Jordan 'Pluralistic corporatism . . .', *op. cit.*, p. 137; and Stein Rokkan, 'Numerical democracy and corporate pluralism' in Robert A. Dahl (ed.), *Political Oppositions in Western Democracies* (New Haven, Conn., Yale University Press, 1966), chapter 4.
25. *Ibid.*, pp. 142–3.
26. *Ibid.*, p. 147; and Lindblom, 'Another state of mind', *op. cit.*, 384.
27. Lehmbruch, 'Concluding remarks', in Schmitter and Lehmbruch, *Trends towards Corporatist Intermediation*, *op. cit.*', 299–308.
28. Schmitter and Lehmbruch, *Patterns of Corporatist Policy-Making*, *op. cit.*, pp.   1–28, 259–80.
29. Alan Cawson and Wyn Grant as outlined in n.1, above.
30. See Crouch, *op. cit.*, 459–60.
31. Cawson, *Corporatism and Political Theory*, *op. cit.*, pp. 80–2.
32. Wolfgan Streeck and Philippe C. Schmitter (eds), *Private Interest Government: Beyond Market and State* (London, Sage, 1985), introduction and chapter 1.
33. On this see: D. C. Hague and B. L. R. Smith (eds), *The Dilemma of Accountability in Modern Government* (London, Macmillan, 1971); Anthony Barker, D. C. Hague and W. J. M. Mackenzie, *Public Policy and Private Interests: The Institutions of Compromise* (London, Macmillan, 1974); and B. L. R. Smith (ed.), *The New Political Economy: The Public Use of the Private Sector* (London, Macmillan, 1985).
34. On the history of these companies, see: Philip W. Buck, *The Politics of Mercantilism* (New York, Henry Holt, 1942).
35. Here one is thinking, in particular, of New Deal America, the period of the First and Second World Wars in Britain, Vichy France and Mussolini's Italy in comparison with present-day state-society relationships.
36. Cohen and Pavoncello, *op. cit.*, make this telling point, 107–22.
37. For this approach, see the articles by Westergaard, Jessop and Panitch, in nn 15 and 16, above.
38. This is the thrust of the argument in Cox, 'Corporatism as reductionism . . .', *op. cit.* But see also the majority of the contributions in the pamphlet: *The Corporate State: Reality or Myth?* (London, Centre for Policy Studies, 1977).
39. This is the approach adopted in D. Willer and J. Willer, *Systematic Empiricism: A Critique of a Pseudo-Science* (Englewood Cliffs, NJ, Prentice-Hall, 1973).
40. Aristotle, *The Politics* (Harmondsworth, Penguin, rev. edn 1983), *passim*.
41. On this see the articles cited in n.4, above.

3 Corporatism and accountability
Patrick Birkinshaw

Introduction

This chapter is written essentially from my position as a public lawyer. A public lawyer's concerns are with the relationship between government and its administration and law, and in establishing or reinforcing appropriate methods of control and accountability. Until recently, most public lawyers set courts at the centre of their enquiry – with predictably barren results in a British constitutional framework – and constitutional conventions, such as *ministerial responsibility*, and their judicial recognition, though not actual operation. There was little attempt to theorise, by lawyers at least, the nature of the state and the public domain in spite of Maitland's heroic efforts.[1] Beyond noting that the state might be larger than the government of the day, except in matters of national security, judicial and legal analysis was content to define the state in terms of 'the organs of government of a national community',[2] the 'organised community',[3] 'the whole organisation of the body politic for supreme civil rule and government'[4] or 'the general community'.[5] Such bland analyses as these were content to posit two distinct realms: the public realm and the private realm. The former was accountable through political channels and processes and by the common law, especially its development of judicial review. The latter saw accountability imposed by the law as it had developed to regulate relationships between private individuals or corporations, and by the efficiency of the market-place. The reality behind the exercise of public power was such that it defied the conventional legal and political processes to achieve accountability in any meaningful sense.[6]

A small but growing band of public lawyers has seen in the work of political scientists and sociologists on the concepts of corporatism and pluralism useful analytical models to theorise about, to identify and explain 'executive power to-day'.[7] That phrase includes, first of all, the expansive use by government, its agencies and partners, as well as local government, of its powers of *dominium* – its proprietorial powers associated with its control of the Exchequer or finance and its contracts, grants or incentives or tax concessions, or the granting of licences or monopolies – and which are to be distinguished from its powers of *imperium*.[8] The latter embodies the traditional power of a government to command and enforce its wish. Secondly, the phrase evokes the reality of the extended state; government by other means through the use of non-departmental bodies, quagos and quangos, and the cosy informal embrace through such bodies and elsewhere between organised interests and officialdom so characteristic of the British way of doing things. 'Executive power today' is the target of what follows as well as the accountability of government and its performance of public tasks through private parts.[9] In our study the role of the courts will not feature in the foreground – though where they can assist will be identified. The Court of Appeal in England, for instance, has recently ruled that the City Panel on Takeovers and Mergers – in legal appearance a private non-statutory body – was in fact a public body, an *alter ego* of the Department of Trade and Industry.[10] 'I should be very disappointed if the courts could not recognise the realities of executive power and allowed their vision to be clouded by the subtlety and sometimes complexity of the way in which it can be exerted';[11] there had, said Lord Justice Lloyd, been an 'implied devolution of power' to the Panel by government: 'Power exercised behind the schemes is power none the less.'[12]

Corporatism

I am well aware of the debate that rages around the concept of corporatism and the varieties in which it is said to exist, and whether it is simply pluralism in another guise. The introductory chapters, written by my two colleagues, illustrate the range and intensity of the debate. Writers have urged us not to make too much mileage out of a concept which has been used as a description of an economic system, a state form and a process of intermediation; other chapters in this book address these points.

If I can take Schmitter's famous definition as a starting-point, I will draw out some pertinent comments for the purposes of this essay:

> Corporatism can be defined as a system of interest representation in which the constituent units are organised into a limited number of singular, compulsory, uncompetitive, hierarchically ordered and functionally differentiated categories, recognised or licensed (if not created) by the State and granted a deliberate representational monopoly within their respective categories in exchange for observing certain controls on their selection of leaders and articulation of demands and supports. The organised interests of civil society are linked with the 'decisional structures' of the State.[13]

Schmitter realises that this definition is an ideal type – with all the associated advantages and disadvantages of that method of inter- pretation of social phenomena. In its ideal or most fully developed form this is what it would look like. However, it is a little simplistic to assert that corporatism is either something you have or do not have – that at one moment it exists and that at another it does not. It is a question of fact and degree involving in relationships between the state and organised interests degrees of relatively exclusive access to state agen- cies and favour; delegation of power to organised interests (OIs) to organise their own affairs either *de facto* or *de lege*; the bartering of outcome by OIs on behalf of their members or interests with govern- ment and the delivery of governmentally approved programmes or policies; the power to formulate their own policies and 'laws' as a surrogate of the state. In other words, where the OI has moved, or is moving, from being a mere suppliant to a surrogate.

The thrust of so much writing in political science on corporatism and pluralism has been to the effect that not only are the claims of the protagonists exaggerated, but that the drawing of clearly defined boun- daries between the two is no easy matter. The view has been canvassed that pluralism and corporatism may represent extreme poles on a con- tinuum.[14] 'The corporatist pole would signify that groups have attained to a regularised and substantial share in formulating and administering Government policy,'[15] while the state for its part has assumed an active role in maintaining particular bargaining systems.[16] This was opposed to a parliamentary pole where parliamentary links provided the optimum level of contact between elected representatives and organised interests. More recent recognition has been afforded to 'arbiter' and 'arena' forms of pluralism where there is respectively a distanced state or the state as an equal partner formulating the rules of conduct with a plurality of other interests.[17]

At the risk of oversimplification, my concern is with the organisation of power. The organisation and exercise (or non-exercise) of power which has an impact upon the public welfare from an economic or social perspective covers the breadth of my enquiry. The organisation and exercise of power inevitably involve problems of accountability. Accountability invariably presupposes a reliance upon openness to ensure that accountability is real, and not a mere shadow of an idea. In conglomerations of power groupings along the pluralist–corporatist axis, accountability is always a problem where there are varying levels of closure, power brokerage, preferential treatment and access to influence which will help to give definition to the public interest or promote a version of the public interest on the state's behalf, whether such a practice or promotion is articulated or left unarticulated. The more one moves along the axis to the corporatist pole, the more closed and exclusive the relationships become; in other words, the more potential scope there is for subversion of constitutional and legal safeguards. Accountability, however, is an issue which precedes corporatism.

Accountability

Accountability is tied in with legitimation of power as well as efficiency and effectiveness. Legitimation has a substantive quality: the perception that people are receiving the slice of the cake that they are entitled to or they are being accorded due concern and respect in the making of decisions affecting their lives or livelihoods; and also a procedural quality: individuals are allowed to participate in or to make their contribution to such decisions either directly or via representatives. In a loose sense, these are democratic ideals of a legal order caught by a universal franchise where political agents operate within the rule of law and/or according to constitutional guarantees of fair play and balanced government.

It is widely argued that corporatist arrangements of whatever degree avoid an appropriate level of legal accountability – if we take 'legal' here in a narrow sense to mean that which operates through an autonomous legal system and autonomous courts of law applying an individualistic rule-based form of law. Although the Takeover Panel case, referred to above, has shown an awareness of the compenetration of state and society and the willingness of the courts to use public law tests to review the actions of ostensibly private law bodies where such bodies are a cipher for state institutions, the basis of *potential* relief in the case, which incidentally the applicants for relief lost, was unusually circumscribed.[18] It might be possible to argue that the particular facts of the case and the volatile nature of the situations which the Panel has referred to it made appropriate only a limited form of relief. However, the test which the Court of Appeal applied to establish whether the Panel was a public body, *de facto* and therefore *de lege*, and not a private one, is very particularistic and will have to be repeated every time a quasi-governmental agency or body is challenged over its exercise of power for the first time. In all events, the British courts have not ventured as far as the New Zealand courts which have held a private club, 'in a position of major national importance', to be subject to the principles of public law review *tout court*.[19]

The avoidance of political responsibility by resort to organised interests to implement government policies or to act as its surrogates is well documented. The secretary of state cannot answer detailed questions in the House on universities as that is a matter for the University Grants Committee (UGC). The UGC cannot give detailed evidence on its advice to the secretary of state to Select Committees as it is given in confidence. Confidentiality, mutual protection of interest, closeted relationships and mutually beneficial bartering are the ingredients of corporatist relationships. As I shall indicate shortly, even though the peak tripartite form of corporatism of the 1960s and 1970s[20] has waned, the features of the corporatist embrace which give cause for concern for the exercise of power on the public behalf have, far from being expunged, undergone a new vitality.

Our task is to review the accountability devices which exist for achieving accountability in the relationships which might, or might not, be corporatist (see above) but which involve degrees of interrelationship between OIs and the state. Normanton's definition of accountability as 'a liability to reveal, to explain, and to justify what one does'[21] will serve as a useful starting-point. As I have explained with Norman Lewis and Ian Harden elsewhere,[22] accountability can be both internal and external. Further, internal accountability can be subdivided into: *democratic* accountability, such as voting, consultation, etc., which has characterised the legislative programme of reform for trade unions in the 1980s, as well as grievance procedures, appeal mechanisms and methods of challenging decisions; and *managerial* accountability, namely that those charged with responsibilities are meeting their objectives efficiently – what was termed programme accountability in Smith and Hague[23] – with process accountability reviewing the general method and procedures of operation by which the delegated assignment is carried out. Fiscal accountability ensures, or seeks to ensure, that money is spent on approved objectives and not unreasonably. Internal democratic accountability is inevitably downward to membership and, as well as elections, will involve rule-making for policies, information and publicity about managerial performance and responsibilities. Internal managerial accountability is vertically upward to supervisors, or horizontal to peer groups. It involves audit, corporate planning, policy analysis and review and publicity for the exercises undertaken.

External accountability is likewise subdivided into democratic and managerial: *external democratic* accountability involves the accountability to the wider community of the relationship between the state and the OI, and the brokerage and delegation of public power, *de facto* or *de lege*. These are not usually voting matters, although they might influence public opinion as in the case of the city and sometimes crucially as in the case of trade unions. Its requirements involve information and publicity: on-the-record contact between government and OIs, open meetings and effective parliamentary oversight of the relationship. In so far as subservience to the law is equally shared by all individuals, personal or corporate, judicial supervision (with the above comments in mind) is relevant. There is also *external managerial*, which is part of a broad matrix. In so far as OIs have acquired a peculiar or distinct represent-ational role and a favoured position in an extended state, they will have to account to political overlords in the sense that they have to deliver their side of the barter in achieving, for instance, a compliant workforce, local employment, a greater contribution to R and D in return for government contracts, technological expertise in the exploration of natural resources, economic expansion and so on. When public finance is involved, fiscal responsibility is the responsibility of the National Audit Office or the Cour des Comptes or their analogues. Ministerial interventions will have to be explained and justified.

With the taxonomy above, we place especial emphasis on the provision of effective devices to achieve the following tasks which we regard as inherent in the concept of accountability:

1. The resolution of grievances and disputes.
2. The provision of procedures and institutions for choosing goals and objectives.
3. The provision of procedures and institutions for implementing policy choices and monitoring their performance and administration.
4. Authoritative (*not* authoritarian) allocation of decision-making.[24]

What must be emphasised is that these tasks are not the preserve of the official legal and political spheres. Indeed their perennial failure to provide effective control and accountability has rendered the provision of other methods all the more necessary, as has been officially recognised. Obviously some of these tasks can be achieved by relatively stable and existing structures; in other areas the practices which are to be regulated are so volatile and subject to such dramatic change and innovation that a very open-ended package will have to be implemented. The City, especially with its growing and well-documented internationalism and dependency on globally based information technology, is an obvious example of this latter phenomenon. What must be insisted upon is the performance of the above tasks through processes that are open, fair, efficient and democratic. Democratic is the most difficult definitional area. It does not mean that on every issue we should all have the right to vote. Where the public interest is at stake, it does entail that I should have the right to know, or that someone has the right to know on my behalf. Where my interests are directly involved, the more appropriate the safeguard of voting.

We have argued elsewhere in detail that the four essential tasks for achieving accountability are part of an expanded concept of law which does not set at its centre a narrow rule-based individualistic or *Gesellschaft* market instrumental form of law.[25] An expanded concept of law would be equally at home with the exercise of wide unstructured discretionary power; with formal and informal processes for dispute resolution; and with the wide variety of devices employed to achieve accountability or to establish aims and objectives. It would be equally at home in pressing for and assessing accountability devices operating within and over non-departmental bodies of the extended state[26] and those non-governmental bodies that stand in especially proximate relationships with the state. An extensive body of literature has detailed how quagos and quangos obfuscate the lines of accountability especially in multi-layered corporatist relationships.[27] This point has not escaped the Cabinet Office itself, which in 1985 published *Non-Departmental Bodies – a Guide for Departments*.[28] This was essentially an internal checklist aimed at improving internal accountability following the spirit of Departmental Financial Management Initiatives[29] and (MINIS) in the Department of the Environment.

Reflexive Law, Soft Law, Responsive Law and Accountability

A lawyer will traditionally concentrate on a narrow, formal concept of law, as described above. It centres on valid rules, or accepted principles applied by the courts of law. Even the most blinkered of lawyers have come to accept the increasing use of substantive rationality as an overriding feature of legal form. This is exemplified by a deliberate pursuit through the medium of law and legislation of specific ends based upon an acknowledged appeal to 'justice', the merits of a case, the greater public good – i.e. inherently vague categories. Judicial acknowledgement of the appeal of substantive rationality in the development of the principles of law has been widely acknowledged as well as stoutly resisted. Also it is, given the enormous delegation of power by the state to its agencies this century to further economic and welfare intervention, a pervasive practice in the form of legislation which gives authority to officials to do what is appropriate, what is fair and just or what is in the public interest. It is the purposive use of law to shape outcomes which are responsive to collective needs, and it is a reaction against the rule-based autonomous model of law associated with a market economy and classical liberalism.[30]

Responsive law, to give it its title, has been criticised because the idea of 'substantive rationality in interventionist law is regarded [as being incapable] of dealing with the increasing complexity of society'.[31] To believe that legislators or judges can assume to comprehend the inner reality of substantive justice and its requirements in contemporary society is fanciful naïvety, the critics allege. To propose that principles of law can be developed to promote articulate consistency in all but a very finite and limited range of relationships and circumstances is to argue for the impossible.[32] The model of law which is seen as developing from the failure of responsive law is called by Teubner and others reflexive law or proceduralised law.[33] Between them these structure: social systems for self-regulation *and* external coordination; and processes of private or governmental decision-making such that all relevant interests affected by the decision are taken into consideration. In Teubner's words:

> The role of reflexive law is to structure and re-structure semi-autonomous social systems, by shaping both their procedures of internal discourse and their methods of coordination with other social systems ... [It seeks the creation of] the structural premises for a decentralised integration of society by supporting integrative mechanisms within autonomous social systems [namely, 'a regulated autonomy'].[34]

The normative element which constitutes accountability is displayed by the shaping of the 'procedures of internal discourse' and the 'methods of coordination with other social sub-systems'. I take this to mean the internal and external forms of accountability, which we have spoken of earlier and which need not be repeated. It is not a reversal to an individualistic free market economy with a limited state, a Diceyan version of the rule of law and efficiency through the optimum allocation of resources and invisible hands ushering people in their freedom of choice. On the contrary, the state is pervasive and yet assiduous in pursuing the idea of self-regulation of private interests, of allowing economic actors (in OIs) a free range within a broad framework of the law, or governmental guidance or statutory regulation. The current preoccupation with self-regulation in the British state may be viewed in a different light from that which is usual as soon as we think of it as being an entrance price for exclusive or nearly exclusive representation. Much of what is termed 'privatisation' may be similarly interpreted.[35] The rationale for much of our increased state activity in promoting self-regulation of OIs, or for privatisation of publicly owned utilities and industries is to increase competition. If corporatism requires exclusivity, or at least oligopoly, then an effective set of instruments for encouraging competition policy would find themselves in a state of tension with corporatist styles of policy delivery.[36] In fact the position, in the UK at least, is that the relationships between the Office of Fair Trading (OFT), the Monopolies and Mergers Commisison (MMC), government and corporate institutions is in itself heavily bargained as evidence by the special pleading which has helped OIs defeat the views of the OFT having made their case directly to the government[37] (see below).

Before I look at examples of the corporatist embrace in a British context, it might be useful to develop Teubner's analysis in relation to the three forms of law, so that the limited utility of formal/autonomous law and substantive/responsive law as accountability mechanisms can be seen in OI – state relationships at whatever stage along the pluralist – corporatist axis. Contract is a useful legal model, as it is the quintessential private law form of obligation in the market economy.

Models of Law

Formal/autonomous law
The idea associated with this model is formal equality between abstract individuals, and it places faith in the overriding importance of objective rules to control behaviour and predict the outcome of disputes. Contract, as with all areas of law, is seen as an objectively valid set of rules which are used to ascertain whether a valid legal agreement has taken place, and, if so, what are its terms. These, in particular, are the rules establishing *consensus ad idem*; offer and acceptance; consideration; express and implied terms; *caveat emptor*, etc.

Substantive/responsive law
Unlike formal law, it is primarily concerned with outcomes such as, substantive equality between differing and unequal individuals, for instance. It cannot rely upon an objective framework of rules applied impartially to settle disputes because the rules are a mere restatement of inequality, it is argued, and to that extent are not value free but a defence of the status quo. What is required is an active intervention by the judiciary and the legislature to rewrite or shape the substantive outcome of contracts to achieve *real* justice, not an abstract shell of it. The case law of the UK and USA is replete with examples of such an approach, though it is probably true to say that it acts as a supplement to

the formal/autonomous form of law. The Unfair Contract Terms Act 1977 in the UK, and the Uniform Commercial Code in the USA give judges considerable scope for rewriting unfair contracts.

Reflexive law

As indicated, reflexive law cannot accept that the aims of responsive law are realisable. To take but one example, one of the most vexed issues in contract law in the UK and elsewhere in Europe concerns the issue of insurance contracts. Contracts of insurance, including life insurance, are 'amazingly'[38] exempt from the terms of the Unfair Contract Terms Act 1977. In fact insurance companies and their representative bodies have bartered to be exempt from the Act and an absence of legal regulation characterises relationships between the representative bodies, their members and government.[39] Agreements between government and such bodies have covered such issues as workmen's compensation, the Motor Insurers' Bureau and rights of sub-rogation.[40] What is not so well known is the extent to which companies agree among themselves to settle disputes, *inter se*, without reference to the courts or arbitration, so that the whole field of judicial law is bypassed and a whole infrastructure of 'internal law' is created.[41] In other words, there is not the opportunity, even if courts were so minded, to invoke responsive law. We are dealing with the brokerage between power bases where the state allows an OI to carry on a practice in the former's perception of the 'public interest', the end-result being an avoidance of effective oversight by legal and political channels. Here reflexive law would seek to structure bargaining relations,

> so as to equalise bargaining power, and it attempts to subject contracting parties to mechanisms of 'public responsibility' that are designed to ensure that bargaining processes will take account of various externalities [namely, the consumer interest in the above example]. However, within the limits of the arena that has been so structured, the parties are free to strike whatever bargain they will. Reflexive law affects the quality of outcomes without determining the agreements that will be reached.[41]

It aims for a procedural legitimacy that does not take prior distribution as given, as in the case of formal law, and it does not insist that certain contractual outcomes are desirable, as with substantive law. It will be appropriate to assess how accurate as a descriptive model it may prove to be. What are its strength and weaknesses in holding OIs to account? Teubner's theory has been criticised for not being capable of fulfilment within an abstract and a political functionalist framework; in other words, that it lacks an adequate political theory of constitution.[42] As a lawyer might say, you cannot avoid the substance by concentrating on the procedure. Or at least not for ever.

It will also be pertinent to illustrate examples of the OI – state interface which pose problems of accountability and which are, it is submitted, part of new or as yet not fully explored corporatist patterns of relationship. I can only make passing reference to the examples here which are catered for more fully elsewhere.[43] There may be a novelty in the specific detail of the relationship, but there is a persistence in its general theme.

Regulation of Business and Competition

Keynes in 1926[44] regarded the limitations – indeed nonsense – of a classical market economy as productive of negative results because of its creation of an unregulated economy. 'The agenda and non-agenda of the State must be modified'; the objective of capitalist expansion is to exercise:

> directive intelligence through some appropriate organ of action over the many intricacies of private business, yet ... leave private initiative and enterprise unhindered. I believe that in many cases the ideal size for the unit of control and organisation lies somewhere between the individual and the modern state. I suggest therefore that progress lies in the growth and recognition of semi-autonomous bodies within the state – bodies whose criterion of action within their own field is solely the public good as they understand it.

This sounds like the maligned area of 'quangoland'. It is a fact that not only has the quango-cull so enthusiastically put in motion by Mrs Thatcher not produced the number of victims to make any significant difference to the area of quasi-government,[45] but the vitality and importance of many have increased while new members have been regularly admitted, not the least to regulate privatised monopolies as in the case of OFTEL and OFGAS.[46]

The Office of Fair Trading (OFT), the Monopolies and Mergers Commission (MMC) and the Secretary of State for Trade and Industry form a triumvirate of overseers/regulators of competition policy in the UK. The secretary of state has overall control of the area and heavy-weight political pacts can be made through his office. However, the OFT's operations are built upon negotiation and compromise which are essentially confidential. Even in the case of mergers, while only the minister may refer to the MMC for its investigation, the OFT actively seeks out the compromise of business organisations. After the MMC reports, the OFT is involved in further negotiation and pressurising to get acceptance of recommendations, a process that can lead to protracted bartering as explained in the Liesner Report of 1978[47] and which can cause complications. The British government has set in motion a review of competition policy with the declared aim of making *competition the* factor of overriding public importance. A Green Paper of January 1988 has promised greater powers to the OFT and the individual consumer.[48] And yet its creation of privatised monopolies in gas and, in essence, telecommunications, and indeed the favourable position in the market-place into which many privatised concerns have been placed, do not bode well for the competitive outlook; and indeed the whole programme of privatisation has been pervaded with special pleading, special favours and the corporatist embrace.[49]

In his patrols over unfair commercial practices the Director-General of Fair Trading has recommended that trade associations should draw up codes of practice which would be binding upon them under a general statutory duty of 'trading fairly'[50] which would remove their present voluntary and unsatisfactory nature. Such a model fits in nicely with Teubner's analysis. But how adequately are the 'externalities', *per* Teubner, catered for? We have examples of this problem elsewhere, where the secretary of state can release OIs from a statutory framework of restrictive practices to settle upon a mutually accommodating form of regulation. Under the Financial Services Act 1986, the financial markets are to be regulated without the possibility of review of *competition policy* by the courts.[51] The first batch of home-spun rules promoted by the Securities and Investment Board were considered in part anti-competitive by the Director-General in so far as they enforced 'polaris-ation' of banks and building societies. This means that they either act as general brokers for life assurance, unit trusts and personal pensions, or they restrict themselves to their own in-house schemes as tied agents. The views of the Director-General were overruled by the secretary of state, who approved the rules which were presented to Parliament. A major factor was political expedience.[52]

As so frequently in the British context, a statutory scheme is bypassed or informality is given maximum sway within a statutory framework.[53] This is not bad *per se*; however one should be alive to the possibility of abuse in a system which does not cater for freedom of information, and where the law and its oversight do not give sufficient attention to the practice of *ex parte*,[54] off-the-record contact between government and OIs. This point, equally relevant in a European framework as a British one where the European Commission prefers to deal directly with OIs rather than single concerns, is examined in the following section.

Government Contracts, Big Business and Trade Associations

One should be careful not to overemphasise the importance of trade associations (TAs) in a British framework. Streeck has noted how German governmental departments discourage individual firms contacting them directly on matters dealt with by TAs.[55] In Britain many of the leading companies have units specialising in rapport with sponsoring departments. Wyn Grant has observed how British civil servants are sceptical about the organisational capabilities of the majority of British TAs. Certainly the British system is characterised by a marked number of informal relationships between individual concerns and government departments, including 'semi-formal representative devices', which do not fit easily into a collective OI–Governmental embrace as seen elsewhere on the Continent.[56] Nevertheless, although the representation of interests through organised concerns might fit more easily within a corporatist pattern, it should not be overlooked that many of the firms with specialist points of contact are multinational conglomerates; this is especially true in pharmaceuticals and armaments. Bentham's old adage that 'in matters of Government, clubs are best' can easily be amended to add: 'and partnerships can be just as good.' Indeed in the British context the element of partnership is one of the most fascinating of governmental – private sector interfaces operating at both central and local government levels. And to repeat: our theme is bartering on behalf of the public interest, exclusivity and government by other means. Procurement and defence contracts are a fascinating example.

In 1985 in the region of £8 billion was spent by the British government on defence equipment by a process of selective and non-competitive tendering.[57] These processes are used because of the degree of specialism that is involved. In government contracting the law has virtually no impact whatsoever if one were to assess the use of the courts to resolve disputes over government contracts. They are simply not resorted to. Nor indeed is arbitration, outside construction contracts in the local government arena. For parliamentary oversight, the Committee of Public Accounts was not informed of the Zircon project which would have cost £500 million – in spite of a Ministry of Defence assurance that it would inform the chairman of projects exceeding £250 million. In May 1987 the government promised to inform the chairman of all projects over £25 million, but the usual timing of release is only when a decision to move to full development or production is taken.[58]

Appropriate price and cost levels for contracts are established by the Review Board for Government Contracts which establishes the profit formula for non-competitive contracts. Its members are jointly nominated by the CBI and Treasury, the latter making appointments. The Treasury has openly admitted that it cannot get all the information it requires from firms to assess levels of pricing. As the MoD has stated, it is difficult to know how to insist without upsetting essential relationships between the state and a private concern.[59]

With pharmaceuticals, similar themes emerge, although not as much money is involved. Prices for drugs are regulated through a jointly agreed pharmaceutical price regulation scheme (PPRS). The state is directly involved as it is the largest purchaser – albeit indirectly – of pharmaceuticals.[60] The government relies upon information from the industries which is invariably inadequate to assess realistically profit levels and therefore establish an 'appropriate price'. When incidentally only 'listed drugs' were allowed to be prescribed by national health service doctors, the British Medical Association (BMA) objected so vehemently that an appeal mechanism involving doctors *alone* was instituted to decide whether the proprietary brand could be used. Arguments that this was a victory for practitioners' independence and not the pharamaceutical industry have to be seen in the context of the economic sums of money expended each year by the industry on GPs in the promotion of its products.[61] Both the above industries possesss trade associations, although the point must be made that industries will have their own contact point with government, as already observed.

In defence the role of the Defence Industry Council was of interest. It meets twice a year at the Society of British Aerospace Companies (SBAC) and comprises senior industrialists of the defence industries and is chaired by one of them. The invitation to be chairman is made by the secretary of state and the Director of SBAC acts as the secretary. The National Defence Industry Council meets twice a year, more often if required, in the MoD. A Joint Research Committee exists between MoD and the society. Defence associations are complaining, in spite of the favourable treatment on pricing, of the increasing placement upon their members of the cost of research and development (R and D) and the increasing responsibility for their members to check the quality of work of primary as well as secondary contractors, i.e. quality assurance. These points are not lost when it comes to the pricing of contracts and profit levels. Of interest in R and D is the recent establishment of a private body to market and license state-produced research and development.

In pharmaceuticals, while similar complaints have been made by the Association of Pharmaceutical Industries (API) about its increasing responsibility to finance R and D by lowering profit levels, a particular

feature of interest with the Proprietary Association of Great Britain has
been its self-policing and 'law-making'. The Committee for the Safety of
Medicines, appointed by the government, approves drugs manufactured
by the API's members and there has been open acknowledgement of the
fact by members of the Committee that they had received paid consul-
tancies from API firms seeking approval of drugs. Self-policing by the
British Agrochemicals Association and the British Aerosol Manufacturers' Association of their respective members and the production
of compulsory codes to comply with state wishes, which exist alongside
statutory requirements, are also interesting examples of a *de facto*
delegation.

Professional Bodies

I cannot here catalogue the accountability and state OI interface concerning professional associations. The control over the entry of individuals to the ranks of their professional bodies and their own
maintenance of discipline are well-trawled areas. The Law Society is to
lose its powers of control and operation over the administration of civil
legal aid, powers which it was given in 1949 because it was not a
'political' body and choice of the society would secure the cooperation
of the legal profession with the legal aid scheme. While this delegation
of state powers may be ceasing, there was a revamping of the complaints
and disciplinary procedures *vis-à-vis* solicitors by way of a process which
still gave solicitors majority control over the disciplinary stages of the
procedures.[62]

The accountancy profession is a very interesting object of study, given
that its activities are now circumscribed heavily by the demands placed
upon it by the state. This was particularly evident in the negotiations
between the Treasury and the Institute of Chartered Accountants in
which the Treasury was seeking to place the profession under a duty to
act as a whistleblower on clients' accounts. The government had gone so
far as to threaten legislation if the professions did not come up with its
own binding code, which in the event it did. The law lays down formal
requirements for accounting, but accounting standards are set by the
profession[63] in the Accounting Standards Committee (ASC). If a complaint is made against an accountant, the matter will be referred to the
ASC to get a 'ruling'. Sometimes big city firms might be asked what
their practice is which is then elevated to 'best practice' in *Accounting
Guidelines and Auditing Guidelines*. Important issues are often raised
after a complaint from a client. The contribution of professional

regulation to the aims of the state is not widely perceived by grassroots membership.

Engineering

Just one further example will suffice. The Engineering Council was created by Royal Charter in 1981 to represent the fifteen engineering bodies and to make their voice effective in government–professional dialogue; to assist in economic development; and to improve credibility in the eyes of overseas customers by having a central register of engineers. The state instigated and supported the Council in financial and other ways, so that it could make more effective the influence, position and financial capacity of the Council. The Council has set in motion a complex regional network of participation and administration, and it is a peculiarly powerful evocation of the corporatist embrace.

Industry and Employment

This represents the classic locus of tripartite corporatism between the state, capital and labour. For those who believe that this is the quintess-ential and only form of corporatism, very little to advance this form has happened since 1979. Or has it?

Middlemas's study, *Industry, Unions and Government*,[64] speaks of the importance of the Sector Working Parties and Economic Develop-ment Committees (EDC) of the National Economic Development Office (NEDO) post-1980. These became

> not just mechanisms to gather information, but as agencies to promote efficiency, first by reducing the level of uncertainty about government policy in different sectors and secondly by prescriptive work intended to improve the international competitiveness of manufacturing industry as a whole.[65]

He described how in the electronics EDC:

> a convergence of state/industry aims can be achieved so that investment support is forthcoming from government quarters in conditions largely identi-fied by representatives of the industries concerned operating through the committee structure.

A similar point has been made by Cawson.[66] When the government announced plans in July 1987 to reduce drastically the role of the

National Economic Development Council (NEDC) and the number of little Neddies, several of them drew support from unexpected quarters'[67]

Also in employment[68] the interface between the Manpower Services Commission (MSC) and a variety of non-statutory industrial training boards was striking. The latter disseminate MSC information and advice in allocating public money and were felt to be particularly interesting because of the proximity between private bodies and the governmental sector. A similar theme manifests itself in the networking between the MSC and Youth Training Schemes and a variety of non-departmental bodies developing employment educational policy or even outright appeals to the private sector to fund jointly technical colleges in urban areas.

Shortage of time precludes discussion of what are essentially joint committees existing between agricultural and house-building consortiums and respective government departments. It is worthwhile highlighting the fact that for several years networks of OIs and departments have begun to replace parliamentary or local elected representatives on the formulation of housing policies.[69] The progress towards the privatisation of the management of publicly owned estates, and the programme of urban regeneration, offer interesting possibilities for the interface of public and private influence promoting the public interest. Before drawing to a conclusion, it will be worthwhile saying a few words on the subject of welfare corporatism.

Welfare corporatism[70]

Welfare corporatism is the offloading on to private OIs of erstwhile public functions, so that insurance companies, medical consortiums, private actors or developers assume responsibility directly for such functions which are rendered attractive to themselves and to consumers by tax concessions, publicly financed incentives, etc. The bodies concerned often stand to make enormous profit, as with the ending of SERPS,[71] after their confidential and selective deals with government. There may be good reasons for some and, possibly, all of these developments taking place. An obvious dimension of political accountability is often lacking. When our lives or interests are affected, do we not have as much right to vote or participate in the private operations affecting the public interest as in those performed by public agencies which are politically accountable? The great issue for the nineteenth century, said Raymond Williams, was who had the vote? Today the great issue is on what issues can we vote? Harrison has written that welfare corporatism may assist legitimation processes because 'Privileged and selective incorporation can be linked with the depoliticisation of issues in such a way that both the incorporated and the excluded perceive the system as just'.[72] Saunders has made not dissimilar claims about the operation of water authorities and different discriminatory treatment of different client groups;[73] Prosser has repeated this point apropos of the privatisation programme.[74] If I may adopt Lloyd LJ's phrase from the beginning of this chapter, public power operating behind the schemes is public power none the less. What suggestions and conclusions can be made about improved accountability devices in our brave new world?

Conclusion

It might be helpful if I make a few suggestions on devices to augment successful accountability in the state – OI interface. First of all, accountability is premissed upon knowing; and knowing is premissed upon information. Britain is a closed society from the perspective of secretive government, and although the picture may not in reality be quite as healthy elsewhere as is generally assumed,[75] there is a much greater role for open government and freedom of information legislation. We do require not only an access to documents statute, but the equivalent of the US Sunshine Act and Advisory Committees Act. These open up to the public meetings of federal agencies and advisory committees. In our research[76] we noted the peculiarly important and privileged position of advisory committees, observing how easily they might be used for purposes of special pleading. We need specialised and relatively independent overseers and interpreters of the information transmitted, especially with technological and complex issues. This point has been pertinently made by Sir Douglas Wass elsewhere.[77]

Secondly, rule-making and policy-making should be made in public and *ex parte* contacts, and details surrounding *ex parte* contacts should be placed on the record unless there is an overriding justification for secrecy. This justification will have to be proved by the party claiming it. If this sounds implausible, it is standard practice in the USA for instance.[78]

Thirdly, we have seen the extension of ombudsmen from the public sector to the private sector. Banking, insurance and building societies (the latter under statute) have ombudsmen. However, the government has consistently refused to extend the power of ombudsmen covering its own institutions, especially *vis-à-vis* contractual and commercial matters. I have written on this topic elsewhere.[79] The Supreme Court of Canada has interpreted the powers of one of its provincial ombudsmen to cover contractual/commercial matters as these are appropriately under the heading of 'administrative' practices when carried out by government.[80] The British statute specifically excludes these matters, and government is not prepared to end the exclusion. It prevents examination of complaints into some of the more important areas which we discussed, especially defence.

Fourthly, much needs to be done to protect adequately the consumer in the privatisation of effective monopolies. Early indications have suggested the relative weakness of OFTEL. For the regulation of gas, we have to wait and see before making an assessment. The position of the consumer as against nationalised industries was pathetic; the story must not be repeated.

Last of all, full consideration must be given to the range of devices required for effective external accountability and internal private accountability. The Financial Services Act 1986 offers some useful future examples of consumer grievance redress within a statutory self-regulated system. Tribunals are provided for disaffected dealers and applicants. One may suspect that little of real substance will change; similar apprehensions attend the reform introduced by the Solicitors Complaints Bureau to provide grievance redress against members of a powerful professional body.

The power brokerage that I have outlined is not susceptible to adequate accountability by detailed central representative political oversight, though it clearly has its role to play. Nor are the courts a suitable mechanism for many of the issues I have examined. On many of the points, it is a question of judgement which courts are prepared to leave to the institutions within broad legal safeguards of fairness. This point was recently exemplified in relation to universities, where the power of the Visitor over internal matters was considered to be exclusive.[81]

Power brokerage will not be eliminated. The above points will help in some small way to ensure, or give greater assurance, that the processes of brokerage and the exercise of power thereunder can be more fully trusted. They can help to ensure that corporatist and pluralist relationships are providers, and not merely consumers, of legitimation.

Notes

This chapter is based on research conducted with Norman Lewis and Ian Harden on 'Patterns of accountability in corporatist arrangements' for the Economic and Social Research Council.

1. F. W. Maitland, Introduction to Otto Gierke, *Political Theories of the Middle Ages* (Cambridge, Cambridge University Press, 1900); 'The Crown as Corporation', *Law Quarterly Review* (1901), 131.
2. *Chandler* v. *D.P.P.*, [1964] AC 763, *per* Lord Devlin.
3. *Ibid.*, *per* Lords Hodson and Reid.
4. *D.* v. *N.S.P.C.C.*, [1978] AC 171 *per* Lord Simon; *per contra*, the British Gas Corporation has been ruled in law not to be a state authority as it did not exercise powers of state: *Foster* v. *British Gas Corporation*, [1987] I.C.R. 52. In English and Scottish law, however, the state regardless of its metaphysical quality, can own property: *Ross* v. *Lord Advocate*, [1986] 3 A11 E.R. 79. And see *R.* v. *Ponting* (1985) Crim. L.R. 318.
5. *'Attorney-General* v. *The Guardian and Observer' The Times*, 26 July 1986.
6. R. Stewart, 'The reformation of administrative law', *Harvard Law Review*, 88 (1975), 1669.
7. T. Daintith in J. Jowell and D. Oliver (eds), *The Changing Constitution* (Oxford, Oxford University Press, 1985), 174–97.
8. *Ibid.*, *Loc. cit.*
9. N. Lewis, in W. Twining (ed.) *Common Law and Legal Theory* (Basil Blackwell, 1986), 99–114.
10. *R.* v. *Panel on Take-Overs ex p. Datafin*, [1987] 1 A11 E.R. 564.
11. *Per* Sir John Donaldson MR.
12. *Ibid.*
13. P. Schmitter, 'Still the century of corporatism?', *Review of Politics*, 36 (1) (1974), 93–4.
14. M. L. Harrison in Harrison (ed.), *Corporatism and the Welfare State* (Aldershot, Gower 1984), chapter 1.
15. N. Lewis in *Journal of Law and Society*, (1985), 87–103.
16. W. Grant, 'Neo-corporatism and the study of business interest associations', *Working Paper No. 35*, Department of Politics, University of Warwick, January 1984.
17. Lewis, *op. cit.*
18. The court held basically that it would give guidance retrospectively rather than quash proceedings.
19. *Finnigan* v. *N.A.R.F. Club Inc.*, [1985] 2 N.Z.L.R. 159 (CA).
20. K. Middlemas, *The Politics of Industrial Society*, (London, André Deutsch, 1979).
21. E. E. Normanton, 'Public accountability and audit: a reconnaisance', in B. L. R. Smith and D. C. Hague (eds), *The Dilemma of Accountability in Modern Government: Independence versus Control* (London, Macmillan, 1971), ch. 14.
22. *The Democratic Dilemma* (forthcoming, 1988).
23. Normanton, *op. cit.*, p. 84 *et seq.*
24. See K. N. Llewellyn, 'The normative, the legal and the law jobs', *Yale Law Journal*, 49 (1940), 1355.
25. *The Democratic Dilemma*, *op. cit.*; and N. Lewis and I. Harden, *The Noble Lie* (London, Hutchinson, 1986).
26. Note the extension over 'non-departmental bodies' of the jurisdiction of the Parliamentary Commissioner (Ombudsman): Parliamentary and Health Service Commissioners Act 1987.
27. For example, A. Barker (ed.) *Quangos in Britain* (London, Macmillan, 1982).
28. HMSO, 1985.
29. The Committee of Public Accounts (CAP) has criticised the operation of FMIs, Thirteenth Report of CAP, 8 July 1987.
30. P. Nonet and P. Selznick, *Law and Society in Transition*, (New York, Harper and Row, 1978).
31. G. Winter, *Bartering Rationality in Regulation: A Comparative Perspective*, ZERP DP 1/84, University of Bremen, 1984.
32. Cf. R. Dworkin, *Taking Rights Seriously*, (London, Duckworth, 1977).
33. G. Teubner, *Law and Society Review*, 17 (1983), 239.

34. *Op. cit.*, p. 255.
35. P. Birkinshaw, N. Lewis and I. Harden, *Patterns of Accountability in Corporatist Arrangements*, Report to ESRC Government and Law Committee, 1986.
36. *Ibid.*
37. See the 'polarisation' episode over the Securities and Investment Board's rules on the same, below.
38. Sir G. Borrie, *The Development of Consumer Law and Policy* (London, Sweet and Maxwell, 1984), p. 110.
39. R. Lewis (1985), Mod. L.R. 275.
40. Which allows the insurer to assume the legal rights of action of the insured.
41. See Teubner, *op. cit.*
42. Kettler, *Law and Society Review*, 21, (1987), 9.
43. See n.22, above.
44. *'The End of Laissez-Faire'*, *Essays in Persuasion* (New York, Harcourt, Brace and Co., 1932), 313–14.
45. *Report on Non-Departmental Public Bodies*, Cmnd 7797 (London, HMSO, 1980).
46. To regulate telecommunications and gas respectively.
47. *A Review of Monopolies and Mergers Policy* (Cmnd 7198); see: *Guardian* 9 October 1987; and *Merger Policy* (London Department of Trade and Industry, 1988).
48. Department of Trade and Industry, *The Department for Enterprise*, Cm. 278 (London, HMSO 1988), and Cm. 331.
49. T. Prosser, *Nationalised Industries and Public Control: Legal, Constitutional and Political Issues* (Oxford, Basil Blackwell, 1986).
50. See Borrie, *op. cit.*; Office of Fair Trading, *A General Duty to Trade Fairly* (London, OFT, 1986), August.
51. Although reviews for natural justice or fair procedure will be possible.
52. To have the rules approved before the dissolution of Parliament.
53. For example, the non-use of powers of direction under the Banking Act 1946, section 4, in favour of informal pressure.
54. *Ex parte* here means the exclusion of an interested party.
55. W. Streeck, *Between Pluralism and Corporatism: German Business Associations and the State* (1982). Unpublished paper cited in Grant *op. cit.*, n.16, above.
56. Grant, *op. cit.*
57. For 1984–5, non competitive contracts, generally of a value of £6,049 million, were placed, *Review Board of Government Contracts – Fifth General Review* (London, HMSO, 1987).
58. *Guardian*, 8 May 1987.
59. Committee of Public Accounts, HC 390 (1984–5), Minutes of Evidence, p. 5.
60. Via health authorities and prescriptions.
61. See H. Teff (1984), Mod. L.R. 303.
62. It was named the Solicitors' Complaints Bureau.
63. For example, the Institute of Chartered Accountants, and the Chartered Institute of Public Finance and Accountancy for the public sector.
64. K. Middlemas, *Industry, Unions and Government* (London, Macmillan, 1983).
65. N. Lewis, 'Book Review' of Middlemas, above, 12 *Journal of Law and Society* (1985), 87–103, 91–95.
66. Cawson, *Corporatism and Accountability News No. 4* (London, ESRC, 1986).
67. Including M. Heseltine MP.
68. Nb, *Training for Employment*, Department of Employment, Cm. 316 (1988).
69. These were the Treasury, DoE, Local Authority Associations, Building Societies Association and the House Builders' Federation.
70. M. L. Harrison (ed.) *Corporatism and the Welfare State* (Aldershot, Gower, 1984).
71. The state earnings-related pensions scheme.
72. Harrison, *op. cit.*
73. See P. Saunders, 'We can't afford democracy too much . . .' Urban and Regional Studies, *Working Paper No. 43*, University of Sussex, November 1984.

74. Prosser, *op. cit.*; and T. Prosser and C. Graham (1987), Mod. L.R. 16.
75. P. Birkinshaw, *Freedom of Information: The Law, the Practice and the Ideal* (London, Weidenfeld and Nicolson, 1988).
76. *The Democratic Dilemma, op. cit.*
77. D. Wass, *Government and the Governed* (London, Routledge and Kegan Paul, 1984) and *Public Law* (1987), 181.
78. K. C. Davis, *Administrative Law Treatise* (San Diego, Calif., 2nd edn with suppl., 1979).
79. P. Birkinshaw, *Grievances, Remedies and the State* (London, Sweet and Maxwell, 1985).
80. *British Columbia Development Corporation* v. *Friedman*, [1985] 1 WWR 193.
81. And therefore courts would not get a look in: *Thomas* v. *University of Bradford*, [1987] 1 A11 E.R. 834 (HL).

PART II
Neo-Corporatism in Practice:
Case Studies

4 From pluralism to pluralism: Italy and the corporatist debate

Martin J. Bull

There is no end to pluralism, for we are never told what is non-pluralism.
(Sartori 1970: 1050–1)

Postwar Italian political history displays a series of apparently 'contradictory' characteristics which cause difficulties for the analyst of
specific, potentially 'corporatist events', and for attempts to locate Italy
along a pluralist-corporatist continuum, difficulties which are compounded both by arguments disclaiming corporatism as a concept distinct
from pluralism (e.g. Martin 1983) and by definitional disputes among
corporatist writers themselves (see Matteucci 1984; Lange and Regini
1987a, 1987b for recent attempts at clarification). As a consequence,
while it has been possible to conclude that Italy is not corporatist and to
cite the likely reasons for this (e.g. Regini 1981; chapter 6; 1982), and to
'rank' Italy in relation to other countries (Wilensky 1976; Schimitter
1981; Tarentelli 1986) different authors have been able to reach directly
opposite conclusions in their analysis of specific periods of 'concentration',[1] and Italy has been identified as being somehow 'midway'
between the 'pure pluralist' political systems (such as the USA) and the
'corporatist' models of northern Europe (Cella and Treu 1986; Treu
1983). A reflection of the problem is the fact that in a period (the 1980s)
when 'corporatist' practices have been clearly in decline across Western
Europe (Carrieri and Donolo 1983; Regini 1986) a trilateral 'corporatist
pact' was reached in Italy. Arguments such as that of Goldthorpe – that
western Europe is becoming divided between those countries experiencing 'dualist' tendencies and those experiencing 'corporatist' tendencies –
are similarly perplexing, in that it could be demonstrated that Italy has
evidenced both. (Goldthorpe 1984). In short, the corporatist debate –
like other debates in political science (e.g. Lange 1985; Furlong 1984) –
reveals Italy to be a hybrid case and thus difficult to classify. Perhaps not
surprisingly this has led some authors to abandon corporatism *and*
pluralism as applicable models to Italy (Golden 1985; 1986), and others
to propose 'a union of corporatism and neopluralism' (*sic*) to resolve
Italy's problems (Dal Co and Perulli 1986: 169).

In this chapter it will be argued that the application of the concept to Italy is not so much difficult as misguided. It is misguided in the sense that while the country has evidently witnessed changes in the relationship between interest groups and the state, the pluralist-corporatist continuum appears unable to capture completely the type of changes which have taken place. The inapplicability of the concept of corporatism to Italy – which in this author's view does not entail a concomitant abandonment of pluralism as an applicable model – will be brought out in two different but related ways. The first part of the chapter approaches the problem historically, by outlining the development of state-group relations in Italy, in order to place the events of the late 1970s and early 1980s (which have been the subject of an application of the corporatist concept) in broader context. The second part then identifies the common factors in this history with a view to determining the limitations of the corporatist concept as a tool for the analysis of the Italian case.

We may take as our starting-point what is probably the most refined and synthesised definition of corporatism to date, which is that given by Cawson:

> Corporatism is a specific socio-political process in which organisations representing monopolistic functional interests engage in political exchange with state agencies over public policy outputs which involves those organisations in a role which combines interest representation and policy implementation through delegated self-enforcement. (Cawson 1986: 38)

For Cawson, there are three 'varieties' of this concept: *microcorporatism*, involving peak associations and Cabinet; *mesocorporatism*, involving interest associations and central departments or regional agencies; and *micro-corporatism*, involving firms and central departments or local authorities, (*ibid.*: chapter 4). More generally, on this view pluralism and corporatism represent end-points on a continuum, with 'corporate pluralism' as a mid-point. The 'independent variable' which Cawson uses to measure this continuum is that of 'the degree of political concentration of political interests'. Corporatism therefore is characterised by a limited number of groups, fixed interest domains, a hierarchical order and no competition; while pluralism is characterised by a larger number of groups, overlapping interest domains, a fluid power structure and pure competition (*ibid.*: 42). The conditions normally cited by corporatist writers for corporatism to flourish are structural. They may be *organisational* conditions (a high concentration of interests (see above), leadership control over members inside groups, an efficient state apparatus); *political* conditions (either stable economic growth providing resources for redistribution, or the need for 'crisis management' of the economy); and *ideological/cultural* conditions (a low level of political polarisation and a political cultural tradition of consensus over conflict) (for a counter view to a structural approach see Regini 1984). Bearing this model in mind, we may now turn to the pre- and postwar history of stage-group relations in Italy, and consider how well the model applies to them. The focus will be the macro level.

Clientelistic, Parentelistic and Political Exchange: Development of State-Group Relations

The reconstruction period 1944–8

As Giugni has noted, 'The Fascist, corporative State was the most systematic attempt of that time to refound the State on the basis of the representation of organized interests' (Giugni 1985: 53). This attempt failed, but the experience was not without its effect on postwar state–group relations in Italy. The fascist period interrupted what was a relatively late development of interest groups in civil society, and forged a strong link between the industrial relations system and the political system. The essential characteristic of fascist corporatism was the dominant role of the state in establishing and regulating industrial relations. A law passed in 1926 laid down rigorously the legal framework of industrial relations, giving legal recognition only to the fascist employers and labour organisations and their exclusive right to represent their appropriate sectors. Confidustria – founded in 1910 as the Italian Confederation of Industry (Confederazione italiana dell industria) and re-launched with its new name after the First World War – did not oppose this policy. On the contrary, the employers' organisation saw in fascism a means of restoring social order and blunting the militancy of the working class – most forcefully exerted in the factory council movement (1919–21) – thus re-creating the climate necessary for capital accumulation. This was in the absence of a strong bourgeois party which that class has failed to organise. Integration between the state and the industrial relations system, however, was not total as Confidustria rejected the fascist project of 1923 designed to organise *all* producer groups (i.e. labour *and* capital) into one organisation through which conflicts could be mediated. (Martinelli and Treu 1984: 264–5). The trade union movement which, before the advent of fascism, had been growing in strength and membership but which was divided along ideological and organisational lines, was not disbanded by the fascist state but marginalised (or reduced to a state of 'formal' existence) by Confindustria's agreement with the state that only the Confederation of Fascist Corporations should be recognised in the collective bargaining process.

The fascist experience has considerable effects on the strength of capital and labour and the strategies they adopted in the crucial years of the reconstruction of the Italian state (1944–8). Before looking at these, reference should be made to the Constitution, drafted in the years 1946–8. This enshrined the 'freedom of trade union organisations' and also accorded them, on registration with the state, legal status which would make collective agreements binding on all members (article 39). One sees here not only a reaction to the fascist experience, but to its origins. The idea of 'registration' raises the spectre of 'state control' as a means of controlling labour conflict and thus guarding against the type of political instability which would generate and justify an authoritarian alternative. In fact the right wing of Italian politics did attempt to activate legislation in the postwar period to implement closely the constitutional provisions relating to state control but without success and they remained dormant. Indeed, Italian industrial relations remained, at least until the 1970s, largely free from legal regulation. Rather than being moulded by a legal framework, the industrial relations system was shaped by the development in practice of collective bargaining, which was shaped by the national environment. The basic characteristics of this environment were determined in the immediate postwar period.

In the mid-1940s Italian business was weak and in disgrace for its collusion with the fascist regime and was confronted with a working class headed by a strong Communist Party (the PCI), whose prestige had been elevated through its leading role in the Resistance Movement. Confidustria was re-founded in 1945, representing approximately 70,000 firms. At first, it presented itself as a non-political, purely technical body (Pasquino 1976: 281). The weakness of Italian business partly explains the failure of the Italian bourgeoisie to found a party in the postwar period which would protect its interests. Indeed, in the absence of such a party and faced with a strong Communist Party, Italian business quickly made a political decision similar to that made in the 1920s when fascism was supported: it gave its support to the new Christian Democratic Party (DC) which looked most likely to be the largest party in the postwar period. A successor to the Popular Party (Partito Popolare), the DC drew its strength essentially from the support of the Vatican and the Americans, both of whom saw the new organisation as a potential bulwark against communism. This developing link between business and what was to become the major governing party for the next forty years was to have significant implications for the development of state–group relations.

Meanwhile the democratic trade union movement was re-founded with three distinguishing characteristics which were to have an influence over subsequent events. First, the new movement was founded on a unitary basis. The influence of the Allied Military government and of leading Italian labour leaders (such as the Communist, Giuseppe Di Vittorio; the Socialist, Bruno Buozzi; and the Christian Democrat, Achille Grandi) prevailed over the attempt to re-create the pre-fascist fragmented trade union movement. In June 1944 a single union, the Italian General Confederation of Labour (CGIL) was established. According to its constitution, the CGIL was a democratic institution which remained independent from all political parties, although it was prepared to associate itself with democratic parties 'in order to safeguard popular liberties and to defend specific interests of the workers' (quoted in LaPalombara 1957: 15). The second characteristic of the new trade union movement was that it constitutionally committed itself to taking a position on all *political* questions which were of interest to the labour movement in general. These included individual liberties, social legislation, the economic reconstruction of the country and 'democratic development' in general (*ibid.*: 18). The third characteristic was largely a corollary of the first two: a high degree of centralisation at the level of organisation and policy.

The union movement re-emerged against the background of a highly unstable political environment. The government of 'national solidarity', which included all the anti-fascist parties, became increasingly riven with internal disputes as the Cold War developed. This caused particular tensions within the CGIL for two interrelated reasons: first, because the union was constitutionally committed to take a stand on all political questions; and secondly, because it became quickly evident that the Communists were the dominant force inside the CGIL. The failure of the Christian Democratic faction of the CGIL (representing 13 per cent of the membership) to remove the constitutional clause relating to political questions at the Congress of Florence in 1947 meant that it was constrained into supporting an essentially Communist and Socialist platform on all national and international questions of the day. Consequently, the internal split, when it occured (as a result of an assassination attempt in July 1948 on Palmiro Togliatti, the leader of the PCI), was along partisan lines. The Free Italian General Confederation of Labour (LCGIL) was founded in October 1948 by the Christian Democratic faction, and less than a year later the Italian Federation of Labour (FIL) was set up by the Republicans and Social Democrats.

These two were fused in March 1950 into the Italian Confederation of Workers Unions (CISL), to form an anti-Communist front. Those who opposed the fusion (besides Republicans and Social Democrats, some Socialists who had left the Socialist Party (PSI) and the CGIL) formed the Italian Union of Labour (UIL), whose purpose was the presentation of an alternative to the Communist and Confessional-based trade unions.

By 1950, then, the combination of the effects of the fascist experience and the Cold War left certain deep-rooted marks on interest group activity during a period in which the state was still in 'embryonic form'. These marks were to have a long-lasting impact on the development of state-group relations in the postwar period:

1. Close ties between interest groups and political parties, with the result of a high degree of fragmentation. Organised business established close links with the DC, while the trade unions divided along partisan lines, establishing close ties with the various political parties (the CGIL with the PCI, the CISL with the DC and the UIL with the lay-centreparties).
2. A commitment on the part of the largest trade union, the CGIL, to political goals rather than the purely economic goal of the material welfare of the working class.
3. A high degree of centralisation of both organised business and the trade union organisations.
4. An ideological and cultural manifestation of conflict over coopera-tion. The events of the reconstruction period in some ways reflected deeply ingrained characteristics of Italian political culture. Deep-rooted territorial and subcultural divisions bred a profound scep-ticism towards associationalism and consultation as a means of representation. Interest group activity was viewed as a means of furthering sectional, particularistic interests rather than as a means of finding the national interest. In short, if, as indicated above, interest groups were fundamentally politicised, political and centralised in nature, they also experienced a low degree of legiti-macy which would become more acute in the 1950s.

'Clientela' and 'Parentela': Italy's model emerges (the 1950s)

The resounding victory of the DC in the first elections of the new Republic confirmed and exacerbated the polarisation of Italian politics into two broad camps, Catholic and Communist. Despite receiving an overall majority, the DC (with De Gasperi as Prime Minister) chose to govern in coalition with the lay parties of the centre (the Republican

Party, PRI; the Social Democratic Party, PSDI; and the Liberal Party, PLI. The PCI and PSI remained in opposition, but without the status of 'responsible' opposition parties: they were regarded as being 'anti-system', thus excluding the possibility of them entering the government. The government pursued an economic policy based on market liberalism, and the combination of the operation of market principles and a tight credit policy led to a large increase in unemployment. Productivity became based on low labour costs and an abstentionist stance towards industrial relations. This gave employers a free hand to maximise the use of labour in the factories and lay off workers when deemed necessary. Industrial production and productivity rose, while the rise in unemployment was not accompanied by commensurate gains in wages. Meanwhile labour militancy was suppressed with severity.

The hostile ideological climate and the delegitimisation of the two main opposition parties were important determinants of a distortion of what might have been the expected modes of interest articulation and aggregation. The state, rather than developing a sense of autonomy from civil society, quickly became permeated by it in the form of a number of sectional interests, while other interests remained excluded. This had particular relevance to labour and capital. The process took place according to two criteria defined by LaPalombara as *clientela* and *parentela* (LaPalombara 1964: chapters VII and VIII). 'Clientelistic' relations were those by which certain interest groups gained privileged access to the bureaucracy to the exclusion of other groups in the same sector. 'Parentelistic' relations were those by which certain groups gained privileged access to the policy-making process via the mediation of the dominant political party, the DC. The basis of both relationships was an 'exchange' determined by the resources the relevant groups could offer the bureaucracy and the dominant party. The resources at the base of clientelistic relationships were the group's representativeness and control over its sector; its political or ideological 'respectability'; its organisational strength; and its technical expertise. Parentelistic relationships were determined by a group's basic commitment to Catholicism and furthering the interests of Christian Democracy; its ability to 'deliver votes' to the dominant party; and its financial resources.

The combination of clientelistic and parentelistic relations resulted in a situation of privileged access to the state being accorded to business, while labour was largely excluded. Confindustria, in the period until the late 1950s, was able to achieve privileged access to the state machinery via both modes: on the one hand, it established a strong clientelistic relationship with the Ministry of Industry and Commerce, largely through its monopoly of technical expertise and information; and, on the other hand, it was able to establish a parentelistic relationship with the DC (which, as noted earlier, it had anyway chosen to support) through the provision of financial resources (both to the DC and the PLI) and through its control over a wide part of the media. The 'exchange' for these resources was favourable legislation passed under the guise of the 'national interest'. This position was further strengthened by the state's abstentionist stance towards industrial relations and a slack labour market which weakened the trade union movement. Finally, the strength of its position enabled the business community to contain potential internal divisions. Pasquino has described the early 1950s as 'the gilded phase of Confindustria', a phase which witnessed 'an organic identification of *Weltanschaunng* and class interests on the two levels of political leadership (Costa, De Gasperi) and bureaucratic-administrative implementation'. (Pasquino 1976: 283). Martinelli has noted that employers in this period effectively 'disappeared' as an interest group (Martinelli 1979: 71).

The trade union movement, on the other hand, was confronted with a slack labour movement; a low degree of unionisation of the workforce (approx. 20 per cent); a low level of organisation at the factory level; a policy of 'labour exclusion' operated by the state; and severe internal fragmentation. As a result, the trade union movement became divided in its relationship with the state. The CISL developed a parentelistic relationship with the DC since, as already noted, the union had been founded on Catholic and anti-Communist principles. However, the resources exchanged did not concern the protection of workers' interests inside the party. This was not only because of the CISL's small membership and weak organisation, but because its philosophy was based on 'social Christian' principles rather than those of 'class conflict'. The former viewed trade unions as serving a pluralist society through the harmonisation of social classes around Christian values (Lange, Ross and Vannicelli 1982: 114). This *was* the CISL's resource, although the more cynical regarded it as straightforward subordination of members' demands to party policy.

The CGIL, with its close connections to the PCI, was delegitimised in an analogous way to the party: it was not recognised as a legitimate bargaining partner by the state and employers alike. Of note, however, is that in the aftermath of the split of the trade union movement the essential character of the CGIL – a highly centralised body with a fundamentally political conception of its role which reduced the emphasis of activity at the level of the workplace – led it to attempt to involve the state in industrial relations. Freed of the constraints of balancing contrasting opinions and able to act as a unitary actor, the CGIL developed a long-term 'Plan of Work' (*Piano del Lavoro*). The Plan was aimed at prompting governmental intervention on a wide range of measures (including agrarian reform, development of the south, control of prices and taxation policy) to increase employment and develop infrastructures in exchange for control over worker militancy and an increase in productivity. This was, as already indicated, in stark contrast with the principles of the government's and employers' economic policy and the attempt to promote political exchange was rejected by government and employers alike.

None the less, the formulation and presentation of the Plan confirmed the essential characteristics and strategy, forged in the reconstruction period, of the main body of the trade union movement. First, there was a stress on broad macro-economic goals to be achieved in the political – as opposed to economic – market. These goals concerned the furthering of the interest of the proletariat as a whole, rather than just the members of the trade union movement. Bargaining at the plant level, which would diversify the struggle and allow adaptation to different plant conditions, was discouraged. Secondly and perhaps paradoxically, the presentation of the Plan, while demonstrating the CGIL's attempt to deal directly with the state, at the same time, emphasised its increased dependence on the PCI. The Plan's analysis and goals were very much in keeping with the PCI's own strategy. Indeed the CGIL's activity in this period was chiefly concerned with mobilising its members around certain political objectives of the party. In the absence of other resources – state recognition, organisational strength and favourable economic conditions – the CGIL was constrained into maximising its partisan ties. Thirdly, the Plan revealed the high degree of centralisation of the CGIL and the degree of control exercised by the leadership over its members. Finally, it should be noted that the outright rejection of the Plan by the government indicated the weakness of the CGIL and the union movement in general. By the mid-1950s the CGIL was in severe crisis: it was suffering from a declining membership, a widening gap between the action taken at the confederal level and the needs of the plant level, and a consequent low degree of bargaining power with employers.

To summarise this phase, the model of industrial relations which developed was characterised by a system of collective bargaining which was tightly controlled at the top by the trade union confederations and Confindustria. This, as Martinelli and Treu point out, tended to favour the latter because outcomes could be kept at the level of the 'slowest unit of industry' (Martinelli and Treu 1984: 267). Political, economic and organisational conditions favoured a largely homogeneous business community both in its relations with the state and with the trade union movement. The state became a vehicle for obtaining economic policies favourable to capital accumulation, essentially via the state's 'dominant party', the DC. The trade union movement was divided and its strategies were hardly conducive to maximising the interests of the industrialised worker in a situation characterised by the dominance of market principles. From an early stage, then, the Italian case was a 'hybrid' one: an absence of state regulation of industrial relations was coupled with, on the one hand, a close identification between the state and the business community, and on the other hand, the exclusion of the main part of the labour movement. Finally, political parties took on an early important role. In the absence of a high level of organisation at the level of civil society, political parties quickly assumed the major role of mediating demands from society to the state. Moreover, this took place in a 'distorted' way because of the nature of the competition between the parties. Because the PCI and the Neo-Fascist Party (the MSI) were delegitimised, a coalition of parties was necessary to keep the extremes out; and because the DC was the largest of these parties, it became indispensable to any government coalition. This fact had important implications for the way in which state-group relations would develop from the late 1950s. The model described above, in fact, was inherently unstable because of the presence of certain latent contradictions which would be exposed in the course of the subsequent decade.

Beyond labour exclusion? (the late 1950s to the Hot Autumn)
The factors which began to undermine the model of state-group relations, described above, were of an external nature and one that was internal to the actors themselves. The external factors were both economic and political. First, rapid economic growth led to a tightening of the labour market as the economy approached full employment. This had the effect of strengthening the trade unions' bargaining power with the state and employers. Secondly, Stalin's death in 1953, and the Twentieth Congress of the Soviet Communist Party in 1956, marked the beginning of *détente*, and thus an attenuation of the Cold War climate. This coincided with a third factor, a growing crisis of the centrist governing coalition formula, after the Republican Party refused to enter the coalition in June 1955. This opened the prospect of a centre-left alternative (through the incorporation of the PSI into the government), this prospect being heightened by a growing rift between the PSI and the PCI, after the latter's condonement of Soviet intervention in Hungary in 1956. The emergence of the centre-left in 1962 created wider scope for trade union action. These external changes partly caused, and were

partly accompanied by, changes with respect to the actors themselves.

The divisions between the CGIL and the CISL were exacerbated by the growth inside the latter of a new conception (which also had its effects on the UIL) of the role of trade unions based on the American model. This model viewed the trade union movement as an organisation which should look after the interests of its members exclusively and not be concerned with the interests of the working class as a whole. This meant that the focus of the labour struggle should be the workplace and objectives economic rather than political. This conception represented a radical challenge to the CGIL's strategy of pursuing broad political objectives at the national level to look after the interests of the working class as a whole. As a consequence, the new conception was rejected by the CGIL on the grounds that it was 'collaborationist' and would undermine the trade unions' bargaining power by its fragmentary effect. Yet it was also becoming clear to the leadership of the CGIL that an adaptation of strategy to take account of the workplace was becoming increasingly necessary for two reasons: first, because the CISL was gaining an increasing hold over the workforce at that level; and secondly, because the effect of the high growth rate and the disparities generated by it was a *de facto* decentralisation of bargaining (*contrattazione articolata*). Employers often granted high wages and bypassed the protracted union bargaining at the confederal level. In this situation, national negotiations were providing no more than a framework within which groups at the plant and industrial category level exercised their *market* power to obtain greater benefits. These developments pushed the CGIL into devoting greater attention to the plant level, while insisting on the importance of a harmonisation of political and economic objectives at the plant and national levels. One can detect in the contrasting positions of the CISL and the CGIL an evident influence of their respective links with a party entrenched in government and a party marginalised in opposition. None the less, the actual development of decentralised bargaining had the effect of loosening union-party ties, a trend which would become significant only in the late 1960s.

Accompanying the trend towards a decentralisation of bargaining and a strengthening of trade union bargaining power was a change in the Confindustria/DC political and social bloc. This had its origins in two interrelated factors. First, with changes in the economic environment divisions emerged in the business community. These divisions were reflected in a power struggle inside Confindustria between those firms (led by the electrical industry) which were largely capital intensive and thus not sensitive to labour problems, and those firms which were labour intensive and favoured a more flexible approach to labour as a means of controlling tension. This split was exacerbated by the second reason: a change in attitude on the part of the government towards the state's role in industrial relations. The entrance of the PSI into the governing coalition was partly responsible for this. The birth of the centre-left was predicated on the introduction of a system of planning which would cater for the representation of previously neglected interests. As a result, the early 1960s saw attempts by the government to encourage 'tripartism' both generally and in the context of a proposed five-year plan. The birth of the centre-left, however, is not a sufficient explanation for these developments. They also had their origins in developments inside the DC from the mid-1950s onwards.

The dilemma for the DC in the 1950s was that the social coalition which had brought the party to power was made up of both progressive and reactionary elements. This was reflected in the political composition of the party. The government's policy in the early 1950s, as described earlier, reflected the wide support the DC received from the traditional agrarian interests in the south and from big business in the north (represented by Confindustria). By the mid-1950s the dangers of this policy were becoming evident. The DC was in danger of moving rightwards, depriving itself of a potentially reformist image, alienating a large section of its social base and increasing its dependence on the traditional conservative interests and the clientelistic system of the south (for analyses, see Tarrow 1967; Di Palma 1979).

The DC's response to this dilemma (a response largely identified with Fanfani, the new party secretary elected in 1954) was to strengthen the party organisation, particularly in the south and build the DC into a modern mass party which would no longer be dependent on the traditional conservative interests which dominated Confindustria. A crucial method of doing this was to forge an alliance with the more modern wing of the employers (see above), expand the state sector of the economy (the *parastate*) and utilise it to promote a modernisation of industrial relations. In 1956 a Ministry of State Participations was set up and state enterprises and firms which were owned by a public body (such as the Institute of Industrial Reconstruction, IRI) were instructed to break their links with Confindustria and practice more modern industrial relations policies. The introduction of the 'IRI formula' (i.e. using ownership of a series of private firms by a state body to pursue public interest targets) to break the hold over the DC of the more reactionary groups in Italian society was successful but it had a further, originally unintended, consequence. By undermining the homogeneity of the business community the DC was effectively attempting to forge a modern middle class. The 'new class' therefore had its origins in, and thus dependence upon, a political factor, the 'centrality' of the DC in the political system. The effect of this interdependence was that what began as a 'strategy of modernisation' developed into what Bianchi has described as 'a vicious circle for the mutual promotion of the interests of politicians and public managers' (Bianchi 1987: 27). The old type of clientelism and patronage based on the individual was gradually replaced with the DC's own brand, based on the party organisation. This trend was enhanced by the internal factionalisation of the DC which occurred as a result of Fanfani's modernisation attempts. The infiltration and control by different political groupings of vast areas of the bureaucracy and *parastate* became an important aspect of the factional struggle inside the DC and, later, the PSI. Public managers received political protection in exchange for support for economic policies (and primarily investment and employment policies) which were politically motivated. In short, this period saw not so much a collapse of the old state-group model, but rather a restructuring of its essential paradigm: 'The once close links between a unified party and a rather homogeneous business class became instead a fragmented network of influences in which different party factions were allied to different centres of economic power' (Martinelli and Treu 1984: 284).

The 1960s saw an expansion of these centres to the point of the creation of a politically controlled public financial sector which included banks, state agencies, state-controlled firms, the traditional bureaucracy and local authorities (see for analyses, Furlong 1986; Martinelli 1979). The significance of the restructuring of the old state-group model was that what was an alleged policy of reformism became in fact a major explanation for the Italian political system's dwindling stability of performance. The fragmentation and decline of the business sector left the Italian republic as a regime based not on a form of 'class solidarity', but rather on a heterogeneous coalition of political groupings. This had two effects: first, economic policy, rather than following a coherent line, became too often tied to the criteria of obtaining political resources for particular factions of the party; and secondly, government instability and immobilism increased as competition between governing parties increased for positions and resources, particularly with the expansion of the governing alliance in the 1960s. Government crises became determined not by parliamentary defeats, but by inter- and intra-party struggles. Finally, the institutional structures within which the parties operated consolidated the above developments. A fully bicameral Parliament, highly developed committee systems in each Chamber, the secret ballot as the most common voting procedure and no formal limitation to private member legislative initiatives were preconditions for the development of a parliamentary system where the majoritarian principle could not prevail. Heterogeneous and conflict-ridden government coalitions, a lack of government control over the parties in Parliament, a high number of party factions and 'permanent' opposition parties completed the picture. It might be suggested that Italy was suffering from a fundamental crisis of representation. Perhaps it is more accurate, however, to view the problem as one of the system representing and reproducing too faithfully the fragmentation of Italian society: the system was articulating interests but failing to aggregate them.

It is in the above context that attempts at 'tripartism' via the introduction of a planning system should be viewed. Planning was one of the major issues of Italian politics in the 1960s. Its goals were multifarious and changing, including redistributing the effects of economic growth, restoring economic growth, reforming the state machinery and attenuating the militancy of the working class through incorporating its representatives into the policy-making process (see LaPalombara 1966 for a general survey). What was proposed to the labour movement was a self-limitation of wage demands, first, in exchange for trade union participation in policies aimed at removing the distortions generated by economic growth, and secondly (after the recession of 1964), in exchange for the *restoration* of economic growth. These attempts failed for various reasons to do with the environment, described above. In the first place, the business community was divided such as to preclude its effective representation by Confindustria, and therefore a commitment on its part to keep to the agreement. There was no longer a locus of business interests because they were fragmented among various competing institutions and enterprises which conducted their own lobbying and financing of different political parties and factions. Secondly, the CISL and CGIL refused to accept the exchange. For the CISL, entering into any form of political exchange ran counter to the principles on which trade unions should operate (see above). The CGIL objected to the Plan's emphasis on a limitation of incomes and to what the union regarded as a largely consultative role for the trade unions. More important, it viewed the plan as a 'neo-capitalist' attempt to rationalise Italian capitalism, isolating the PCI and splitting the working class in the process. Thirdly, the state proved unable to meet the conditions necessary to an effective launch of the Plan. The first Five-Year Plan was approved by Parliament in 1965. The text of the document itself, however, appeared to concede that the institutional requirements for an effective system of planning did not exist. Indeed, in the absence of an institutional framework, the plan's proposals with respect to incomes policy amounted to little more than an appeal to the labour movement to 'act responsibly' in the area of collective bargaining (see *ibid.*: 152). Activation of the Plan was delayed until 1967 and it rapidly collapsed. In short, the changes in the industrial relations system in this period did not alter the basic characteristics of the postwar model. That model was essentially based on a form of privileged access to the state and the changes which took place were largely the result of the manoeuvrings of different actors to maximise their own interests. The failure of planning was symptomatic of the static nature of the system and was a harbinger of the dramatic changes which the industrial relations system was about to undergo.

The end of the postwar model: the 'Hot Autumn' and its consequences (1967–75)

The immobile and 'closed' industrial relations system and the low capacity and stability of the political system gained explosive significance with the modernisation of civil society and the consequent growth of new and demanding constituencies. Whether or not the centre-left split the working class (through incorporation of the PSI into the government), it none the less did not rationalise, even stabilise, Italian capitalism. Worker militancy, which began in 1967 and peaked in the 'Hot Autumn' of 1969 should be seen therefore in the context of a general growth of social and political militancy, sparked off by the student movement in 1967. If there was a common element to this militancy, it was a rejection of the traditional modes of interest intermediation (i.e. the trade unions and political parties), which were regarded as being insufficient to protect and advance workers' (and other) interests (Petta 1975; 206; Mammarella 1978: 453).

The rejection saw its expression in the development of extra-parliamentary groups, factory councils and other forms of direct democracy and the positing of demands of a qualitatively different nature to those normally espoused by the trade union movement. These demands focused on 'political-economic' aspects such as the division of labour in factories and the reduction of wage differentials between different categories of workers. The militancy had significant effects on the relationship between the state, capital and labour, and on the internal nature of the actors themselves.

Unlike its French counterpart, in May 1968, the Italian trade union movement did not attempt to suppress the workers' demands. Rather it took up these demands and attempted to channel them towards longer-term issues of social and economic policy. This represented an attempt to exploit labour's 'clout' in the market arena to obtain objectives in the political arena, which contrasted with the policy of the 1950s in using the political arena to compensate for an absence of power in the market arena (see above). It had the further benefit of healing the split between the trade union leadership and the rank-and-file. The leadership attempted to obtain government action on issues such as schooling, housing, transport, welfare and the south as well as more immediate factory-related issues. This new strategy was called 'the struggle for reforms' (la lotta per le Riforme'). The heart of this strategy concerned the goal of the structural reform of Italian society, primarily through workers' control over investments within the framework of a plan which would be negotiated at all levels of the economy. Therefore, planning was to be linked to industrial democracy via the trade union movement's control over the economy (see Lange, Ross and Vannicelli 1982: 158).

The new strategy had two closely interelated consequences. First, it led to close collaboration between the CGIL, the CISL and the UIL. For the first time in twenty years, the representation of the labour movement by one body appeared to be a realistic prospect as a time-table was drawn up for the reunification of the three unions. Secondly, the 'struggle for reforms' expanded the role of the trade unions beyond their traditional place in the political economy to a point at which they began to usurp the political parties as chief mediators of working-class interests and as the base from which radical reformism could be launched. The trade unions, then, were encroaching on the political parties' traditional aggregative functions in view of the latter's failure in this area. The combination of the above two trends resulted in a dis-tancing of the three unions from their respective political parties, the breaking of official links being approved by the CGIL and CISL in 1969.

The response of the state and capital to the 'Hot Autumn' was a divided one. Farneti has argued that the Italian ruling class was divided in the late 1960s between those wishing to disperse the political and social conflict and those wishing to accentuate the tension, opening the prospect of a right-wing governmental solution (Farneti 1976: 99–100). The division between the capital-intensive and labour-intensive firms inside Confindustria was exacerbated. For the latter, a more open approach to the trade unions was all the more pressing in view of the failure of the state-controlled enterprises to promote more progressive collective bargaining policies. They also viewed the continued centrality of the DC in the political system as inhibiting such a change. The publication of the Pirelli Report by the 'young entrepeneur' repre-senting the labour-intensive firms represented the victory of this group – as far as official policy was concerned. The report constituted an attempt to modernise the image of entrepeneurs and reverse their declining social prestige. Amongst other things the trade unions were recognised as legitimate bargaining partners in the industrial relations system: their cooperation was deemed essential not only for dealing with immediate issues in the factory, but for resolving the major problems of Italian society (see Pasquino 1976: 291–2).

The governing parties were similarly divided, particularly with the collapse of the centre-left after the 1968 elections, which seemed to confirm that this was not the coalition formula that could carry through what most perceived to be essential structural reforms. The parties of the right, plus the PSDI and the right-wing of the DC, favoured a centre-right alternative or a form of 'strong government', through provoking the dissolution of Parliament and going to the electorate on a law and order platform. The parties of the left, plus part of the Socialists, the progressive wing of the DC and the Republicans, favoured a more open stance towards the labour movement and the possible incorporation of the Communist Party into the governing coalition. The result was a series of short-term, caretaker governments until the elections of 1972.

The late 1960s, then, saw the collapse of the basic model of industrial relations which had predominated until then. The stablility of that system had depended upon the operation of the mechanisms of the market and collective bargaining in conjunction with a system of 'privileged access' to the political system for certain groups unrepresentative of their sector as a whole, and mediated via the political parties. The breakdown of this system saw a more united trade union movement bypassing the political parties and negotiating directly with a weak and divided political system, using national and regional strike action to back up their demands. The new relationship between the industrial and political systems was one of negotiation and conflict. The 'closed' nature of the system did not give way to cooperation and political exchange. However, the extent to which the attempt to wrench reforms from the political arena through pressure in the market arena yielded results was more open to question. There is no doubt that the trade unions made significant gains with respect to workers' rights, working conditions and wage differentials, most of the legislative aspects of which were contained in the Workers' Statute which was passed in 1970. However, the bargaining over long-term reforms, such as housing and health reform, did not produce the expected results (see Lange, Ross and Vannicelli 1982: 139–40). Divided and weak governments and an unreformed bureaucracy proved unable and increasingly unwilling to respond to the needs of reform. Meanwhile the employers deeply divided over the position of an open dialogue with the labour movement, became primarily concerned with resisting the workers' wage push.

The positions of the state and business were intensified after the 1972 elections (which resulted in a centre-right government), and the 1973 oil crisis. These events – coupled with the failure to reunify the three unions due to opposition from the political parties and within the unions themselves – also determined a change in emphasis on the part of the trade union movement. A more defensive posture was adopted, the essential aim of which was to protect wage gains against inflation. This is not to say that the 'struggle for reforms' was abandoned. General problems, such as unemployment and the south, continued to be high on the agenda, but were negotiated largely at the factory or sectoral level. Moreover, issues which were pursued at the political level were no longer subject to direct negotiation with the government, but mediated through the political parties, which were anxious to reassert their predominance within the political system. These developments probably explain why the trade unions, in obtaining in 1975 the full protection of wages from inflation that they had been seeking, did so in the absence of the state. The 1975 agreement – which increased the protection of the wage indexation system (the *scala mobile*) to 100 per cent – has mistakenly been identified either as being 'corporatist' in nature (Martinelli and Treu 1984: 287) or as involving 'political exchange' (Dal Co and Perulli 1986: 161). This is probably because, on the one hand, it had a 'corporatist goal' of establishing a more stable pattern of industrial relations through removing the issue of wage dynamics from the conflict/negotiation agenda; and, on the other hand, it occurred in the context of a dramatic electoral increase on the part of the PCI. Yet, it was an agreement concluded between Confindustria and the trade unions alone. The state did not 'exchange' anything. On the contrary, it could be argued that it was concluded at the state's expense (Regini 1987: 196). It did help to pave the way for an experiment in political exchange was to stabilise industrial relations, its chief significance in fact was that it was to become the very bedrock of dispute on which the stability of the system would founder in the mid-1980s.

Political exchange and political conflict: The years of 'National Solidarity' (1976–9)

In 1978 the trade union movement, at its national assembly, formally launched the so-called 'EUR' strategy (named after the Roman district where the meeting took place), which entailed a shift back to a position reminiscent of the 1950s in offering the state restraint in the market arena in exchange for government macro-economic action. This resulted in the signing of the first Italian tripartite pact on macro-economic policy. The origins of this agreement were mixed. The trade union movement was subject to various pressures to adopt a change in strategy. First, the unions' success in contractual bargaining had caused them problems of both an internal nature (due to complaints of groups not covered by indexation and complaints from some workes about the levelling of wage differentials) and an external nature (in that wage indexation restricted the scope for free collective bargaining, yet the unions' disruptive power in the market remained high in a period of economic crisis, which had implications for political stability). Secondly, their success at the contractual level had not been matched by achievements in areas of political and social reform. Thirdly, developments in the political situation were conductive to a shift of focus to the political arena. The dramatic rise in support for the PCI registered at the 1975 regional elections, and the 1976 national elections, in an atmosphere of economic crisis and rising social tension (caused by terrorist activity) led the party to present its candidature for government as being the only solution to Italy's crisis. The party proposed an 'austerity' policy whereby workers would make sacrifices on the wages front in exchange for certain commitments on the part of the government. The 'National Solidarity' experiment which followed involved the PCI continually abstaining in Parliament, in 1977 which allowed the government to remain in office, and actually voting for the government in 1978. This action was based on the signing of a series of programmatic accords acceptable to the PCI. The 'EUR' strategy launched in 1978 resembled, to a large degree, the PCI's austerity proposals.

On the part of the employers and the government, a containment of the militancy of the trade union movement, specifically on the wages front, was deemed essential to surviving the economic crisis and restoring political stability. The exchange which followed was based on self-restraint in the wage market and other aspects of the labour market in return for the government's commitment to, and labour participation in, the re-programming of investments and policies to increase employment. The trade unions proposed bargaining at the firm and sectoral level over investment plans; a reform of the 'state participation' system; a decentralisation of state responsibility for the allocation of resources to local and regional levels; and a reform of the social services sector, breaking the hold over it of the patronage system (for detailed coverage of these points, see Lange, Ross and Vannicelli 1982: 165 *et. seq.*). Two points should be noted about this exchange.

First, it was brought about primarily as the result of pressure from the trade unions, with employers and the government in a defensive position. The new stance of the trade unions represented a clear abandonment of the idea, prevalent since the 'Hot Autumn', of the pursuit of political objectives through a maximisation of market potential, and its replacement with the idea that *containment* of contractual demands might further the goal of political objectives. Evidently part of the thinking behind this change was the recognition that the continued maximisation of market potential in a period of intense economic and social crisis could have political implications for Italy's stability. Yet it would be wrong to interpret this as some form of benign sacrifice on the part of the labour movement in the interests of Italian capitalism. On the contrary, it should be seen as a shift in strategic resources to change the framework within which industrial relations issues were resolved such as to protect – if not advance – the interests of the workers. This is evidenced in the fact that the *scala mobile* was not open to negotiation; that pressure was to be maintained at the workplace and at sectoral levels over investment policy; and that the unions retained complete autonomy at the national level to pressurise the government in the absence of any institutional arrangements through which tripartism would be conducted. Seen in this context, the unions were driving quite a hard bargain:

> ... unions were proposing a series of limited changes which, while making economic change and growth more possible by removing unwarranted restraints on decisions, would maintain pressure on capital and protect the fundamental gains made by the working-class. (*ibid.*, 173)

Maintaining unrestrained pressure in the market arena during a period of high social and political tension and economic recession was likely to provoke a right-wing or 'strong' government alternative, which would not be in the interests of the trade union movement. Indeed the back-drop of the political situation is the second general point about the exchange which should be considered.

It would be simplistic to argue that the tripartite agreement was simply the result of the reassertion of the 'transmission belt' principle between the PCI and the CGIL, i.e. that the 'EUR' line was simply an adjunct to the PCI's strategy of entering government. This of course overlooks the other two unions, the CISL and the UIl, the former of which opposed stating coalition preferences and the latter of which resolutely opposed the PCI's 'Historic Compromise' of a DC–PCI governing alliance. It also overlooks the fact that incorporation of organised labour into the decision-making machinery of the state, in conjunction with the incorporation of the PCI into the government, was a part of the Christian Democratic leader Moro's 'third phase' (Cassano 1979: 108–10). None the less, it remains true that all three unions regarded the success of their new line as being dependent upon a change in the coalition formula at the centre which – in view of the exhaustion of other alternatives – meant the incorporation, in some way, of the PCI into the government. This fact meant that the experiment in political exchange was inextricably tied to the party political struggle. The outcome of this represented an implicit element in the exchange, and constituted a source of division inside the actors.

The above two points help to explain why the exchange failed. The government and employers proved increasingly unwilling to make the commitments necessary to making the agreement work as union strength began to decline and the 'national solidarity' experiment proved to be failing. There was considerable opposition to the experiment not only from the PSI, but from inside the DC itself. Certain legislative aspects, such as the pension reform, never emerged from the parliamentary floor, having been sunk through sectional interest group pressure on individual political parties. Where legislation was passed, the government often failed to activate the process of implementation. Where the process of implementation was activated, the bureaucracy – dominated by vested interest groups – proved itself unable and unwilling to activate policies in the fast and innovative manner required of them. Finally, trade union pressure on the state proved to have little effect because of the fragmented and compartmentalised nature of decision-making (on the above points, see Regini 1987: 200–1; 1984: 40–1).

The employers were as divided. Agnelli had become head of Confindustria in 1974, and under his presidency and that of his successor, Carli (1976–80), there was an attempt to re-establish the employers' organisation as an important and autonomous actor. This involved consolidating the position of the large-scale private firms inside the organisation, loosening the ties between the private sector and the DC, breaking the trend towards using the *parastate* and restoring the bargaining system which had been shaken in 1969. This generated considerable opposition from the smaller industrialists who still constituted a majority inside the business community, and who feared that a position of 'openness' towards the labour movement would advance the prospects of the Communist Party. Finally, the trade union movement became increasingly divided over its new line. This was partly because of dissent from the base which feared the leadership being 'co-opted' into managing the capitalist state, and partly because the CISL and UIL became increasingly concerned that the line represented little more than an attempt by the CGIL to increase the hegemony of the Communist Party.

In short, the experiment in political exchange of the mid-1970s was unstable from the outset. It was the result of the changing strengths and strategies of different actors in a particular economic, social and political environment. That environment was undergoing rapid change, and was most clearly signalled in the electoral defeat of the PCI in 1979, which marked the beginning of a new phase in Italian industrial relations.

Deregulation and neo-liberalism: the 'new consensus' (the 1980s)

Developments in Italy since 1980 have been part of a general trend in western Europe, where state and employers have favoured an undermining of traditional forms of collective bargaining and a shift to a deregulation of institutional procedures and a more 'flexible' labour market as solutions to the problems of economic growth and unemployment (see Goldthorpe 1984, and Rhodes 1987, for general analyses). In Italy the elections of 1979 saw the emergence of a five-party coalition (the *pentapartito*). The chief concern of this government, and subsequent governments, has been the control of inflation. The adjustment of the *scala mobile* has been a major focus of attention in this regard. The election of Vittorio Merloni (a Christian Democrat) to succeed Guido Carli as head of Confindustria in 1980 marked the beginning of a shift back towards a tough line on the trade unions because of the need for a reduction in the labourforce and a restructuring of industry. It also suggested the likely return of the DC as the major supporter of organised business interests. The changing labour market and political environment has seen a decline in strength of the labour movement, particularly in the market arena, the first sign of which was the defeat of the strike at Fiat in 1980 (Jacobi 1986; 47–8), and a crisis of representation, effectiveness and strategic orientation on the part of the trade unions (Carrieri and Donolo 1986: 207).

However, these trends were, in the early 1980s, mitigated by evidence of apparent counter-trends, which obscured the analysis and prognosis of some authors of the direction in which industrial relations were heading. First, the appointment of Romano Prodi as head of IRI marked the beginning of an attempt to modernise the public sector and to use it to carry through required restructuring without suffering major societal dislocations. There has been much discussion over proposals for the creation of 'joint management committees' (consisting of representatives of labour and capital) to carry through these changes in return for the trade unions' acceptance of a suspension of their constitutional right to strike. It should be stressed, however, that the attempt to modernise the public sector has been closely associated with the secretary of the DC, De Mita, in his attempt to 'modernise' the DC. Reform of the public sector requires its depoliticisation, and this has met with considerable opposition not only from inside the DC, but from the PSI under Craxi. The

1980s has witnessed an electoral decline in the position of the DC, and an attempt by the PSI to gain the DC's position of 'centrality' in the political system. The appointment of Craxi to the premiership in 1983 enhanced this attempt. Its significance is that it requires continued governmental control over public shareholdings, something justified by Craxi in terms of being essential to the maintenance of 'social order'. Prodi has consequently experienced great difficulties in breaking the public sector's essential characteristic of *lottizzazione*. Hence the pursuit of more progressive industrial relations policies remains problematic.

The second piece of evidence of an apparent counter-trend was the signing in 1983 of a trilateral agreement on the *scala mobile*. This second apparently 'corporatist' achievement led to some optimistic prognoses of Italian industrial relations, based either on the idea that this was a major 'turning-point' or on the view that the two agreements (of the late 1970s and early 1980s), seen together, constituted an evident trend towards 'institutionalising conflict' in Italy (see, for example, Carinci 1983). Subsequent events, however, found these views to be ill-founded: 1984 witnessed a dramatic clash between the trade unions and the government, and between the political parties and inside the trade unions themselves. This clash was the direct result of an attempt to renew the trilateral agreement of 1983. Two aspects were underestimated in immediate analyses of the agreement. First, the environment in which negotiations took place was considerably unstable: the economic situation was worsening after the second oil crisis in 1979; the trade unions, weakened by the prolonged recession, were finding it more and more difficult to present a united front; the political situation had become re-polarised with the exclusion of the PCI from office; and the employers and the government had little intention of limiting their autonomy through an institutionalised relationship with the labour movement (on the contrary, as already noted, they wished to begin deregulating such aspects). Finally, both the employers and the government had threatened to resort to unilateral action unless there was some prospect of an agreement being reached. The second aspect which was underestimated was the exact nature of the agreement itself. Analyses conducted in the light of subsequent events show that the agreement was little more than an *ad hoc* exchange focused on incomes policy which did not limit the actors' future behaviour, nor involve long-term benefits (Regini 1985; Dal Co and Perulli 1986; Lange 1986). Lange, for example, concludes that:

Rather than reflecting the ambitions of the union movement to play an institutionalised role in the restructuring of the economy through government and firm policies [the 1983 agreement] . . . represented a series of short-term trade-offs intended to ease wage-push pressure without damaging workers' purchasing power. (Lange 1986: 31–2)

Indeed it could be argued that the agreement reflected a clear shift in the balance of power between capital and labour to the latter's disfavour: on the part of capital even such a long-term and indirect aspect such as the reduction of inflation was viewed to be part of the exchange because of its effect on purchasing power. Therefore, it was not altogether surprising that the employers wished to harden their line the following year and decided not to renew the agreement. The attempt to draft a new text failed, however, more as a result of the trade unions' response. The Communist faction of the CGIL, in opposition to the UIL, the CISL and the Socialist faction of the CGIL, refused to accept the new draft. The Socialist Prime Minister, Craxi, announced an 'exchange' based largely on the agreement, except that it would be implemented by decree: the *scala mobile* was to be cut by three points in exchange for a freeze on a number of prices and rent increases, and the introduction of a number of measures to restrain inflation and promote growth. As with previous periods, it is impossible to evaluate this breakdown outside the context of the party political struggle, as the union division along party lines indicates. The PCI was opposed to the agreement, yet this became a secondary concern to its opposition to the government's action in implementing a decree on an issue traditionally subject to collective bargaining. Indeed the decree can be seen as part of Craxi's goal of Socialist 'centrality' in the political system: it was meant to show that economic policy should not be subject to the need of seeking the consent of the Communists. The PCI obtained enough signatures to call a referendum on the decree, and the referendum campaign reflected the intensely political nature of the clash. The trade unions campaigned along party lines, and Craxi staked the future of his government on the outcome of the vote. The limited economic costs and benefits of the activation of the decree were overshadowed by a general debate over how economic policy should be conducted, and this, at its deepest, concerned a debate over the distribution of power in the political economy (see *ibid.*). The defeat in the referendum of the PCI and the Communist faction of the CGIL indicated the way in which that distribution had altered.

Conclusion: Corporatism and its Limits

For the corporatist 'gold-digger', the case of Italy may appear to be highly problematic: are the 'seams' of 'corporatism' discovered in the late 1970s and early 1980s, the real thing or simply 'fools' gold'? This chapter's outline of state–group relations in the postwar period suggests that (on the assumption that the question itself is not a misguided one) the latter would evidently appear to be the case. When placed in a broader historical perspective, the agreements of 1977 and 1983 might be seen to be little more than the result of converging, or diverging, strategies of the different actors attempting to maximise their interests by shifting the framework within which industrial relations problems are resolved. The failure of some authors to recognise that 'corporatist practices' might be simply ephemeral products of the pluralist game is indicative of the degree of influence that corporatist thinking has enjoyed. The history of state-group relations in Italy suggests that analysing the Italian political system in corporatist terms is limiting and consequently not very fruitful. This chapter concludes by indicating why this is so. This will be done by drawing on the findings of this chapter to look, first, at the internal nature and external goals of the relevant *actors* in Italy, and secondly, at the type of *conditions* cited by corporatist writers and how they relate to the Italian case.

The actors

Cawson claims that the 'major element' which the new corporatist writing added to the earlier insights of writers such as Beer and Rokkan was a conception of 'the state' as distinct from 'government', and the recognition that the relationship between the state and corporate groups was very different from that between pressure groups and elected governments (Cawson 1986: 45). Yet it is perhaps precisely this assumption which is highly problematic when it comes to empirical analysis. Whatever the theoretical nuances or qualifications, the essential assumption remains that 'it makes sense to speak of a "state interest"' (*ibid.*: 57). One might finish this phrase by stating, 'which is distinguishable from a "business interest" and a "labour interest"'. The strength of this contention lies in its contrast with a 'pure' pluralist approach which views the state as a mere 'arena' lacking an independent interest. It fails, however, to account for states which do not fit neatly into either category.

The Italian state has been described as 'available' (Di Palma 1979), as an 'archipelago' (Donolo 1980) and as a system of 'spoils allocation' (Amato 1976). If there is a common element in these analyses, it is that the state has been 'occupied' or 'colonised' by private interests which have not had a common interest in maintaining an efficient mechanism of capital accumulation. As this chapter has shown, the weakness and disunity of the private interests has resulted in their 'cohesion' being

maintained through a diverse *political* coalition, the DC, which has used
the resources of government to further such interests and consolidate its
own position or, more accurately, the positions of its various factions.
Economic policy has consequently been haphazard and dependent upon
political criteria rather than being the result of a coherent 'outlook' on
the part of 'the state'. The consequences have been, first, an expansion
of institutions and actors responsible for state tasks, and secondly, an
increasing level of conflict between those institutions and actors. The
bureaucracy, the *parastate*, the government, Parliament and the parties
are all dominated by a high level of internal political conflict and
interference from one another in most aspects of policy-making. This is
not to reduce the DC to a pure vehicle of patronage. On the contrary, as
an unwieldy coalition of factions representing business, the church, the
'small man' and anti-communism (Pasquino 1979), the DC prevented a
clear distinction emerging between capital, labour and the state. A
policy of 'privileged access' *was* operated, but – as we have already seen
– according to a number of criteria which led to a partisan appropriation
of the state, and which was not exclusive to one party, faction or
interest. Policy outcomes are, then, highly dependent upon the parties'
abilities to interfere with the policy-making process at almost all levels
of the political system, from inputs to outputs.

Much of the above also explains the internal fragmentation of the
business and labour communities. As this chapter has shown, Confindustria since the late 1950s has had continuous problems in representing a
business community fragmented in its access to the state and by the dual
nature of Italy's economy (labour intensive/capital intensive firms, large
firms/small firms, the north and south, etc.). The divisions inside the
trade union movement run deeper, along the interlinked lines of
partisanship and access to the state. This, coupled with a low degree of
concentration and representational monopoly, has meant a continual
degree of dependence upon political parties. In short, if the corporatist
instrument of analysis assumes a clear distinction between labour, capital and the state, it is difficult to see how it can usefully be applied to the
Italian case.

Of course, where a clear line *has* emerged which is representative of a
single actor, then that line has generally not been conducive to the
pursuit of policies of political exchange. If there is a common factor
which unites the business community, it is a 'fear of the left' in both its
political and union forms. This has acted as a constant constraint on the
business community's willingness to open dialogue with the union movement; it has tended to reinforce the view that the 'centrality' of the DC
in the political system is essential to preventing the Communist Party's

advance; and it has meant that the business community is most united when it is following a hard line towards labour. The trade union movement's position in the postwar period has also had a certain consistency. This has been reflected in a constant attempt to squeeze reforms from the government, and in the post-1969 period to protect the gains made in the 'Hot Autumn'. Moreover, the undermining of these gains has been perceived as being the core of strategies of the state and business. Finally, the state's activism in industrial relations has been, as we have seen, a major political source of economic problems and mismanagement rather than a stimulant to political exchange. In short, if the corporatist instrument of analysis assumes a sacrifice of the individual actors' interests in pursuit of a common interest, then it is difficult to see its applicability to the Italian case.

It is in the above context that political exchange in Italy must be seen in a different light to that of strategic actors coming together to pursue a common approach with an aim to stabilising the system. Political exchange in Italy can be viewed as the result of changing methods of (often not clearly defined) actors who remain faithful to the goals of pluralistic pressure, with the consequent possibility of *destabilising* consequences. 'Consensus', then, can be the result of the changing balance of power in a conflictual situation. This introduces the final question of whether a change in structural conditions would result in a 'corporatist' system in Italy.

The conditions
Italy's case would seem to demonstrate that the positing of certain 'universal' structural conditions for the flourishing of corporatism is highly problematic both because of the 'peculiarity' of national environments and the inherent instability of any forms of political exchange. This point will be illustrated by briefly analysing the Italian case with reference to five conditions, which are seen to be characteristic of corporatism.

First, it is unlikely that the cited organisational condition of a high level of concentration of interests and representational monopoly would promote more experiments in political exchange. The trade union movement was able to promote and activate a strategy of political exchange in the absence of this condition in the mid-1970s. Moreover, it was a failure on the part of the state and not the trade union movement that contributed to the collapse of that strategy.

Secondly, the Italian case shows that the cited political condition of a 'pro-labour' government is too simplistic to be universally applicable. Citing this as a condition overlooks the type of effects generated by the

interaction of political parties in different political systems. In Italy the
following points come to light: a change in the composition of the
government may become an *implicit element* of political exchange rather
than a condition for it; governments may attempt to bring trade unions
into the policy-making machinery as part of a partisan manoeuvre to
preclude the importance of the main pro-labour party; the main pro-
labour party may remain excluded from office but 'compensated' by its
participation in the formulation of labour policies; the entrance into
government of the main pro-labour party may actually make exercises in
political exchange more problematic both because of the tensions it
causes inside the governing coalition and the frictions it causes inside a
trade union movement divided essentially along party lines; and in a
system of 'rule by parties' (*partitocrazia*) any 'corporatist-style' negotiations will suffer from interference from parties at all levels of the
policy-making process (on the rate of parties in general see Pasquino
1984, 1987).

Thirdly, the Italian case shows that the economic conditions conducive to the emergence of experiments in political exchange are considerably complex. Economic growth may foster political exchange
arrangements but may also provide an incentive to the participants to
obtain more by resorting to conflictual action. An economic recession,
or crisis, may also foster political exchange experiments. Continued
recession, however, can have the effect of making these arrangements
unstable because it makes the materialisation of long-term benefits
more unlikely.

Fourthly, the cultural conditions cited by corporatist writers are not
necessarily always clear-cut. The Italian case shows that a political
exchange agreement may be the result of a conflictual struggle, the
agreement representing a form of compromise as a result of the changing balance of power between the state, capital and labour. It is possible
for such arrangements to have a temporary stabilising effect in the
absence of a consensual culture.

Finally, an efficient state machine, one that can 'deliver', would
appear to be an important condition for political exchange to exist and
persist. Yet citing the 'nature of the state' as a condition for corporatism
has an implication of considerable significance. Any serious move
towards a corporatist style of policymaking has *institutional* implications. In other words, if this style of policy-making were to be a
distinctive trend, then institutional reform – involving changes of a
particular type – would be on the political agenda. In Italy, where
institutional reform has been a major political theme of the late 1970s
and early 1980s, institutional changes of a corporatist type have hardly

been countenanced (Pasquino 1986: 121). Yet this argument leads inexorably to the question of exactly what type of institutional implications are involved in a shift to a 'corporatist' system. For it might be argued that corporatism is unlikely to develop in Italy without a Sartorian 'lurch to the right'. But that of course would have little to do with the 'corporatism' that corporatist writers have claimed to have discovered.

Note

1. See, for example, the conclusion reached by Golden (1986:293) on the 'National Solidarity' period, 'more an ad hoc product of external pressures than a genuine commitment by any of the relevant actors, each of which has remained deeply distrustful of the others', with that of Regini (1987; 204): 'an ambitious attempt to create a genuine concertation, similar to the North European settings of the 1950s and 1960s.' There have also been erroneous identifications of corporatism as constituting an agreement between labour and business in the absence of the state; see Martinelli (1979: 85), and Martinelli and Treu (1984: 287).

References

Amato, G. (1976), *Economia, politica e istituzioni in Italia* (Bologna, Il Mulino).

Bianchi, P. (1987), 'The IRI in Italy: strategic role and political constraints', *West European Politics*, **10** (2) (April).

Carinci, F. (1983), 'La via italiana all' istituzionalizzazione del conflitto', *Politica del Diritto*, **3**, 14 (September), 417–29.

Carrieri, Mimmo and Donolo, Carlo (1983), 'Oltre l'orizzonte neo-corporatista. Alcuni scenari sul futuro politico del sindacato', *Stato e Mercato*, **9**, (December), 475–503.

Cassano, Franco (1979), *Il Teorema democristiano* (Bari, De Donato).

Cawson, Alan (1986), *Corporatism and Political Theory* (Oxford, Blackwell).

Cella, Gian Primo and Treu, Tiziano (1986), 'Collective and Political Bargaining', in O. Jacobi, B. Jessop, H. Kastendiek and M. Regini (eds), *Economic Crisis, Trade Unions and the State* (London, Croom Helm), ch. 8, pp. 171–90.

Dal Co, Mario and Perulli, Paolo (1986), 'The trilateral agreement of 1983: social pact or political truce?' in B. Jessop, O. Jacobi, H. Kastendiek and M. Regini (eds), *Economic Crisis, Trade Unions and the State* (London, Croom Helm), ch. 7, 157–70.

Di Palma, Giuseppe (1979), 'The available state: problems of reform', *West European Politics*, **2** (3), 149–65.

Donolo, Carlo (1980), 'Social change and transformation of the state in Italy' in Richard Scase (ed.), *The State in Western Europe* (London, Croom Helm), ch. 5, 164–96.

Farneti, Paolo (1976), 'I partiti politici e il sistema di potere' in AA. VV. *L'Italia Contemporanea, 1945–1975* (Torino, Einaudi), ch. 5.

Furlong, Paul (1984), 'Italy' in F. F. Ridley (ed.), *Policies and Politics in Western Europe* (London, Croom Helm), ch. 5, 115–53.

Furlong, Paul (1986), 'State, finance and industry in Italy' in Andrew Cox (ed.), *The State, Finance and Industry* (Brighton, Wheatsheaf), ch. 5, 142–71.

Giugni, Gino (1985), 'Concertazione sociale e sistema politico in Italia', *Giornale di Diritto del Lavoro e di Relazioni Industriali*, 25, VII, 53–64.

Golden, Miriam (1985), 'Neo-corporativismo ed esclusione della forza-lavoro dalla rap-presentanza politica' in Gianfranco Pasquino (ed.), *Il Sistema Politica Italiano* (Bari, Laterza), 208–31.

Golden, Miriam (1986), 'Interest representation, party systems and the state in comparative perspective', *Comparative Politics*, **18** (3) (April), 279–301.

Goldthorpe, John (1984), 'The end of convergence: corporatist and dualist tendencies in modern western societies' in John Goldthrope (ed.), *Order and Conflict in Contemporary Capitalism* (Oxford, Oxford University Press), ch. 13, 315–43.

Jacobi, Otto (1986), 'Trade unions, industrial relations and structural economic ruptures' in O. Jacobi, B. Jessop, H. Kastendiek and M. Regini (eds), *Economic Crisis, the Trade Unions and the State* (London, Croom Helm), 32–60.

Lange, Peter (1985) 'Semiperiphery and core in the European context. Reflections on the post-war Italian experience' in Giovanni Arrighi (ed.), *Semiperipheral Development Politics of Southern Europe in the Twentieth Century* (London, Sage), ch. 8, 179–213.

Lange, Peter (1986) 'The end of an era: the wage indexation referendum of 1985' in R. Leonardi and R. Nanetti (eds), *Italian Politics: A Review*, vol. 1 (London, Frances Pinter), ch. 3, 29–46.

Lange, Peter and Regini, Marino (1987a) 'Regolazione sociale e politiche pubbliche: schemi analitici per lo studio del caso italiano', *Stato e Mercato*, **19**, 1 (April), 97–121.

Lange, Peter and Regini, Marino (eds) (1987b) *Stato, mercato e regolazione sociale: nuove prospettive sul caso italiano* (Bologna, Mulino), Introduction, 9–41.

Lange, Peter, Ross, George and Vannicelli, Maurizio (1982) *Unions, change and Crisis: French and Italian Strategy and the Political Economy, 1945–1980* (London, Allen and Unwin).

LaPalombara, Joseph (1957) *The Italian Labour Movement. Problems and Prospects* (Ithaca, NY, Cornell University Press).

LaPalombara, Joseph (1964) *Interest Groups in Italian Politics* (Princeton, NJ, Princeton University Press).

LaPalombara, Joseph (1966) *Italy: The Politics of Planning* (Syracuse, NY, Syracuse University Press).

Mammarella, Giuseppe (1978) *L'Italia dalla caduta del fascismo ad oggi* (Bologna, Mulino).

Martin, Ross M. (1983) 'Pluralism and the New Corporatism', *Political Studies*, 31, 86–102.

Martinelli, A. (1979) 'Organised business and Italian politics: Confindustria and the Christian Democrats in the post-war period', *West European Politics*, 2, 3, 166–86.

Martinelli, A. and Treu T. (1984) 'Employers associations in Italy', in John P. Windmuller and Alan Gladstone (eds), *Employers' Associations and Industrial Relations: A Comparative Study* (Oxford, Oxford University Press), ch. 10, 264–93.

Matteucci, Nicola (1984) 'Corporatisvismo', *Il Mulino*, 2 (March–April), 305–13.

Pasquino, Gianfranco (1976) 'Capital and labour in Italy', *Government and Opposition*, **11**, 3, 273–93.

Pasquino, Gianfranco (1979) 'Italian Christian Democracy: A party for all seasons', *West European Politics*, **2** (3) (October), 88–109.

Pasquino, Gianfranco (1984) 'Party government in Italy: achievements and prospects', Paper presented to the 1984 Summer School on Comparative Politics, European University Institute, Florence, 18 June – 13 July).

Pasquino, Gianfranco (1986) 'The debate on institutional reform' in R. Leonardi and R. Nanetti (eds), *Italian Politics. A Review, Vol. 1* (London, Frances Pinter), 8, 117–33.

Pasquino, Gianfranco (1987) 'Regolatori sregolati: partiti e governo dei partiti', in Lange and Regini, 1987b, 53–81.

Petta, Paolo (1975), *Ideologie Costituzionali Della Sinistra Italiana (1892–1974)* (Roma, Giulio Savelli).

Regini, Marino (1981), *I Dilemmi del sindacato. Conflitto e partecipazione negli anni settanta e ottanta* (Bologna, Il Mulino).

Regini, Marino (1982) 'Changing relationships between labour and the state in Italy:

towards a neo-corporatist system?' in Gerhard Lehmbruch and Phillippe C. Schmitter (eds), *Patterns of Corporatist Policy-Making* (London, Sage), ch. 3, 109–32.

Regini, Marino (1984) 'The conditions for political exchange: how concertation emerged and declined in Italy and Great Britain' in John Goldthorpe (ed.), *Order and Conflict in Contemporary Capitalism* (Oxford, Oxford University Press), ch. 6, 124–42.

Regini, Marino (1985) 'The three attempts at concertation in Italy and the reasons for their failure', *Occasional Paper No. 49*, Research Institute, Johns Hopkins University Bologna Centre, February.

Regini, Marino (1986) 'Political bargaining in western Europe during the economic crisis of the 1980s' in O. Jacobi, B. Jessop, H. Kastendiek and M. Regini (eds), *Economic Crisis, the Trade Unions and the State* (London, Croom Helm), ch. 3, 61–76.

Regini, Marino (1987) 'Social pacts in Italy' in Ilja Scholten (ed.), *Political Stability and Neo-Corporatism. Corporatist Integration and Societal Cleavages in Western Europe* (London, Sage), ch. 8, 195–215.

Rhodes, Martin (1987) 'The regulation and de-regulation of Labour Markets in western Europe; a comparison of Britain, France, West Germany and Italy', *European Consortium of Political Research Conference Paper*, April, 1–48.

Sartori, Giovanni (1970) 'Concept misinformation in comparative politics', *American Political Science Review*, **LXIV** (4), December, 1033–1053.

Schmitter, Phillippe C. (1981) 'Interest intermediation and regime governability in contemporary Western Europe and Northern America' in Suzanne Berger (ed.), *Organizing Interests in Western Europe. Pluralism, Corporatism and the Transformation of Politics* (Cambridge, Cambridge University Press), ch. 10, 287–330.

Tarentelli, Enzo (1986) *Economia politica del lavoro* (Torino, Utet).

Tarrow, Sidney (1967) *Peasant Communism in Southern Italy* (New Haven, Conn., Yale University Press).

Treu, Tiziano (1983) 'L'intervento del sindacato nella politica economica', *Giornale di Diritto del Lavoro e di Relazioni Industriali*, 5, 67–92.

Wilensky, H. L. (1976) *The New Corporatism. Centralisation and the Welfare State* (London, Sage).

5 Corporatism in Germany in historical perspective
V. R. Berghahn

Research on the history of corporatism in Germany greatly benefited from the fruitful, though precarious, *rapprochement* between historians and social scientists which occurred in the 1970s. On both sides the preceding decade had seen a revival of interest in the links between politics and economics. At the same time, neo-Marxists, and the Frankfurt School in particular, had given a fresh impetus to theorising about the role of the state in advanced industrial societies.[1] There was also the influence of orthodox 'Stamocap' interpretations of modern industrial capitalism.[2] Admitting that historians, in analysing socio-economic strutures of the past, cannot do without prior concep-tualisation, but also convinced that orthodox Marxism was unsuitable for understanding systems of power and domination in modern Ger-many, scholars like H.–U. Wehler and J. Kocka of Bielefeld University explored the usefulness of 'organised capitalism' as an analytical con-cept.[3] The result was a lively debate between the 'Bielefelders' and a number of West German political economists.

A similarly animated exchange started a little later between a number of historians of modern Germany and political scientists. Some of the latter had been uneasy for some time about the way the notion of pluralism had come to dominate political analysis in their discipline since the 1950s and were searching for alternative ways of comprehen-ding the wielding of power and influence in advanced industrial societies. It seemed obvious to them that competition among divergent interests was not as open and power not as diffuse as the pluralists had asserted. Certainly this dissatisfaction would appear to go some way to explain why Schmitter's article on 'Still the century of corporatism?' generated so much spontaneous interest within the discipline.[4] And just as a number of West German political scientists quickly began to toy with the corporatism paradigm, it was also picked up by some West German historians who had grown sceptical of the value of 'Organised Capitalism' as a framework for analysing the past structures of the German political economy.

The unfolding of this particular exchange was somewhat retarded by the fact that it took participants in the Schmitter debate sometime to clarify the meaning of corporatism. Schmitter himself, though not unaware of earlier uses of the concept, may not have fully appreciated how problematical it had become as a result of the experience of the 1930s.[5] But it was, above all, J. T. Winkler who muddied the waters when he defined corporatism as 'an economic system in which the state directs and controls predominantly privately-owned business according to four principles: unity, order, nationalism and success'.[6] What made this definition so controversial was that it subsumed both the fascist systems of the interwar period and the western systems of the postwar era, even if ironically it had been Winkler's intention to detach the concept from its historical legacies and thus make it available again for contemporary political science analysis. Clearly, Schmitter's hesitant differentiation into a state corporatism and a societal corporatism had to be refined.[7] One of those to attempt this was G. Lehmbruch when he began to focus on what he called the 'liberal' variant of corporatism which, to him, reflected 'the large measure of constitutional autonomy of the groups involved; hence the voluntary character of institutionalized integration of conflicting groups . . . [and] a high degree of cooperation among these groups themselves in the shaping of public policy'.[8] Unlike 'authoritarian corporatism', he added elsewhere, the liberal variant had remained embedded 'in a system of liberal constitutional democracy, comprising institutional rules such as freedom of association'.[9] In the meantime Schmitter, too, had given the concept greater precision.[10]

A further step was subsequently taken by Lehmbruch when he proposed a differentiation between research concentrating on the centre of national politics and peak interest groups on the one hand, and work concerned with 'sectoral corporatism' and a more limited interaction of government and interest representation in certain fields on the other.[11] The former would be dealing with the peak associations and 'the granting to these associations of privileged access to government' connected with 'the growth of – more or less institutionalized – linkages between public administration and such interest organizations'. He also pinpointed as a distinguishing feature, 'the "social partnership" of organized labour and business aimed at regulating conflicts between these groups in coordination with government policy'. Here in a nutshell was the triangular relationship between the 'state' and the two sides of industry which became known as 'tripartism' or, as Lehmbruch put it, 'liberal corporatist concertation' which, at the same time, is not antiparliamentary.

In the meantime and without immediately taking these refinements

on board, a few historians of Germany who had followed with interest
the debate among political scientists, had begun to apply the concept to
their analysis of the evolving structures of the German political economy since the late nineteenth century. They were particularly intrigued
by the way in which the Prusso-German monarchy had set out to
incorporate emergent interest groups and tried to use them from the
1870s onwards as counterweights to the influence of Parliament which
was being elected on the basis of universal (manhood) suffrage. When
they extended their approach to the First World War, they discovered
the beginnings of a triangular relationship between the state
bureaucracy, the trade unions and the peak employers' associations.
Although he did not explicitly deploy the corporatist paradigm, G. D.
Feldman's pioneering study of *Army, Industry and Labor in Germany,
1914–1918* was in fact concerned with the genesis of tripartist arrangements between the military as the actual political rulers of the time and
the two sides of industry from 1916 onwards.[12] His sources showed how
an institutional framework was created outside the Reichstag in which
basic compromises relating to the development of the German wartime
economy and society were hammered out. These compromises may not
have been all too durable. Nevertheless, they pointed to new depar-
tures. For the first time, state officials and military bureaucrats who took
an interest in the active management of the economy could be seen
sitting around the table with weary employers and willing trade
unionists. For the first time also, these trade unionists had gained official
recognition by their partners.

In the light of these findings by Feldman as well as his later work on
Zentralarbeitsgemeinschaft of 1918,[13] it is not surprising that one of his
students, U. Nocken, should link up with the debate on corporatism and
seek to apply the concept to German history between 1871 and 1945.[14]
Taking over Schmitter's subtypes, Nocken argued that the period 1850–
1914 was characterised by 'a mixed system of state corporatism and
pluralism ' – a description which raised a number of problems to which
we shall shortly return. According to Nocken, the First World War then
became 'the most important single cause for the various changes in the
system of interest representation in Germany. Its immediate impact
provided a great victory of the state corporatist idea.' Further changes,
he asserts, came in 1918–19: 'It was the negative reaction of the entre-
preneurs against the state corporatist system, and the fear that it might be
continued and expanded indefinitely, which largely helps to explain the
early rise of societal corporatism in Germany'. What emerged in the
early years of the Weimar Republic was, Nocken believes, 'a confusing
pattern of societal corporatism', which to confuse matters further, was

'gradually replaced by state corporatism, placed in a constitutional structure which was largely conceived as a framework for a pluralist system'. Fortunately there is no need to ask what kind of system this could possibly have been, for it was replaced from 1924 onwards by another pattern which 'was built largely on a societal corporatist system coexisting within, and next to, pluralist structures'. Much of the rest of Nocken's analysis is devoted to outlining the mechanisms of this pattern and to demonstrating that it continued to be opposed by powerful heavy industry. Ultimately this opposition was so effective that 'the possibility of a new societal corporatist alliance between labor and industry was sabotaged by the confrontationist policy of heavy industry', although 'the divisions within the ranks of labor also contributed significantly' to this failure. Thenceforth and propelled by the heightening tensions of the Great Slump and its search for authoritarian solutions, the 'state corporatist' approach was once again 'activated' and successively strengthened once Hitler had come to power. It disappeared only with the collapse of the Third Reich in 1945. Nocken merely alludes to a tenuous link beyond 1945. For the depressing outcome of the Weimar experiment notwithstanding, the repeated efforts 'to reach . . . a societal corporatist structure and the recognition of its various progressive groups in industry' was to provide: 'some of the important lessons of the Weimar Republic and a fore-shadowing of events in the Federal Republic'.

It was only several years later that this idea of a continuity beyond 1945 was picked up by the West German economic historian, W. Abelshauser.[15] His 1984 article in the *European History Quarterly* starts off with a discussion of the long-term historical roots of the postwar system, and since he diverges from Nocken at various points, it seems worthwhile to deal with this discussion before moving on to Abelshauser's interpretation of corporatism in the Federal Republic.[16] He proposes to treat state corporatism as 'a defining element of the pre-liberal, delayed capitalist, authoritarian state'; societal corporatism, by contrast, 'appears to be a concomitant, if not the essential, component of the post-liberal, advanced capitalist, democratic welfare state'. According to Abelshauser, 'the differences in structure and behaviour' between the two types, 'depend first on whether the nature of the interest-reconciliation process is more a product of general socioeconomic developments and voluntary arrangements than of state imposition; and secondly, on whether the state's control is the result of a reciprocal consensus or of an asymmetric imposition by the state'.

In line with this typology, Abelshauser finds that 'both variants are to be seen in German history', so that the corporatist paradigm is extremely useful for analysing modern German social and economic history'. However, unlike Nocken, he regards the year 1879 as 'the birth-point of the modern system of corporatist interest mediation'. Subsequently he 'contrasts Bismarck's efforts to establish state corporatism with the emergence of societal corporatism as the dominant feature of the Wilhelmine economy'. Nevertheless, the rejection of Bismarck's idea of 'corporatist anti-parliaments' did not imply 'that corporate structures were absent from the interest politics of the Empire'; indeed,

> the process of incorporation of the free associations into the welfare-state bureaucracy of Prussia-Germany was well advanced – whether through the interplay with the expanding network of Chambers [of Commerce, Crafts and Industry], through the conferment of authority on nominally voluntary associations, or through the responsiveness of association officials to the ideal of the state bureaucrat and to the idea of the paternalist social state. In the Bismarckian project of a comprehensive corporate system for the whole of society it was only the authoritarian form of corporatism that had failed. This was not least because corporatism in a societal and open form – that is to say based on freedom of contrast and association – had already long dominated the constitutional reality of the Empire.

But in justifying this conclusion, Abelshauser adds a rider which – as we shall see shortly – reveals a flaw in his scheme of periodisation: 'Trade unions, one of the pillars of the tripartite pattern of modern corporatism, were not of course [!] much involved as yet in the process of "wheeling and dealing" characteristic of Wilhelmine Germany's interest politics.'

There is little disagreement between Nocken and Abelshauser that societal corporatism definitely emerged in Germany in the second half of the First World War. But while explicitly rejecting 'Organised Capitalism' as a possible explanatory device of developments, he implicitly takes issue with Nocken's analysis of the Weimar system. To him, the 1920s embody 'the heyday' of German societal corporatism, though by the late 1920, 'organized labour no longer achieved its gains within a framework of consentient tripartite interest policy but in growing confrontation with industry and with other sectors of the economy'. Consequently, 'Weimar Germany, which at the beginning of the 1920s was indeed characterized by class collaboration and consensus rather than by class conflict and repression, was by the end of the decade no longer a working model of modern, tripartite corporatist interest policy'. Nor, according to him, could 'the challenge of the world depression . . . restore the co-operative pattern of German industrial relations'. Conflicts between the two sides of industry had just become too

serious. Worse, there was also the rebellion of the 'unorganized middle
class – whether the old middle-class artisans, shopkeepers, small producers, marginal farmers burdened with debts, or the new middle class
of clerical workers and office employees [which] felt crushed between
organized labour and big business'. Above all, together with the conservatives in heavy industry, these groups came to believe that only a
renewed state corporatism would offer a way out of the crisis. And: 'the
Third Reich seemed to match this desire. After 1933 the Nazis established an authoritarian version of corporatism which differed as much
from the Weimar model as from the theory of the corporative state
which was developed during the romantic epoch of German philosophy
and economics', i.e. in the first half of the nineteenth century.

However, Abelshauser's main concern is to analysis the development
of the West German political economy with the help of the corporatism
paradigm. Here the 'Concerted Action' which was inaugurated in
January 1967 under the chairmanship of the Economics Minister, Karl
Schiller, provided the meeting-point between historians and political
scientists. Lehmbruch and others made the 1967 experiment the
starting-point of an analysis of West German liberal/societal corporatism and its vagaries in the late 1960s and 1970s.[17] For Abelshauser,
on the other hand, the 'Concerted Action' represented the culmination-
point of a development whose postwar roots he traces back to 1951.[18]
Following the collapse of Nazi state corporatism in 1945, he believes the
economic reform of 1948, 'established the view that neo-liberal principles, diametrically opposed to those of the corporatist model, should be
extensively embodied in the "social market economy" of the Federal
Republic'. And yet the neo-liberalism of Ludwig Erhard allegedly lasted
no more than a few years; according to him, 'it is possible to date the
return of a traditional and . . . an altogether more modern pattern of
German interest politics'. The rest of Abelshauser's analysis is therefore
devoted to showing 'that as early as the Korean crisis of 1950–52 the
umbrella organizations of business and the trade unions not only won a
decisive share in the formulation of German economic policy but also
regained important planning and control functions in autonomous self-
government and in close co-operation with [the] state authorities'.

The trigger for this drastic shift, he argues, was a letter by US High
Commissioner John McCloy of 6 March 1951 to Chancellor Adenauer
which, by reference to the economic impact of the Korean War on the
western economics, demanded, '"a significant modification of the free
market economy" in order to measure up to the "dramatic international
developments and the related efforts of the United States for a strengthened defense expenditure"'. Hence, for Abelshauser, there is only one

conclusion to be drawn from his discovery of this letter and a number of other documents relating to the 1951 situation:

> The framework of German societal corporatism, which had come into being under the Empire, taken full shape during the Weimar Republic and been deformed in an authoritarian direction during the Nazi regime, began to re-establish itself. With the Korea boom and its economic and political effects on Germany, the phase of the 'free' market economy in the Federal Republic came to an end three years after it had begun. It gave way to a market economy with unmistakeable features of societal corporatism.

It is the purpose of the rest of this chapter to re-examine, against the background of such far-reaching conclusions and by reference to the corporatism paradigm, the evolution of interest group politics and the state in modern German history up to the most recent period.

There is no question that the policies of the 1870s and 1880s and the institutions which Bismarck tried to create can be usefully analysed within the framework of an authoritarian or state corporatism. Once the boom of the years immediately after the founding of the German Empire had begun to give way to an extended period of retarded growth and even depression, agriculture, commerce and industry responded by getting more highly organised.[19] Pressure groups emerged in large numbers outside the party political and parliamentary sphere. Some of their lobbying activities were directed at the Reichstag parties which were in the process of transforming themselves from loose associations of notables – local *Honoratiorenparteien* – to centralised organisations with professional politicians and permanently employed functionaries.[20] But given the relatively minor powers granted to Parliament under the Bismarck Constitution, and the growing importance of a centralised Reich bureaucracy operating within the authoritarian command structure of a monarchical executive appointed by the emperor,[21] it is not surprising that business and agriculture should see the government as their primary addressee. It was, after all, from within the bureaucracy that laws and decrees were formulated.

Conversely, Bismarck and the state machinery which he directed in autocratic fashion became interested in incorporating the mushrooming extra-parliamentary corporatism.[22] Evidently with this in mind, he expanded and created an increasingly elaborate system of councils and other advisory bodies, many of which were charged with the management of public functions, such as the training and examining of apprentices, an important task of the Chambers. Therefore, the Reich Chancellor deliberately promoted the establishment of an institutional framework at regional and national level by which private pressure groups were able to participate in government. In this context, the creation of the Prussian Economic Council, composed of government-picked representatives from agriculture, commerce and industry and called into being in January 1881 by royal decree, is of particular interest. Its purpose was to 'scrutinize and report upon legislative bills . . . in order that they might receive the seal of "expert" approval before being passed on to the "political" [Prussian Diet]'.[23] As Paur added,

> the obvious intention was that the legislative proposals should receive the endorsement of both the government, indicating that they were necessary for reasons of state, and of the major interest lobbies, demonstrating that they met the real needs of the people. The doctrinaire parliamentarians would thus find themselves in a corner, robbed of any pretext for refusing their assent.

Being a staunch monarchist, Bismarck was keen to extend that idea to Reich level. Indeed, the need to provide there a counterbalance to 'doctrinaire parliamentarians' was felt even more acutely. Unlike the Prussian Diet, which was elected on the basis of a restricted 'three-class' franchise, a suffrage system existed in the Reich which, its many complexities notwithstanding, was nevertheless essentially universal. By the 1880s – if not before – Bismarck had come bitterly to regret this universality. Therefore, he – and even more so his successors – were constantly on the look-out for means of undermining it. Time and again, radical solutions like abolishing the suffrage altogether were mooted together with ideas of copying the Prussian Economic Council at Reich level. The barely veiled intention was to strengthen the link between the representation of business and agriculture and the monarchial government in order to weaken further the constitutional ties between the government and the national Parliament. Unfortunately for Bismarck, a Reich Economic Council never got off the ground, ultimately because both the non-Prussian princes and the Reichstag deputies were shrewd enough to recognise 'the twin threat to the federal character of the Reich and to the status of the Reichstag that they believed it to represent'.[24] Still it is quite clear that the whole scheme was part of a more general tendency to reinforce state-corporatist collaboration, once the axis between the government and the organised interests of business and agriculture had begun to develop. The council structure was designed to strengthen this axis and to erode the position of Parliament.

However, there is a related aspect to be considered. On closer inspection, the anti-parliamentary thrust of Bismarckian corporatism is inseparable from its anti-Socialist design. What worried the Reich Chancellor and many other conservatives in late-nineteenth-century Germany more than anything else was the growth of an industrial

working class that had emerged in the wake of industrialisation and a
veritable demographic explosion.[25] Increasingly this working class
began to turn to the Social Democratic Party, which had been founded
in 1875 and which, by competing at the polls, could expect to attract a
growing number of voters. The universal suffrage thus contained a good
deal of political dynamite for the established order in view of the fact
that the Social Democrats presented themselves as a radical opposition
party. By 1879 perceptions of this threat among other social groups had
become so great that Bismarck succeeded in pushing the anti-Socialist
laws through the Reichstag which proscribed Socialist organisations and
press organs, though it did not ban Social Democrats from standing for
election.[26] But when in 1890 Bismarck failed to obtain a parliamentary
renewal of the anti-Socialist laws, the Social Democrats quickly recon-
stituted themselves. Thenceforth they went from strength to strength.
By 1912 they had gained 4,250 million votes and 110 seats (27.7 per
cent) in the Reichstag.[27] No less significantly for our context was the
mushrooming of Socialist trade unions. Despite many discriminations
and hostility by employers and authorities, these had 2,549 million
members in 1913.[28]

Faced with these numbers, a possible strategy for both government
and business would have been to try to incorporate the various working-
class organisations, and the unions in particular, in the same way as the
other economic interest groups had been incorporated by Bismarck and
his successors. However, so great was their fear of the 'revolutionary'
Social Democrats that they refused to have any contact with them.
Consequently the advocates of 'incorporation' always remained in a
small minority. The German working-class movement was forced to
remain in the ghetto to which the anti-socialist laws had first officially
consigned it. It was quite unthinkable for government bureaucrats to
have dealings with allegedly subversive socialists.[29] With a few exceptions this was also true of employers' attitudes towards the unions.[30] In
other words, containment rather than incorporation remained the predominant strategy. Putting up dams against 'the Revolution' was more
important than trying to forge links between the two sides of industry
and to develop mechanisms for the institutionalisation of industrial
conflict. The latter policy would have involved recognition of the unions
and this alternative most German employers were quite unwilling even
to contemplate. Their hope was rather the same as that of the state
authorities: that it would be possible to roll back the growth of unions by
means of harassment and blacklisting of known members and activists.
In the 1980s, when the right of associations is constitutionally
guaranteed in the Federal Republic, it is often difficult to imagine just

how authoritarian and 'punishment-centred' (A. Gouldne) German industry continued to be. There were, it is true, a few signs that the conservative phalanx of state and employers might have weakened in the long run, as a few branches of industry and enlightened employers began to negotiate with the unions about wages and conditions. But it is significant that all collective bargaining arrangements remained strictly limited. Moreover, under constant attack from the patriarchs, especially in heavy industry, they were at risk when a recession loomed on the horizon and when, as happened in the last two years before the outbreak of the First World War, the general domestic situation worsened.[31] By that time politics in Germany had become markedly more polarised. Anti-parliamentarianism and anti-socialism were on the increase.

These findings are of some importance to the periodisation argument put forward by Abelshauser. There is little evidence that the Wilhelmine Empire was on its way towards a societal corporatism. By defining societal corporatism as a post-liberal phenomenon and Germany as the 'first post-liberal nation', he in fact overlooks Lehmbruch's argument concerning the liberal-democratic and parliamentary-constitutional essentials of this type and ignores the distinctly *illiberal* features of corporatist politics in pre-1914 Germany. One does not have to go as far as Bob Jessop, who described liberal corporatism as the 'highest stage of Social Democracy';[32] but we are in danger of being led astray if we leave out the position which the organisations of the working class occupy in the total picture. Certainly, Alan Fox would see the incorporation of the unions as a fundamental precondition of this corporatist variant.[33] In the same vein, R. Heinze has argued that liberal corporatism emerged in postwar western Europe wherever Social Democratic movements played a prominent role in the debate and desision-making on basic questions of economic management and social policy.[34] It has thus become a *sine qua non*[35] to examine how, and how far, the two large blocs of 'capital and labour' are included in a corporatist framework. This variant is characterised by the links which exist not only between the 'state' and business, but also between the two sides of industry as well as between the unions and the government – hence the notion of a triangular relationship, a tripartism. By contrast, the existence of a government-business tie with the implicit or explicit purpose of eroding the powers of a parliamentary-democratic assembly and of ostracising or totally emasculating a free working-class movement constitutes, if anything, a state corporatism. And this – whether defined as a network of institutions or as an ideology or as a system of domination – was the corporatism that grew up and persisted in pre-1914 Germany.

It was only under the exigencies of total war that these realities began to change. Thanks to Feldman's study,[36] there is little disagreement among historians interested in testing the corporatist paradigm that it was the threat of defeat which moved the German government, the employers and the unions towards a triangular structure of consensus-building and conflict resolution. Now the unthinkable happened: the unions were drawn to the negotiating table to sit next to military bureaucrats and industrialists. The revolution of 1918 then strengthened these wartime arrangements, in that it facilitated, for the first time, the creation of an institutionalised link between employers and unions at national level:[37] on 22 October 1918 a number of prominent industrialists met the leader of the Allgemeiner Deutscher Gewerkschaftsbund (ADGB), the Social Democratic peak association, to work out the Stinnes-Legien Agreement. Under the terms of this agreement, the employers recognised the right of association for all workers and promised to stop supporting company unions. They also promised to speed up the re-employment of soldiers returning from the front and to support the setting-up of labour exchanges. Firms with more than fifty employees were to have a Works Committee and there would be a system for the arbitration of labour disputes. Last but not least, the eight-hour working-day was to be introduced. In return, the unions promised to curb all pressures for a programme of nationalisation and to cooperate with government and industry to restore order and stability in a situation which appeared to be getting out of hand. The Stinnes–Legien Agreement remained in force after the collapse of the Hohenzollern monarchy on 9 November and was reinforced in the middle of that month by the establishment of the Zentralarbeitsgemeinschaft (ZAG) as the forum for the top representatives of the two sides of industry.

Avoiding a development similar to the one in Russia in the previous year was not the only calculation behind the ZAG 'working community', though. Certainly industry had become quite alarmed over the extent to which the imperial government had been drawn into the economy during the war. At war's end there was a strong desire to bring about a disengagement of the 'state' from this sphere, not least in the field of wages and prices. Obviously one way of achieving this and of reviving liberal-capitalist market mechanisms was to invigorate the axis between 'capital and labour'. However, what made the situation so confusing was that there were other businessmen who wanted to go back to the pre-1914 state–corporatist model and were hence opposed to the ZAG idea. Worse, there was a third faction, of which the AEG director, Walter Rathenau, was probably the most prominent representative.[38] He was the advocate of a system which in fact amounted to a

continuation of the wartime tripartism. He believed that the many
daunting problems of postwar reconstruction could not be mastered
without the involvement of the 'state' in the economy and the participation of the labour movement. Macro-economic planning seemed
inevitable and vital to him, if a revival of industry without destructive
industrial disputes was to be achieved.

In the face of these currents and cross-currents it is admittedly not
easy to make sense of the early 1920s in terms of the corporatist
paradigm. Nocken has criticised Charles Maier for having operated with
the 'unclear' concept of 'corporative pluralism' which, he feels, 'has not
been rigorously defined or distinguished from the elements constituting
organized capitalism'.[39] But it seems doubtful if Nocken's own interpretation of this phase in the development of the German political
economy is any more convincing. At least it is not easy to be convinced
by his argument that, after a short and confused spell of societal corporatism, there reemerged a state corporatist solution. It seems more
plausible to follow Abelshauser and to assume that a less formal societal
corporatism continued for a number of years, until all arrangements,
including the ZAG, became swallowed up by the total chaos of the year
1923.

However, few people would disagree with Nocken and Abelshauser
that the years 1924–9 may be analysed fruitfully in terms of a pre-
cariously balanced societal/liberal corporatism. This was the period
when the peak associations of business came to be dominated by industrialists who preferred a policy of collaboration and compromise with
the trade unions. It was also the time when the Republican government,
egged on by Heinrich Brauns, the Catholic Labour Minister, far from
wishing to ostracise the unions, pursued a tripartist consensus and
promoted the further expansion of the still rudimentary welfare state.[40]
But there were oppositional forces as well. Heavy industry, which had
retained much of its 'veto power' (B. Weisbrod) used its position of
influence in politics more and more openly after 1927. In 1928 the Ruhr
steel managers locked out some 250,000 workers and thereby re-
inaugurated a blatantly confrontationist style which was directed not
merely against the Metal Workers' Union, but also against the liberal
corporatist experiments of the mid-1920s. And soon this confronta-
tionism was, once again, to become the hallmark of industrial politics in
Germany. If a strong government-industry/agriculture tie, together with
anti-parliamentarianism and anti-socialism, are salient features of a
state corporatism, then the country was sliding back into this pattern
well before 1933 and the establishment of the Nazi dictatorship. The
years of the Brüning chancellorship were still a period of often barely

perceptible transition; but when in 1932 the Cabinet of Franz von Papen enunciated its 'New State' concept, policy and ideology would appear to meet all the criteria of an authoritarian solution.[41] A few months later, Hitler did no more than to carry it to its logical conclusion when he destroyed both Weimar constitutionalism and the German working-class movement.

To be sure, it would barely be adequate to define the 'German dictatorship' (K. D. Bracher) simply as a state corporatism and both political scientists and historians would deploy other analytical tools in order to explain the peculiar structures and the unprecedentedly destructive dynamism of German fascism in the 1930s. But the notion does help us to understand a number of important characteristics and institutions of the regime in its relationship with industry, commerce and agriculture.[42]

The final destruction of the Third Reich by the Allies in 1945, and the emergence of the West German state in 1949, leaves us with the question raised earlier in this chapter of where the roots of Schiller's liberal corporatist 'Concerted Action' of 1967 might be found. Obviously the starting-point here must be Abelshauser's hypothesis that Erhard's neo-liberal market economy was replaced by a societal corporatism as early as 1951 and that the origins of later developments may be located at this point.[43] The problem with his interpretation is that he himself wrote that: 'the industrial business associations grasped the chance, in the crisis situation of 1951, of strengthening their influence again and of preventing a direct state intervention in the economy in that they themselves offered the Federal Government and in particular the Chancellor "their good services" – as Adenauer put it.'[44] The unions, on the other hand, do not appear as part of these moves, and this suggests that something rather different was happening during the Korean crisis. This was certainly the impression of Professor Franz Böhm who, in the wake of the McCloy letter of March 1951, produced a report for the Economics Minister.[45] Should, he wrote, this development continue,

> we shall have a completely different political and social structure from that which is foreseen by our Constitution. Parliament, parties, in short the whole method of legislation and administration built on general elections, will be replaced by a kind of organic structure of community in which the making of political decisions falls into the hands of bodies organized according to interest and profession with their private bureaucracies competing with the government bureaucracy.

Böhm was an expert on *ständestaatliche* ideas and, in the 1930s, had in fact himself written in that vein. And now, in 1951, looking at the behaviour of the peak associations of business, he, who had meanwhile been converted to neo-liberalism, was reminded of those earlier years. Abelshauser actually provides some further evidence that the tendency among influential sections of West German industry was for a re-formation of a state corporatist system of the interwar period.[46] This perspective is confirmed by H. Adamsen's study on the origins of the 1952 Investment Support Act. This piece of legislation arose, as he puts it, 'from a collusion of State and Business'. He quotes, it is true, Walter Raymond, the president of the West German Employers' Federation who, in words typical of his particular integrationist approach, appealed to his fellow industrialists 'to come to a reasonable cooperation with the trade unions in the parity-committees'. The reason why Raymond saw a need to make this appeal emerged a moment later. As he admitted in the same breath, the task was to 'bridge an enormous gap between the ideological standpoints' of business on the one hand, and the unions on the other. In view of these exhortations, Adamsen finally reached the conclusion that there had been no 'trade union influence on the genesis of the Investment Support Act'. On the contrary, 'the Federal govern-ment and the economic associations put "the screws" on the trade unions which helplessly faced the situation'. All in all, the cooperation between the government and the business associations in the early 1950s reminded him, like Böhm, of a 'quite well-proven German tradition' – a continuity 'which had survived the end of the Nazi economy and the Currency Reform [of 1948] virtually unbroken'.[47]

It looks therefore as if there were influential forces in the peak associations which wanted to use the crisis of the early 1950s for a bilateralisation of the relationship between state and industry and for a return to the system of the 1930s. Naturally the trade unions were to be excluded from this relationship, and it was Viktor Agartz, an economic adviser to the Deutscher Gewerkschaftsbund (DGB), the federation of West German trade unions, who drew attention to these tendencies. Speaking before the Economic Policy Committee of the Social Demo-cratic Party, he referred to 'the multitude of commissars around the federal chancellor' and described them as a 'peculiarity' which violated the principles of parliamentary democracy.[48]

What Agartz and Böhm did not say (and perhaps were not fully aware of) was that the Economics Minister, Erhard, was himself anxious to avoid a relapse into the system of the 1930s. The same is true of one of the 'commissars', the industrialist Otto A. Friedrich, whom the Federal government had nominated as raw materials coordinator.[49] His nomina-tion was Adenauer's response to the McCloy letter of March 1951 and American pressures to have clearer priorities in the allocation of raw

materials at a time when these had become scarcer as a result of the
Korean War. Friedrich was an opponent of the prewar German system
of raw materials allocation, and in so far as he was corporatist, he
advocated a modern tripartism. In 1951 his strategy was therefore to
give the impression of decisive action by initiating a survey of the raw
materials situation in the Federal Republic, but to leave the economy
more or less untouched in organisational terms. Looking back on his
activities years later, he concluded that:

> we in fact succeeded in maintaining the social market economy even in the
> face of world-wide restrictions; apart from a few formal concessions to the
> Americans in the field of iron and steel, [we also succeeded] in initiating the
> march towards an even greater expansion of the economy, towards constantly
> growing employment and towards the abolition of the remaining chains
> imposed by the occupying powers.

In the long run men like Friedrich asserted themselves over the
authoritarian corporatists who reared their heads in the crisis of 1951.
Nevertheless, societal corporatism was not put into place at that
moment, as Abelshauser believes; rather the opposite was the case. The
roots of the 'Concerted Action' of 1967 are more tenuous, and in tracing
them it is important to bear in mind that the three partners of West
Germany's later liberal-corporatist concertation had to adapt themselves to the changed conditions of the postwar world and thus to create
the attitudinal preconditions of the 1967 experiment. This applies to the
unions; given their early postwar commitment to nationalisation and a
democratic socialism, they had to make a slow and sometimes painful
transition to a framework of liberal corporatism. The first beginnings of
this shift can be detected by the early 1950s. Here the positions of Fritz
Tarnow are of particular interest. During the Weimar period, he had
been one of the leading economists of the ADGB and at the height of
the Great Slump, in December 1931, he had put forward, together with
W. Woytinsky and F. Baade, the so-called WTB Plan, essentially a
proto-Keynesian programme of economic crisis management.[50] Having
travelled widely in the west during the 1920s, Tarnow spent the Second
World War in Swedish exile. No doubt, these experiences contributed
to a deepened knowledge of the modern welfare state in theory and
practice. So here was a representative of a tradition on the union side
which made a gradual *rapprochement* with liberal corporatists like
Friedrich on the employers' side easier and paved the way for the
tripartism of the future.

Even greater were the mental adjustments which West Germany's
industrial élites and the ministerial bureaucracy had to make, both of

which had once cooperated, after the proscription of the unions, in the state-corporatist arrangements of the Nazi economy. As many of them had survived the collapse of the Third Reich and had regained their former positions, it would seem wiser to assume that their transition towards concertation was slower than Abelshauser has postulated. Eventually the three sides did meet around the table and a formal institutional framework did come about, and it is fruitful to examine developments of the late 1960s and 1970s with the help of the liberal-corporatist paradigm.[51] Schiller's 'Concerted Action' was an attempt to coordinate policy for dealing with the brief recession that hit the Federal Republic in 1966–7. One element in the planned revival of the economy was that the unions would voluntarily agree to reduce their wage claims. Once the expected upturn of the economy had occurred, this 'social asymmetry' was to be recitified. The ground lost in previous years on the wages front was to be recovered by the unions.

The DGB did not subscribe to Schiller's strategy with enthusiasm, nor was it openly resisted. The recession was overcome with remarkable speed, and high growth rates were achieved in 1968 and 1969. Profits rose sharply and the incomes of the self-employed rose by 17.5 per cent, with workers' incomes trailing behind by more than 10 per cent! The shopfloor became restive, and Germany was affected by a wave of spontaneous unofficial strikes in September 1969. Inevitably these strikes, directed as much against the moderation shown by the DGB as against the employers, put a strain on 'Concerted Action'. Later the situation was reversed, and it was for the employers to feel increasingly unhappy with economic and social policy-making in the Federal Republic. In 1977 'Concerted Action' was formally abandoned, but informal trilateral contacts have continued and have survived even the harsher economic climate of the 1980s. The recent West German experience with liberal corporatism has therefore been similar to that of other countries: all too often interests were too divergent for stable compromises to be achieved. On the other hand, there remained an at least unspoken assumption that the problems of the advanced industrial societies of western Europe had become so complex as to require the consensual cooperation of the government with the main power blocs in the economy. Only Prime Minister Margaret Thatcher in Britain took a different view on this; her West German counterpart certainly did not.

Notes

1. See e.g. J. Habermas, *Legitimationsprobleme im Spätkapitalismus* (Frankfurt, 1973); C. Offe, *Strukturprobleme des kapitalistischen Staates* (Frankfurt, 1972).

2. See e.g. B. Guggenberger, 'Politik und Okonomie' *Neue Politische Literatur*, 4 (1974), 427 ff.

3. For a summary of the debate, see: H. A. Winkler (ed, *Organisierter Kapitalismus* (Göttigen, 1974). See also K. J. Bade, 'Organisierter Kapitalismus', *Neue Politische Literatur*, 3 (1975), 293–306; V. Hentchel, *Wirtschaft und Wirtschaftspolitik im Wilhelminischen Deutschland* (Stuttgart, 1978), 9 ff. For a reassessment ten years later, see the special issue of *Geschichte und Gesellschaft*, 10 (1984), 163 ff.

4. P. C. Schmitter, 'Still the century of corporatism?' *Review of Politics*, **36**, (January 1974), 85–131.

5. See R. H. Bowen, *German Theories of the Corporative State (New York, 1947)*.

6. J. T. Winkler, *'Corporatism', Archives Europeennes de Sociologie*, 1 (1976)), 103.

7. First mention of the two types is in Schmitter, 'Still the century of Corporatism', *op. cit.*, p. 105.

8. G. Lehmbruch, 'Consociational democracy, class conflict and the new corporatism' in P. C. Schmitter and G. Lehmbruch (eds.), *Trends towards Corporatist Intermediation* (Beverly Hills, Calif., 1979), p. 53 ff.

9. G. Lehmbruch, 'Liberal corporatism and party government', *Comparative Political Studies*, **10**, 1 (April 1977), 92.

10. See P. C. Schmitter, 'Modes of interest intermediation and models of societal change in western Europe', *Comparative Political Studies*, **10**, 1 (April 1977), 11. G. Lehmbruch, 'Concertation and the structure of corporalist networks'.

11. J. H. Goldthorpe (ed.), *Order and Conflict in Contemporary Capitalism* (Oxford, 1984, p. 61. See also: G. Lehmbruch and P. C. Schmitter (eds), *Patterns of Corporatist Policy Making* (London, 1982); A. Cawson (ed.), *Organized Interests and the State* (London, 1985); W. Grant (ed.), *The Political Economy of Corporatism* (London, 1900).

12. G. D. Feldman, *Army, Industry and Labor in Germany, 1914–1918* (Princeton, NJ, 1966); Feldman spoke of 'collective capitalism'.

13. See e.g. G. D. Feldman, *Iron and Steel in the German Inflation, 1916–1923* (Princeton, 1977).

14. U. Nocken, 'Corporatism and pluralism in modern German history' in D. Stegmann *et al.* (eds), *Industrielle Gesellschaft und politisches System* (Bonn, 1978), pp. 37–56, and *passim*.

15. W. Abelshauser, 'Ansätze "korporativer Marktwirtschaft" in der Korea-Krise der frühen fünfziger Jahre', *Vierteljahrshefte für Zeitgeschichte*, 4 (1982), 714–56.

16. W. Abelshauser, 'The first post-liberal nation: stages in the development of modern corporatism in Germany', *European History Quarterly*, **14**, 3 (1984), 285–318, and *passim*.

17. G. Lehmbruch and W. Lang, 'Die Konzertierte Aktion', *Der Bürger im Staat*, 3 (1977), 202–8. See also W. Bonß, 'Gewerkschaftliches Handeln zwischen Korporatismus und Selbstverwaltung. Die Konzertierte Aktion und ihre Folgen' in V. Ronge (ed.), *Am Staat vorbei* (Frankfurt, 1980), pp. 125–69; U. von Alemann and R. G. Heinze (eds), *Verbände und Staat*, (Opladen, 1979); K. H. F. Dyson, 'The politics of economic management in West Germany' in W. E. Paterson and G. Smith (eds), *The West German Model, Perspective on a Stable State* (London, 1981), pp. 35–55; A. Markovits (ed)., *The Political Economy of West Germany* (New York, 1982), and *The Politics of the West German Trade Unions* (Cambridge, 1986).

18. Abelshauser, 'The first post-liberal nation', *op. cit.*

19. See e.g. H. Böhme, 'Big business pressure groups and Bismarck's turn to protectionism, 1873–79', *Historical Journal*, 2 (1967), 218–36.

20. See e.g. S. Neumann, *Die Parteien der Weimarer Republik* (Stuttgart, 1965), p. 104 ff.; see also G. Eley, *Reshaping the German Right* (New Haven, Conn., 1980).

21. See H.–U. Wehler, *The German Empire, 1871–1918* (Leamington Spa, 1985), p. 52 ff.

22. P. Paur, 'The corporatist character of Bismarck's social policy', *European Studies Review*, 4 (1981), 427–60.

23. *Ibid.*, p. 439.

24. *Ibid.*, p. 441.
25. See K. J. Bade, *Population, Labour and Migration in 19th- and 20th-Century Germany* (Leamington Spa, 1986).
26. See e.g. W. L. Guttsman, *The German Social Democratic Party, 1875–19 33* (London, 1981); V. Lidtke, *The Outlawed Party* (Princeton, NJ, 1966).
27. See e.g. G. Roth, *The Social Democrats in Imperial Germany* (Totawa, NJ, 1961); C. E. Schorske, *German Social Democracy, 1905–1917* (New York, 1972).
28. See e.g. J. A. Moses, *German Trade Unionism from Bismarck to Hitler*, Vol. I (London, 1982).
29. See e.g. D. Groh, *Negative Integration and revolutionärer Attentismus* (Frankfurt, 1973); K. Saul, *Staat, Industrie und Arbeiterbewegung im Kaiserreich* (Düsseldorf, 1973).
30. See e.g. E. Spencer, *Management and Labor in Imperial Germany* (New Brunswick, 1984); L. Schofer, 'Modernization, bureaucratization and the study of labor history: lessons from Upper Silesia, 1865–1914' in H.–U. Wehler (ed.), *Sozialgeschichte Heute* (Göttingen, 1974), pp. 467–78.
31. See F. Fischer, *War of Illusions* (London, 1975); V. R. Berghahn, *Germany and the Approach of War in 1914* (London, 1973), p. 145 ff.
32. B. Jessop, 'Corporatism, parliamentarism and social democracy' in P. C. Schmitter and G. Lehmbruch (eds), *Trends, op. cit.*, p. 207, with qualifying footnote.
33. A. Fox, 'Corporatism and industrial democracy', ms, University of Oxford, 1977, p. 48 ff.
34. R. G. Heize, *Verbändepolitik und 'Neokorporatismus'* (Opladen, 1981), p. 84. See also A. Cawson, 'Pluralism, corporatism and the role of the state', *Government and Opposition*, 2 (1978), 178–98.
35. L. Panitch, 'The development of corporatism in liberal democracies', *Comparative Political Studies*, **10**, 1 April 1977), 93.
36. See n.12, above.
37. V. R. Berghahn and D. Karsten, *Industrial Relations in West Germany* (Leamington Spa, 1987), p. 154 f.
38. See e.g. H. Pogge von Strandmann (ed.), *Walther Rathenau. Industrialist, Banker, Intellectual and Politician* (Oxford, 1985), p. 16 ff.; D. E. Barclay, 'A Prussian socialism? Wichard von Moellendorff and the dilemmas of economic planning and Germany, 1918–19', *Central European History*, 1 (1978), 50–82.
39. U. Nocken, *op. cit.*, p. 38 f., with reference to C. S. Maier's statement in H. Mommsen *et al.* (eds), *Industrielles System und politische Entwicklung in der Weimarer Republik* (Düsseldorf, 1974), pp. 955–6. But see also C. S. Maier, *Recasting Bourgeois Europe* (Princeton, NJ, 1975), p. 9 ff.
40. See e.g. B. Weisbrod, *Schwerindustrie in der Weimarer Republik* (Wuppertal, 1978), and 'Economic power and political stability Reconsidered: heavy Industry in Weimar Germany', *Social History*, **4**, 2 (May 1979), 241–63; H. Mommsen *et al. op. cit.*, D. Abraham, *The Collapse of the Weimer Republic* (New York, 1986); M. Schneider, *Unternehmer und Demokratie* (Bonn, 1975).
41. See e.g. D. Abraham, *op. cit.*; R. Neebe, *Grossindustrie, Staat und NSDAP, 1930–1933* (Göttingen, 1981); H. A. Turner, *German Big Business and the Rise of Hitler* (New York and Oxford, 1985).
42. On the state–industry system under Nazism, see e.g. W. A. Boelcke, *Die deutsche Wirtschaft, 1933–1945* (Düsseldorf, 1983); I. Esenwein-Rothe, *Die Wirtschaftsverbände, 1933–1945* (Berlin, 1965); J. Gillingham, *Industry and Politics in the Third Reich* (London , 1985); L. Herbst, *Der totale Krieg und die Ordnung der Wirtschaft* (Stuttgart, 1982); A. Schweitzer, *Big Business in the Third Reich* (Bloomington, Ind., 1964); M. Y. Sweezy, *The Structure of the Nazi Economy* (Cambridge/,Mass., 1941). On the wider question of the structure of the Third Reich, see: K. D. Bracher, *The German Dictatorship* (Harmondsworth, 1973); M. Broszat, *The Hitler State* (London, 1981); E. Fraenkel, *The Dual State* (London, 1941); F. Neumann, *Behemoth* (New York, 1942). For useful summaries of the debates, see: J. Hiden and

J. Farquharson, *Explaining Hitler's Germany* (London, 1983; I. Kershaw, *The Nazi Dictatorship* (Londo, 1985).

43. See above.
44. W. Abelshauser, 'The first post-liberal nation', *op. cit.*, p. 307 f.
45. Quoted in *ibid.*, p. 310.
46. *Ibid.*, p. 308 ff.
47. H. Adamsen, *Investitionshilfe für die Ruhr* (Wuppertal, 1981), p. 32, 167, 249, 178.
48. Quoted in W. Abelshauser, 'Korea, die Ruhr und Erhards Marktwirtschaft', *Rheinische Vierteljahrsblätter*, 3 (1981), 313.
49. See V. R. Berghahn, *The Americanisation of West German Industry, 1945–1973* (New York, 1986), p. 275 f.
60. On the WTB Plan, see R. A. Gates, 'Von der Sozialpolitik zur Wirtschaftspolitik?' in H. Mommsen *et al.*, *op. cit.*, p. 2127 ff. and M. Scheider, 'Konjunkturpolitische Vorstellungen der Gewerkschaften in den letzten Jahren der Weimarer Republik in *ibid.*, pp. 226–37.
51. See Berghahn and Karsten, *Industrial Relations*, *op. cit.*, p. 205 ff. See also the studies cited in n. 17, above.

6 Spain after Franco: from corporatist ideology to corporatist reality

J. Martinez-Alier and Jordi Roca[1]

In the years which immediately followed the death of Franco in 1975, policies and practices developed in Spain which, it will be argued here, may plausibly be interpreted as neo-corporatist. In order to understand the nature and significance of these policies, it is necessary to relate them to the more general problems presented by the political and social transition to the post-Franco era, and in particular to the most extraordinary feature of that transition. This was the high degree of continuity it displayed with the previous regime. In this respect, the process of democratisation in Spain contrasts markedly with for example, that in Western Germany, Italy or Vichy France after 1945, or even in Portugal after 1974.

A description of the transition as a recasting of bourgeois Spain would be disliked by most of the political élite. They would prefer to describe it, neutrally in class terms, as a change from an authoritarian regime (or from a dictatorship) to a parliamentary democracy. The mainstream on the left did not entertain a view of the Franco regime as a form of bourgeois rule to be succeeded by a new political regime which would change property relations. The revolutionary left of the 1930s no longer existed in the 1970s, and those few who disagreed with such a tame transition have been politically defeated with the exception (up to now) of the Basque Country. The purpose of this chapter is to explain how different streams of the left came to agree with the type of political transition which has taken place. There was some talk on the left in the 1960s and early 1970s about land reform and about nationalisation of the banking system (Muñoz 1969), but somehow such socio-economic changes were left aside after 1975. Land reform has surfaced again as political rhetoric after 1982 but not in practice. Changes in the structure of property have been successfully separated from political changes, while on the other hand there has been a change towards a neo-corporatist pattern of labour relations, consistent with an increasingly unequal distribution of income since 1977 as between wages and property income.

123

Recasting Bourgeois Spain?

Was Franco's rule a form of bourgeois rule? The answer does not only
depend on the facts, and on the political point of the view of the analyst,
but also depends on the disciplinary perspective. Some types of political
analysis would deny or leave aside the question as lacking interest or
relevance. Since the mid-1960s, Juan Linz characterised the Franco
regime as an 'authoritarian' regime, with 'limited pluralism', a third
term in the dichotomy 'totalitarianism', – 'democratic' pluralism. The
Franco regime (and subsequently many other regimes, as other authors
followed Linz's steps) was an authoritarian regime and not a pluralist
democracy because it lacked a system of political parties which would
compete in elections, the winning party or parties forming a government. It was not, on the other hand, a 'totalitarian' regime because,
although there was a single 'party' or 'movement' (the Falange, later
Movimiento Nacional), there were other political groups or tendencies
which also had power (the ACNP, Asociación Católica Nacional de
Propagandistas, the Opus Dei). The single political party never did
direct all socio-economic life: there were Chambers of Industry, for
instance, and other socio-economic groups outside the framework
Falange–*sindicatos verticales*. Many politicians and civil servants did not
agree with the Falangist ideology (this was so, for instance, with the staff
in the planning office in the 1960s, under Lopez Rodo, an Opus Dei
member), and many of them from the beginning would call themselves
'apolitical experts', which would be unthinkable in a totalitarian regime.
Finally, there was a low degree of political mobilisation, and the regime
made no serious attempt to create a wave of open political support,
except perhaps in moments of crisis, as could be termed 1947 or December 1970, at the time of the first important trial of ETA members.

Linz was concerned to show that the Franco regime could not be
classified as a totalitarian regime. There was a single political party, but
there was also a certain degree of pluralism – limited, however, to some
political groups (often disguised as non-political) and to some interest
organisations. Also the regime lacked any will (after the first few years)
to mobilise the population, and preferred to let it slumber in a state of
political apathy. 'Apathy' was one issue on which one could easily
disagree with Linz: it was not so much a defining trait of the regime as a
consequence of it, and it should be called 'fear' rather than apathy
(Martinez-Alier 1975). The regime had called itself 'organic democracy'. But according to Linz, the regime lacked a precise ideology; it was
a pragmatic regime and this is why an élite of administrative and
economic experts, who did not belong to the Falange or Movimiento

Nacional or, in any case, did not feel any loyalty to it, had become ministers and high government officials. Against Linz, however, one could say that there was a clear ideology of 'national solidarity', the language of which shifted from old-fashioned Catholic corporatism (and Falangist *nacionalsindicalismo*) to the 'modern' language of economics. Reality was distant from the ideology because although it was true that the regime allowed a 'limited pluralism', the basic question was: pluralism for whom? Economic policy options could be publicly discussed but *nobody could genuinely present options at central level as spokespersons for the working class*, and one could argue that even the capitalists, although increasingly pleased with the economic administration under the so-called 'technocrats' of the Opus Dei, were also suffering from a lack of voice. Charles Anderson (1970) emphasised the breadth of the economic debate in Spain in the 1960s, but did not dwell on the lack of workers' representation at central level. The question was not an unwillingness to take part in 'social pacts', or in 'concerted planning', as in France, but the exclusion of representation.

There was certainly a measure of pluralism, but it was not wide enough to include the possibility of a corporatist agreement with workers' organisations. An incomes policy signed inside the corporative organisation would have been a joke. Thus whether 'class harmony' and 'national solidarity' under the disguise of macro-economic guidelines and incomes policy would be accepted by the working class was an unanswered question until after Franco's death because they had no representatives empowered to give an answer.

There is an analogy with Brazil in the late 1970s and early 1980s, where the lack of state recognition of the authentic workers' leaders (such as Lula) made impossible an agreement on economic policies and on a wage norm. In Brazil, however, even a central corporatist agreement on wages linked to redemocratisation, which after 1985 was a distinct possibility, would still leave out the unorganised poor whose means of political expression is the food riot or the public transport riot. One other parallel comes to mind: if the Polish government had succeeded in separating the 'radicals' from the Solidarnosc leadership, there might have been a macro-agreement on economic policy between the union and the party bureaucracy (which performs the double role of employers and government), also in the context of 'limited pluralism'.

While for a formal political analysis, such as that of Juan Linz, the class content of the Franco regime was irrelevant, for the Marxist left it was important to characterize the regime in class terms. Was it an expression of bourgeois rule (despite the reluctance of part of the Catalan bourgeoisie to join in Franco's praise), or was it rather a

manifestation of typically Spanish social backwardness? Was it a hin-
derance to the accumulation of capital? Victor Pérez-Diaz has written
that 'Spanish culture lacked two great historical processes: protestant
reform and empirical science, which had to a large degree fashioned
the spirit of Great Britain and the continent of Europe in modern
times' (Pérez Diaz 1987: 220). One cannot but agree. However, Prussia underwent both historical processes, and it also had Bismarck (and
Hitler). But neither Prussia nor Spain had a land reform against the
landed élite. Britain also lacked a land reform: did this peculiarity
make it 'backward'?

For the dominant current in the left, the depicting of Spanish society
as backward, indeed as 'semi-feudal' in the countryside, was of the
essence in order to characterise the Franco regime *not* as a form of
bourgeois rule (or of military rule *on behalf* of the bourgeoisie), but as
the rule of a *camarilla*, and of a financial and agrarian 'oligarchy'. The
description was consistently put forward by the Communist Party in
the 1950s and 1960s, and it was the brilliant piece of analysis needed in
order to sustain the policy of 'national reconciliation' from 1956
onward, a policy in which both Carrillo and Claudin concurred, even
after their split of 1964. In fact unemployment (a most unfeudal
phenomenon) was the main workers' grievance in the latifundist
countryside – both *before* as well as after the Civil War. 'Land hunger'
did exist, because land was seen as a means to secure employment. But
although the countryside was capitalist, the economy was backward. It
was not until the 1970s that the number of tractors exceeded the
number of mules. In the 1940s and early 1950s Spanish agriculture
gave some sort of employment to over 50 per cent of the active population, the share being higher in the 'hungry' forties' than in the 1920s
and 1930s. It was still based on human and animal work, and on dung
as fertiliser. A part of the left which was in the 1960s to the left of the
Communist Party, and has since then provided intellectual sustenance
to the Socialist Party (a party almost non-existent in the Franco
period), argued that the Franco regime should be interpreted not so
much as the expected form of bourgeois rule against the revolutionary
threat of the 1930s as an 'exceptional regime' which, perhaps more by
luck than by design, had fulfilled the long-delayed bourgeois task of
industrialisation, carried forward by the European boom of the 1950s
and 1960s. In a way, the discussion was still whether the Civil War
should be seen as 'Fascism against Social Revolution' or as 'Fascism
against Democracy', whether the Spanish bourgeoisie had become fascist against a revolutionary working class or whether it had been
inherently weak. A 'weak' bourgeoisie was less responsible for the

Franco regime. This interpretation (Viñas 1972) was, or became, a call to the bourgeoisie to discard an outmoded regime and adopt instead a cooperating or even a leading role in instituting a democratic form of government.

In the 1960s and early 1970s there was a debate in Spain (similar to debates in Brazil) on whether the latifundist agrarian structure was an obstacle to the growth of production. This is not the place to enter (again) this debate (Martinez-Alier 1967), which requires empirical studies in agriculture. In any case, in Spain (as also in Brazil) the debate receded because in the 1960s and, at least, until the mid-1970s the growth of agricultural productivity (chrematistically measured, though not ecologically) proved that the 'feudal' side was in the wrong. Not that this changed the terms of the general political debate: the feudal image was used for political tactics, to signal the willingness on the part of the left to reach a pact with the bourgeoisie. In the 1930s the land reform was a failure because the Republicans and the Socialists, taken in by their own verbiage, had believed that the confiscation of the landholdings of the nobility would suffice for the settlement of a substantial part of the landless (Malefakis 1970; Martinez-Alier 1973). In the late 1970s this same willingness to come to terms with the bourgeoisie (a potential ally against Franco's *camarilla* and the so-called agrarian and financial 'oligarchy' was no longer expressed in the language of a common anti-feudal struggle, which had become too ridiculous, but in the language of consensus politics, modernisation, social pacts, austerity policies, national solidarity: Eurocommunism became indistinguishable from social democratic Eurocorporatism. This conciliatory policy was easier than in the 1930s because of the increase in the standard of living, and because the threat from a non-domesticated landless proletariat had disappeared since their number (as also that of the peasanty) had gone down dramatically in the 1960s and 1970s. In the Spanish debate on land reform the ultra-leftists had made the point that the bourgeois revolution had long taken place, since bourgeois property in the land, and also a free labour market, obviously existed in the mid-nineteenth century (the Carlist Wars being motivated by the defence of a 'moral economy' against the market, and against the liberals who won the wars). The ultra-leftists also made the point that land redistribution was a good thing, not in order to remove obstacles to growth since the existing agrarian structure seemed quite capable of promoting growth (as conventionally measured), but because agricultural workers, threatened by unemployment, wanted to have either land or assured employment. This argument still stands, reinforced by the doubts on whether 'production' is adequately measured, not from an economic but from an ecological point of view (Naredo and Campos, 1980); but this is altogether another question. Macro-economics (and not ecology) provides the common language and the ideological cement for Spanish politics.

State Corporatism, 1939–75

As we have seen, the Franco regime was catalogued as an authoritarian regime by Linz. It could also be classified as a case of state corporatism since there was compulsory membership in the occupational corporations (*sindicatos verticales*) grouping both workers and employers, there were no political parties apart from the Falange (later Movimiento Nacional), and the Cortes were organised as a corporative Chamber, although with some territorially based members. However, state corporatism should be considered a political ideology without historical reality. In the Spanish case the doctrinal character of corporatism under the Franco regime can be shown by focusing on the determination of wages and conditions of work at the level of the individual firm or work centre. In the period 1939–58 wages and conditions of work for each branch of the economy were determined by government regulation and not by negotiation, although research is needed on whether the minimum wages laid down by the government were improved upon in particular cases. Strikes were a criminal offence. Real wages reached prewar levels only in the mid-1950s in industry, and in the early 1960s in agriculture. The working class had suffered a great political defeat (executions going on for three or four years after the end of the war in 1939), and in the 1940s there was also a true crisis of subsistence, with 'years of hunger' still in 1946 and 1949.

All workers and employers formally belonged to the *sindicatos verticales*, but the officials of these corporations were government appointees and had to belong to the Falange. Some research has been done on the roles they played (Molinero and Ysàs 1985). In general, they exercised little bargaining power on behalf of their members. This was the case for 'worker' officials, perhaps also for employers' officials, and the employers' pressure on the government often went not through the *sindicatos verticales*, but through the Chambers of Commerce and Industry which, somewhat incongrously, were allowed a secondary role. Catalan industrialists had little use for the officials in the *sindicatos verticales*, of petty bourgeois and rural origin and strongly Spanish nationalist in orientation. The Basque Country was at the time the other big industrial region. Andalusia is an interesting case, because here the agricultural *sindicatos verticales* got off to a late start in the second half of the 1940s as far as nominal membership by the workers is concerned, when landowners had joined them from the beginning. Such *sindicatos verticales* kept at the provincial level the name of Chambers of Agriculture, and worked as a meeting-place and coordinating body only for landowners, carrying out studies of interest to them and making representations on their behalf to government agencies. In this case, at least one half of the state-corporatist system worked rather well.

Despite their basic satisfaction with Franco as the winner of a Civil War fought on their behalf, many industrialists were in Spain in the 1940s and 1950s in disagreement with the way the economy was run, with an extremely high degree of government intervention, partly out of principle and partly out of necessity, since there had to be a rationing system until the early 1950s. The capitalist class and their different sectors would have needed representatives to argue their own cases against government policies. To some extent, they certainly used the channels of the *sindicatos verticales*, and the topic requires further investigation. The bankers, for instance, had their own association which was not a part of the official corporative structure. A sign that lack of representativeness persisted even in the more liberal 1960s is that, after Franco's death, the head of the new Confederation of Employers' Organisations (CEOE), Ferrer Salat, had had little to do with the official corporative organisation, although this is not the case of his successor, José Maria Cuevas. Lack of representativeness applied, *a fortiori*, to the workers. Acting in a social vacuum, many Falangist officials of the *sindicatos verticales* made a career out of economic corruption, which did not help their position as the assumed representatives of organised social interests.

The introduction of collective bargaining in 1958 at all levels (work centre, firm, county, provincial and national) made clear the contradictions of state corporatism: the state appoints the top officials of the bodies which are supposed to represent organised interests, but a union whose top officials are appointed by the state is a dead union. The legislation on collective agreements of 1958 and 1973 stated that collective bargaining would further 'the integration, in a community of interests and objectives, of the elements who take part in the economic process, and it will contribute to strengthening social peace'. At the same time, there was a new emphasis in the fact that collective bargaining would contribute to 'the increase in productivity'. The period of 'primacy of the economy' (and of the economists) was then starting, in the late 1950s, with nearly twenty years of the Franco regime still to go. It has not yet ended.

Economics was to be pressed into service as a theory of social harmony more convincing than the 'old' corporatist ideology. While the economicism of Opus Dei ministers has often been noticed, the evolution of the ideology of the ACNP is more revealing. This was a small society of Catholics (never more than 600) founded in 1909 and recruited by co-optation with the explicit intention of occupying high administrative and political posts (Sáez Alba 1974). They provided many members of the government during the dictatorship of Primo de Rivera (1923–9), they were the mainspring for the CEDA, the right-wing party or Confederacion española de derechas autónomas during the Republic (1931–6), and they gave several decisive figures (Osorio, Lavilla and Oreja) to the political transition after Franco's death. Under the Franco regime (1939–75) they had supplied more ministers than any other group but the army. In the 1920s and 1930s the ACNP had a clear-cut Catholic-corporatist line which can be seen, for instance, in Herrera Oria's comment to *Quadragesimo Anno* in 1933. He wrote:

> Leo XIII saw – in *Rerum Novarum* – employers and workers, against each other, divided into two groups of very unequal fortune and as mutual enemies . . . The Pope wanted to unify these two classes as members of the same body, through links of justice and by the life-giving spirit of Christian charity. (Herrara Oria 1933:15)

Pius XI, in the new encyclical, was not satisfied with just making brothers in the workplace out of employers and workers, he sought also a harmonic order of the different occupations: '*Quadragesimo Anno* has value as a political encyclical, in the sense that we see in it the main lines of a theory of the state.' Corporatism was to be the main element for the 'New State' (Herrera Oria 1933: 15). The Catholics, in Spain as elsewhere, believed in the so-called 'subsidiarity' principle, and before the Civil War had always proposed 'free unions inside the corporations', hoping for genuine Catholic workers' unions which would enter into collective contracts with the employers of the same 'corporation'. By virtue of the subsidiarity principle (which gives grounds, for instance, for the defence of subsidised private Catholic education), wages and conditions of work were not to be regulated in detail by the state, and this is why the 1958 collective bargaining law had Catholic support which would be expressed in the corporatist language of common interests and national solidarity. In the Civil War, the Falangists, who disliked the subsidiarity principles, had won points, but after the Civil War, and especially after 1945, Falangists and Catholics worked together in the 'New State', the Catholic politicians paying the price of having to don the flamboyant Falangist uniform. In 1946, Larraz, the

Minister of Finance (and member of the ACNP), complained bitterly about the Allies' (short-lived) 'mistreatment' of the Franco regime: 'in this hour of passion, people think that a corporative regime is an idea belonging to totalitarianism, and therefore to be condemned *a priori*. Some would like to make of it a sort of war criminal.' This was pure ignorance, because corporatist ideas came back time and again, after the clearance sale made by liberalism. There was corporatism in Sismondi, in the first socialists, in social Catholicism, in the English Guildists, and 'the transformation of revolutionary syndicalism into a constructive enterprise, as Duguit proposed', was also corporatism. It was a natural and spontaneous product of social life (in Aznar 1946: xi–xii).

Severino Aznar, one of the first Spanish Catholic corporatists, was aware that the doctrine of corporatist political representation grew in the reaction against the French Revolution. Corporatism could be traced back to Adam Heinrich Müller (1779–1829), who was born in Berlin, joined the Catholic Church, entered the Austrian civil service and was the author of *Elemente der Staatskunst* (1809). He became the first of the line of German and Austrian Catholic corporatists. Adam Müller was influenced by Burke, who had complained that in the National Assembly there was not the slighest sign of the 'natural interest' of landed property (1790: 132), while Paine agreed with the Abbé Sieyès's motion by which the Tiers Etat called themselves the representatives of the nation, and the two Orders were to be considered merely deputies of corporations, with only a deliberative voice (1791: 127).

Aznar quoted not only the Catholic corporatists (Ketteler, Vogelsang and Hintze), but also Durkheim and Duguit. Durkheim was the spokesman for 'a scientific, positivist sociological school' which had reached the same conclusions as the Catholic social reformers, though he had no religion. Duguit, who felt for Catholicism 'una hostilidad siniestra de hugonote', held nevertheless views similar to the Catholic corporatists (Aznar 1946: 214). Duguit's work was introduced in Spain by the Krausist, non-Catholic, Adolfo Posada, who translated *La transformación del estado* (1909). Two of Duguit's ideas proved most fruitful for corporatist ideology: (1) the change from a Roman-law conception of ownership rights to ownership as a 'social function', and (2) the notion that class struggle would be calmed down by establishing *contractual* regulations between classes. This was more useful than the extremist liberal view impracticably contrary to unions, if one had to cope (in Spain and other countries at the time) with a growing revolutionary syndicalism based on the idea that 'la propriété, c'est le vol', and on the principle that unions should always use direct action. La Charte d'Amiens dates from 1907. The state, by providing the legal framework for such collective bargaining, might disactivate revolutionary syndicalism. The Spanish Catholics would have liked accordingly a 'spontaneous and natural' corporatism to develop. But, of course, after killing so many workers from 1936 onwards, after repressing out of existence the workers' unions, after doing away with or putting into twilight even the employers' organisations, they had no right to expect a genuine corporatist system to function. State corporatism suppressed its necessary social base.

The course of events after the introduction of collective bargaining in 1958 highlighted this deficit in social corporatism, even at the micro level of the individual firm. Between 1958 and 1975 the governments of the day wanted collective agreements to be signed at decentralised levels, keeping powers in reserve to disallow them should they be considered to be inflationary. Given the legal restrictions on firing workers, decentralised collective agreements were seen as a means to link wage increases to productivity gains. The economy grew consistently in the 1960s and early 1970s, and there was a great shakeout of labour, with massive migration to industrial areas and also to Europe. Collective bargaining was to be carried out by employers' and workers' representatives inside the *sindicatos verticales*. The growth of so-called *comisiones obreras* out of collective bargaining has often been explained. The workers tried to give themselves true representatives at workplace level, especially in the Jurados de Empresa (a sort of works council) (Amsden 1971; Ibarra 1987). The procedure of mass meetings, to which proposals were put, developed spontaneously, and from the mass meetings at the workplace grew the notion of electing temporary workers' delegates whose job it would be to negotiate the agreement, whether they belonged or not to the more permanent Jurado de Empresa. A para-legal system developed, which some employers came to prefer (and even publicly stated so) because they could get firm agreements with responsible partners. When the political change came after Franco's death, one such employer, legitimised by his former support for the Workers' Commissions and moved by the need to reassert control in the factories, demanded strong measures against the mass meetings at the workplace which, according to him, would make the new unions unrepresentative (Durán Farrell, *La Vanguardia*, Barcelona, 6 November 1977).

Before the transition, the growing *comisiones obreras* were not legal, and therefore coordination between workers' representatives from different firms was difficult, and indeed illegal. To this one should add the political infighting within the Workers' Commissions in the 1960s. Little by little, the Communist Party took over and provided a leadership to the Workers' Commissions. In 1973 (in December, precisely when ETA gave a big push to the political transition by blowing up the Prime Minister, Admiral Carrero Blanco) the leaders of the Workers' Commissions were sent to gaol, re-emerging a few months after Franco's death in November 1975. The Communist Party, fearing competition on the left, had refused to acknowledge ETA's spectacular success, and the respected Socialist leader, Tierno Galván (1981: 460), would still dare doubt ETA's achievement some years later. In the 1970s there were no less than ten general strikes in the Basque Country (including Navarre), but not elsewhere, in defence of ETA's prisoners or against police repression (Ibarra 1987).

The insistence from the government in the 1960s on the need for collective bargaining was clear, even in agriculture. Officials in the corporative organisation were pestered by the authorities to get landowners and labourers to negotiate wages, hours of work and piecework rates. Thus, in the province of Cordova, in the two or three villages with the most militant working class the labourers refused to take part (in the 1960s) in elections for representatives in the corporatist unions. On the other hand, they dared not hold mass meetings and elect extra-legal delegates who would bargain by direct action because repression was easier than in industrial areas. Therefore, quite often genuine agreements could not be negotiated. This is a case of lack of even micro-corporatist arrangements, caused precisely by the forced introduction of state corporatism (Martinez-Alier 1971).

The 1960s and early 1970s were a period when there was undoubtedly a 'primacy of the economy' at the ideological level inside the regime, nevertheless a general incomes policy proved impossible. One example in the change in vocabulary from doctrines of 'social harmony' to economic reasoning in the issue of the distribution of income will clarify what is meant by the 'primacy of the economy'. The banker Ignacio Villalonga (who was also treasurer of the ACNP) explained in1961 that

> many innocent people and others who are demagogues assume that by syndical pressure or by social legislation one can improve the situation of the economically weak classes . . . But if employers are forced to pay wage rates higher than marginal productivity value, unemployment follows sooner or later. (Cited by Muñoz 1969: 357)

This could be compared to Herrera Oria's vocabulary: 'from the income that his properties produce, the owner has the right to take what he needs for the sustenance, the improvement, and the *decorum* of himself and his family, but the rest he should give out as alms'; and this after 'capital would have been reintegrated a portion of the product to compensate for risks, as commutative justice demands' (1933, Preface).

Already during the 1950s inside the regime one could find modern economic views on the need for an incomes policy. Thus in one of the 'Social Weeks' organised by the ACNP there was a communication by Carlos de Inza (1952), before an audience where bishops were well represented. Inza explained marginal productivity theory, reaching the conclusion that there was no 'entirely satisfactory justification in order to establish that the part of the product which, in conscience, corresponds to each factor of production can be found by making its remuneration or price equal to its marginal productivity'. However, economics could help, after all, and Inza went on to explain that economic growth depended on investment, and that therefore there was a right to profits, although it was difficult to say in exactly what proportion of total production.

In Spain, in the 1960s and 1970s, the required economic vocabulary was available for the prospective *Sozialpartner*. Nevertheless, *there was no way in which a central agreement on incomes could be established because there were no valid interlocutors, at least on the workers' side*. An incomes policy signed inside the state-corporatist organisation would have been a joke. The *sindicatos verticales*, though they were sometimes used as a legal platform, were a shell often unable to contain collective bargaining at plant level. They were much emptier at a higher level. This is why the state resorted to compulsory arbitration (the so-called *normas de obligado cumplimiento*, setting wage limits in particular cases), and this is also why decrees were enacted giving a wage norm, but they were not complied with. The government was successful in slowing down real wages by decree in 1968–9, but in the following years up to 1977 other such attempts failed completely, most notably so in 1973–6. (Proveda Anadón 1974; Cuadrado and Villena 1979).

After 1977: From Corporatism to Corporatism

In Franco's Spain the political-economic system was assumed to function according to corporatist principles. In fact it did not do so. On the other hand, 'corporatist structures' have developed in the post-Franco political-economic system, though not a single one of its politicians, employers' leaders or union leaders would call himself a partisan of corporatism. This is why one could write on 'the old corporatist ideology and the new corporatist reality in Spain ' (Martinez-Alier 1977, 1978,

1981, 1985a, 1985b; Lang 1981; Giner and Sevilla 1984).

Genuine corporatist arrangements were impossible under a system of 'state-corporatism'. They are now possible in the sense that there are valid interlocutors and intermediaries. Which are, however, the ideological basis for such agreements? Would doctrines of 'social harmony' be compatible with the intellectual traditions of left-wing unions, and with the images of society held by the working class? Would the ideology of corporatist arrangements as *scambio político* take root among the social agents and their membership? Mainly, in 1975–7, how did the macro-economic orientation of the unions get roots? After 1977, the consolidation of the new corporatism advanced greatly in Spain. Thus, Nicolas Redondo, the head of the Union General de Trabajadores (UGT), would argue that trade unions must opt for one of three alternative courses of action (*El País*, 11 June 1983): Either to help come into being a 'liberal solution with a clear anti-union content', or 'free and sectorialized bargaining which inevitably will give rise to corporatist practices' or, lastly, 'a policy of great agreements, with balanced sacrifices and counterparts', at the level of the whole economy. Redondo opted for the last alternative, keeping the word 'corporatism' – in Italian or French fashion – for practices which seem not to have a settled name in the scholary literature (*Betriebs-Egoismus* has different connotations from the British 'free collective bargaining', although perhaps corresponds to similar practices. 'Syndicalism' should not be used because it was pre-empted in a different sense by Schmitter in 1974).

In the last years of the Franco era the labour movement had been marked by two main characteristics. First, a considerable degree of mobilisation, largely due to the practice of 'direct' action and bargaining (the word 'direct' is used to indicate the absence of permanent intermediaries). Secondly, a general identification with a single labour organisation, the Comisiones Obreras or Workers' Commissions (born in the early 1960s) which, again with the exception of the Basque Country, gradually became ever more controlled by the Communist Party, which used this control to work its way into elective posts within the official trade unions. Following Franco's death, the Communist Party tried to promote a single labour organisation (similar to the Portuguese Intersindical), based on the prestige and tradition of the Workers' Commissions and the position of some of its members in the official unions. This would not be a typical trade union with voluntary membership, but it would act as the organised representative of the entire labour movement. By monopolising worker representation it would therefore be entitled to the financial resources accumulated by the 'vertical' unions which collected compulsory fees from both the employees and employers. From the outset, the Communists made it clear that in the new political context they would refrain from confrontation and would opt instead for the agreement of pacts with the business interests in exchange for an anti-Franco political pact.

The Communist leaders were sincere in offering their party as the cornerstone of a new corporatist relationship between capital and labour in which the sole labour union would be the unquestioned representative of all workers and would negotiate solutions to the economic recession which was then starting. Nevertheless, there were a number of reasons why this idea stood little chance of success. First of all, the radical background of the Workers' Commission had little in common with the European social-democratic unions which had successfully engaged in the practice of negotiating social pacts. Secondly, in order to acquire full legitimacy, the proposal should have been discussed openly, but such an open discussion might have had unforeseen results. This is because many militant workers understood the union as a 'socio-political' movement, an alternative to the bureaucratised style of the European labour organisations. Lastly, the idea failed to take into consideration the possibility that other 'historical' trade unions, such as the UGT and the CNT, might enjoy a revival despite the fact that they had been only on the fringes of the resurgent labour movement of the 1960s. Ideological differences apart, these unions were obviously not about to agree on a single labour organisation which would, in practice, both spell the end of their independent existence and ensure Communist control of the labour scene.

In the months following Franco's death, in November 1975, there were heated discussions on whether there would and indeed should be a single labour organisation or a variety of unions. The government's position was clear: although the UGT was still illegal, the government allowed it to hold a public conference in April 1976 (when Arias Navarro was still Prime Minister), while in contrast the congress of the Workers' Commissions, held in July of the same year, remained a clandestine affair. It was during this latter congress that the Workers' Commissions decided to turn themselves into an ordinary union with voluntary affiliates and to admit that its original plan was unfeasible. This decision led to a split whereby the factions which were closest to two Maoist parties, the ORT (Workers' Revolutionary Organisation) and the PTE (Spanish Labour Party), decided to set up their own short-lived unions.

The resulting union structure was one of stiff competition between the two leading labour organisations which, at the same time, adopted a joint policy aimed at the elimination of the other smaller unions. The competition between these two major unions was particularly strong in the first years after they had been legalised. The UGT needed to woo members from the Workers' Commissions in order to grow, and the norms governing representatives in the workplace, a debated question, had not yet been established. Afterwards, if one takes the results of works council elections as an indicator, both are about equal in strength, but they are linked to different political parties. Since 1982 these unions have represented one opposition party and the governing party, although in 1987 the UGT is in deep disagreement with the socialist government.

In some regions of Spain union representation is not restricted almost solely to the UGT and the Workers' Commissions. In the Basque Country the leading labour organisation is the nationalist ELA/STV, which gets around 30 per cent of work councils delegates and which has opposed all agreements which are settled at the national level. Despite this, the political positions of the ELA/STV are only moderately nationalist in character rather than left-wing and pro-independence; their opposition to nationwide agreements owes more to their geographic boundaries rather than to other reasons. Other unions with some weight exist also in the Canary Islands, Galicia (INTG, which in 1982 had more than 15 per cent of delegates, and which has now split) and in rural Andalusia, but not in Catalonia. In general, small left-wing unions opposed to neo-corporatist agreements have almost disappeared. The UGT has grown (not certainly in affiliation compared to 1978, but in delegates to works councils), while small unions contrary to social pacts have died, or nearly died. This seems to indicate conformity to neo-corporatism. In the case of the anarcho-syndicalist CNT, disappearance can be attributed to some extent to internal squabbling which was inherited from the bitter exile under the Franco regime, and which took the appearance of a disagreement between a syndicalist faction and a more individualistic faction which was more concerned with new social movements and the unorganised sectors of the population than with union action. But there is also another factor. As R. B. and D. Collier (1979) have explained, corporatism offers inducements and imposes constraints. Recognition by the state and by the employers' organization, and the continuation of a whole series of benefits, depend ultimately on union behaviour which stays within certain guidelines. In the Spanish case the strategy of the UGT until 1987 (and of the Workers' Commissions in 1977 and 1981–3) has been rewarded with measures which tend to make these two unions the representatives of the entire labour force. Thus the labour laws stipulate that no union may participate in bargaining sessions unless it has at least 10 per cent of the delegates of the works councils of the firms affected by the agreement, except that unions with more than 10 per cent of work council delegates at national level (UGT and Workers' Commissions) are always entitled to take part in bargaining sessions. Also public funds have been given to unions in proportion to results to work council elections or through *ad hoc* measures, helping those already strong.*

The Moncloa Pact of 1977

The first important concrete step in the consolidation of neo-corporatism in Spain was the Moncloa Pact of October 1977. In the first place, it was a Pact (setting wage increases for the following year in line with expected inflation, in contrast to the previous practice in decentralised bargaining where past inflation plus productivity increases was the rule), which was signed by the leaders of political parties, but outside Parliament, and with only ex-post and very brief parliamentary debate. Since neither the Employers' Organisation (CEOE) nor the unions signed it, one could perhaps say that it was not an instance of neo-corporatist agreements. However, in 1977 the Employers' Organisation had not yet quite established itself and the elections for president took place only in November of that year. One should also take into account the presence of top businessmen in the first governments after Franco's death (which showed them, at the time, ready to work with Suárez for political democracy and a social pact); and one should remember the close links between the Workers' Commissions and the Communist Party (Carrillo was one of the signatories) and between the Socialist Party and the UGT. Despite a remarkable lack of enthusiasm at the lower levels of both main unions, their leaderships did not speak against the Pact. In fact the leaders of the Workers' Commissions carried out a campaign in favour of the Pact.

There is one further point. Parliamentary elections had taken place in June 1977. In the campaign, the left-wing parties had spoken *against* a social pact, and there was after the Moncloa Pact much verbal juggling in order to explain that it was not properly speaking a 'social pact'. The unions could not show excessive fervour in favour of the Pact. So it was useful to overlap an implicit consensus on a wage norm between organised interests with an agreement between political parties which comprised almost the whole parliamentary spectrum. The new government was the first democratically legitimised in forty years. The elections had had a very high turnout. That the Pact was signed by the leaders of all

*The preceeding paragraphs have been taken from Roca (1987).

political parties (excluding only Basque separatists and almost nobody else) gave it added force over what it would have had if signed only by the major unions and employers' leaders. To make this point clear, we quote from an open letter published in the press by a firm* whose workers were on strike in December 1977 and January 1978, with the explicit intention of breaking the wage norm:

> All workers in Spain could today be on strike on this very same issue (whether collective contracts which had foreseen wage increases according to the inflation rate of the previous year were or were not enforceable). But Spain, through our representatives for whom we all voted on June 15, has also voted this Pact. It is not something that a particular firm might like or dislike, or some particular workers might like to dislike. It is a law for all of us.

In the Pacts in subsequent years there was no need for this supplementary legitimation of corporatist agreements from the parliamentary system. It is something that might be used, if needed. But in principle, in a market economy, wages and conditions of work should be established by bargaining without government interferences, and certainly outside Parliament.

The scope of the Pacts has always been rather wide, but one specific 'counterpart' is rarely mentioned. The unions (and the left-wing parties, particularly the Communist Party) restrained their members in exchange for assurances as to the consolidation of a democratic regime, although around the negotiating table there were not representatives of the one corporation (the army) which represented the real threat.

Social acceptance (as far as it went) shows that in the calculus of costs and benefits the social actors thought they were not overcharged too much, but such a tautological explanation has little value in order to ascertain the reasons for the demise of revolutionary syndicalism (and for the demise both of fascism and state-corporatism) in Spain. In different words, what needs explaining is why union leaders and to some extent their rank-and-file have come to accept a 'macro-economic orientation' for their actions, and to what extent this contradicts the vision of society that (in a country such as Spain) most workers still have. It is interesting that, in a sample of 4,200 workers, in the spring of 1978, around 36 per cent found the Moncloa Pact to be 'harmful or useless' (and nearly 40 per cent did not know or did not answer, while only a quarter found it 'reasonable'). Of those who were against, 60 per cent saw no alternative to it: they were rather perplexed and simultaneously

---

*The firm was 'Bimbo' of Granollers, Barcelona. Most workers were affiliated to the CNT, which was against the Pact.

against and in favour (Pérez Díaz 1979; cf. also Fishman 1984). A 'dual view' of society persists, and opinion polls would find – if they asked such questions – that workers agree, by and large, to the proposition that 'those who work in the hardest jobs earn less than those with lighter jobs, or the capitalists who do not work'. At the same time, there is a feeling of resignation, even accommodation to such a state of things, since it is believed that it will not be easy to change it. This sometimes has been called 'dual consciousness'.

While workers can accept the argument that there might be a trade-off between wage increases and employment, it does not follow from this that they accept the existing distribution of property and income, or that they do not realise that a large portion of profits goes to luxury consumption. 'There is no evidence either that workers would rather have proportional wage increases than across-the-board increases. Wage incomes have decreased in favour of property incomes, and unemployment has *also* increased considerably since 1977 and up to 1986 (whether despite or because of wage-moderation is a moot-point, since wage-moderation depresses effective demand). Some of the officially unemployed work in the 'hidden' economy but, on the other hand, there is a large number of 'discouraged' unemployed workers who do not bother to register because only 30 per cent of the unemployed get unemployment benefits.

In the 1960s, and up to 1977, gross real wages (pre-tax, and not substracting social security contributions) grew by and large as quickly as productivity (Table 7.1), following a 'Fordist' pattern. The increased share of wage incomes in GDP would be explained by an increasing rate of salaried labour (as opposed to self-employed), and also to some extent by the increase in social security contributions (Toharia 1981a, 1981b). In the period after 1977 and until 1986, characterized by increasing unemployment and by neo-corporatist agreements, real wages grew less than productivity, and therefore the share of wage incomes in GDP diminished from about 58 to about 50 per cent, although the part of the employed population which is in wage employment had been practically stable since 1977.

Neo-corporatist Pacts, 1980–7

Despite the avowed intentions of the leaders of the UGT and the Workers' Commissions, they were unable to reach an agreement with business interests for the year 1979, an electoral year (after the Constitution had been drawn up by the first Parliament elected in June 1977).

Table 7.1 Annual average percentage increases in real wages and in productivity

	(1)	(2)	(3)	Increase in productivity
1964–77	2.74	6.69	5.27	5.08
1977–86	−1.08	1.51	−0.22	3.09

Note: Column 1 is increase in wages agreed in collective agreements.
Column 2 is increase in wages effectively paid (includes wage drift) in a sample of manufacturing and building firms with more than ten workers, and banks. This source excludes small firms and the agricultural sector and therefore has an upward bias. Column 3 is increases in legal minimum wage.

Instead the government decreed the range of permitted maximum wage increases based on predicted inflation, and recommended – as did all subsequent Pacts – that increases be proportionate. The Moncloa Pact had still foreseen, on the contrary, that at least half the increase be distributed equally in each firm, as an across-the-board increase to all employees.

The 1980–1 Interconfederate Framework Agreement (AMI), was signed only by the Employers' Association (CEOE) and the UGT. One smaller union, USO, later accepted the agreement. It was also based on the predicted rate of inflation. A statutory *scala mobile*, at times discussed before the political transition, went definitively out of the political-economic agenda with the change to democracy and the simultaneous economic recession. In 1980 the Workers' Commissions and the UGT were locked in serious disagreement over the working of the future labour relations Act, and the Workers' Commissions were edged out of the AMI negotiations. In a climate of political uncertainty and the prospect of new general elections (which would take place in October 1982), CEOE gave UGT a boost by negotiating exclusively with it, and set the two major unions at each other's throat.

The National Employment Agreement (ANE) was signed in June 1981, that is seven months in advance with respect to the bargaining session for 1982. This was because of the threat to democracy in the aftermath of the attempted coup of 23 February 1981. This time, the signatories were the CEOE, the UGT, the Workers' Commissions and the government itself. One of its peculiarities is that it was presented as an agreement on employment rather than just on wages, the actual wage restrictions (which made of 1982 the first year in which all indices of real wages pointed downwards) being seen as capable of generating employment in themselves. In fact unemployment continued its increasing course.

Following the spectacular socialist victory in the general elections to October 1982, 'concertation' again became the byword. A new Interconfederate Agreement between the CEOE, the UGT and the Workers' Commissions, and formally without the government, was reached by 1983. While 1984 was a year without a central pact on wages (and much was made in retrospect of the fact that real wages went down, in order to show that neo-corporatist agreements in a context of increasing unemployment would favour labour rather than capital), the following two years, 1985 and 1986, saw a biannual pact negotiated in October 1984 come into force, the AES (Economic and Social Agreement) signed by the government, the CEOE and the UGT. The Communist Party was by then splitting into three factions, and the Workers' Commissions (which had not split) could not really bring themselves to take part in new agreements. Some of their leaders, who fervently preached the virtues of the Moncloa Pact, do now regret the policy of central agreements, though so far they refuse to use 'neo-corporatism' as a word in the political struggle.

Until 1987 there had been a declining rate of affiliation to unions, and one could therefore argue that the unions whether signatories or not to social pacts, do not represent the workers, but one remarkable feature of neo-corporatist agreements in Spain in an international comparative context is the good fit between wage increases agreed at the top in the pacts and wage increases (without wage drift) agreed in actual collective agreements (Table 7.2). One source (Departamento de Investigaciónes Sociales de la Fundación FIES 1985) gave a rate of affiliation of around 20 per cent for the years 1983–5. Figures for paid-up members have been given before the Congress of the Workers' Commissions of 1987 showing them to have had around 1,800,000 members in 1978, and to be now down to 353,000. Paid-up membership in the Workers' Commissions would now be around 5 per cent of the working salaried population in Spain. The decline in UGT is not so stiff because, in 1978, it was a smaller union. According to a well-known union leader, affiliation to unions is not higher than 14 per cent of the working salaried population (Julian Ariza, *El País*, 15 July 1987). However, the two main unions have a strong presence in political and economic life. In the works councils elections of 1986 the UGT had most delegates, followed by the Workers' Commissions and independents. Works councils elections have been held in 1978, 1980, 1982 and 1986; they were organised simultaneously in all of Spain, and official results were published by the Ministry of Labour. It was the government which first decided that

Table 7.2   Percentage wage increases in collective agreements, compared to social pact provisions

	Social pact provisions		Agreed wages in collective agreements	Consumer prices index
1878	Moncloa Pact	20–22	20.6	19.8
1979	Decree law	11–14	14.1	15.7
1980	AMI	13–16	15.3	15.6
1981	AMI	11–15	13.1	14.6
1982	ANE	9–11	10.5	14.4
1983	AI	9.5–12.5	11.5	12.2
1984	Free bargaining		7.8	11.3
1985	AES	5.5–7.5	7.4	8.8
1986	AES	7.2–8.5	8.1	8.8
1987	Free bargaining		6.5	5.3

elections would be every two years, and now every four years. The involvement of government and unions in such elections is closer to a system of state corporatism than to societal corporatism: one may doubt whether the unions, with such low rates of affiliation, would be able to organise elections by themselves. On the other hand, were they strong, there would be no need for government help. The unions' place in social life is enhanced by the high turnout in such elections, and also by the mass media publicity surrounding the negotiation and, eventually, the signature of central social pacts. It has also been enhanced in the case of the Workers' Commissions by their role in representing the workers against dismissals because of restructuring of some industrial sectors (e.g. naval construction and steel).

Low union density is the main argument against the neo-corporatist interpretation of labour relations and the class struggle in Spain after Franco. If central social pacts are signed by CEOE (which convincingly represents the employers), by the government and the UGT (whose membership is certainly less than 10 per cent of workers), and some years also by the Workers' Commissions, then the pacts cannot be considered as solid institutions of integration of the working class into the capitalist system. But the pacts do actually work, in the sense that the wage norms are complied with.

There have been only three years (1979, 1984 and 1987) since 1977 without a central agreement on a wage norm in Spain. In 1984, for the public sector, a norm of 6.5 per cent was incorporated into the budget, as compared to a foreseen rate of inflation of 8 per cent (which was in fact exceeded). In the private sector the range of disagreement between

CEOE and UGT was small, while the Workers' Commissions held out for an upper level of 10 per cent. In the end, there was no agreement, probably because inside CEOE a neo-liberal current was gaining weight as the rate of unemployment grew (reaching in 1984 nearly 20 per cent), and also because UGT leaders were worried that the Workers' Commissions could appear as successfully outbidding them. Inside the Socialist government there are some believers in a larger wage spread linked to productivity gains, to be achieved by having one year of decentralised bargaining now and then. There are others in the Socialist Party who would like a dirigiste French pattern to emerge, and who can live therefore without social pacts. In general, however, the use of voluntary methods to secure wage moderation and social integration has been much preferred by the Socialists. Felipe González himself, a former labour lawyer, is outspokenly in favour of social pacts. Under the Opus Dei ministers of the 1960s, a managerial concept of the state prevailed. Nowadays proposals such as that put forward by Felipe González in 1987 for a social pact for three years in which even the state budget would be negotiated with the Employers' Organisation and with the two main unions, outside Parliament, as part and parcel of a social pact, reveal also the managerial style: a pact based on *the macro-economic guidelines produced by the 'experts'* would take precedence over parliamentary politics (and over the market). Felipe González has also proposed that the government submit legislation to institute the Economic and Social Council foreseen in the Constitution, and he favours workers' investment funds, on the Swedish pattern, in exchange for wage restraint. There is, then, no specific Spanish contribution to the theory and practice of neo-corporatism, unless the helpful role of sporadic army rumbling sounds (at least up to 1982) is catalogued as such. Army complaints have not been against labour unrest, but against the 'democratic system', ineffective in order to prevent ETA's violence. (There have been hundreds of deaths of military and police after 1977, and also an increasing number of civilian victims in incompetent bombings by ETA: the effects that the Basque bid for independence will have on Spanish politics is, however, outside the scope of this chapter.)

There were conjunctural political factors in the absence of a central corporatist agreement in 1979, 1984 and 1987. Also up to 1987 there seemed to be long-term factors, mainly the increase in unemployment, and the weakness of the unions (possibly induced not only by unemployment, but also to some extent by the corporatist practice of previous years which empties negotiations at lower levels of meaning). The unions' weakness tempts the employers to do without a general wage norm. On the other hand, one way for the unions to recover some muscle is to give them some sort of role at the local and firm level, and one year of decentralised bargaining certainly improves their much weakened position, which makes them dependent on state support because of a low rate of affiliation. In 1987 the government was aiming at a wage norm of 5 per cent, but even UGT refused to play along. The wave of labour unrest in 1987 showed that a pattern of free collective bargaining could result in 'excessive' wage increases (as it would happen in General Motors and Ford, which are nowadays the largest 'Spanish' exporters). Neo-corporatist pacts have perhaps been good for the economy of Spain and for the stability of its democracy. They have certainly been good for the new General Motors factory in Saragossa. In 1987 there was a long labour conflict at General Motors (publicly underplayed by the mass media and by the unions themselves, in contrast to similar situations in Britain under Wilson and Callaghan), with a wage demand of over 9 per cent increase in monetary terms, compared to a government norm of 5 per cent for the public sector. New factors bearing on the feasibility of a central neo-corporatist agreement might now be therefore, after 1987, the renewed growth of the economy and the success of the unions in 1987, in a year of free bargaining, in securing wage increases in collective agreements which exceed the inflation rate. The government may fear labour con-flicts, but unions seem to be acquiring a more sanguine disposition, perhaps also because of some decrease in unemployment. The govern-ment's insistence at the beginning of 1987 that wage settlements in excess of a 5 per cent increase would necessarily imply an inflation rate greater than 5 per cent has proved counterproductive, in that it has discredited the managerial, class-neutral abilities of the economists in the Cabinet, and despite Felipe González's efforts, 1988 will also be a year without a social pact, as the UGT drifts apart from the socialist government. However, one should emphasise that the unions basically accept that the objectives of economic policies are suitably quantified in terms of balance-of-payments constraints, and in terms of aggregated variables such as the volumes of investment and production. Despite its apparent neutrality, there are in fact strong ideological implications contained in this sort of language, and it is different from talking about *what* to produce in response to *which* necessities.

A school of political economists who see capitalist development in terms of a 'theory of regulation' have used the concept of 'Fordism' (Aglietta, 1979; Toharia, 1986) in order to explain the relation between wage increases and productivity growth (taking 'productivity' at its face value in conventional economic accounting). The reference to Henry Ford does not arise from a particular liking for cars but rather from Ford's view that wages should be high enough so that the workers would be able to buy the cars they were themselves producing: wages are labour costs for the particular firm, but in the aggregate they are also demand of consumer goods. Mass production requires mass consumption (although from an international and inter-generational point of view, one may doubt whether mass consumption of 'positional' goods such as cars will ever be possible). In the Spanish economy, as in many other economies, the period from the early 1960s up to 1975 or 1977 was characterised by a 'Fordist' relation, while in 1977–86 growth of wages lagged behind productivity growth. Whether in the absence of corporatist pacts, the lag would have been greater or smaller is difficult to tell – but, as we have seen, the experience of 1987, a year of free collective bargaining, would favour the view that corporatist pacts worked against wages.

Reference to Henry Ford is suggestive also on other grounds. Thus a discussion of the valuation of cars ought certainly to be appropriate if we are to speak of 'Fordism'. Many economists would agree that there is an element of arbitrariness (or rather there are certain decisions which come from outside economics in the strict sense) not only in the evaluations, but also in the selection of negative and positive externalities. Synchronic externalities are difficult enough for the chrematistic outlook. Moreover, when we are dealing with irreversible events which affect our descendants (such as depletion of oil reserves), valuations in money cannot arise by taking into account, even notionally, the expression of their preferences because they are not yet alive and so cannot be economic agents now. We are ready to concede that ecological economics is not relevant for actual neo-corporatist agreements, but we find it nevertheless remarkable that unions have not only abandoned a Marxist view of exploitation, but also refuse to join in the ecological critique of macro-economic magnitudes, and on the contrary, adopt uncritically an orthodox macro-economic orientation which adopts market valuations as an article of faith.

The Legitimation of Neo-corporatism

This brings us to the last point, which is how neo-corporatism which implies refraining from exercising union power at lower levels, can be legitimised from a social democratic point of view. One possibility is that of agreeing to permanent wage moderation in exchange for a greater voice for workers' organisations in the running of the economy. This is where Otto Bauer's comments of 1933 come to mind, when he argued that the distance between Catholic corporatism and 'industrial' or 'economic democracy' was not that large. It is perhaps a case, understandable in the circumstances, of 'if you can't beat them, [try to] join them'. But his remarks preserve their interest. The Spanish Socialists have adopted them in the 1970s and 1980s, although with embarrassment and without acknowledgement, since the word 'corporatism' implies a system of permanent, structured inequality.

Otto Bauer wrote that the 'class struggle' in Austria at the time was a struggle on the interpretation of *Quadragesimo Anno*. Despite the Pope's praise for Italian fascism, one should trace a fundamental distinction between the fascist corporative system (with appointed officials; and without freedom of association or the right to strike or parties and Parliament), and what we would call now 'liberal corporatism', *berufsständische Selbstverwaltung*, 'corporative autoregulation' or 'self-administration', a concept which, as he explained, was similar to 'organised capitalism' or to 'economic' or 'industrial democracy'. Capitalists and workers would collaborate in a range of new institutions, with wide competences (which he discussed in detail). Such institutions would be like those which had grown out of collective bargaining (*Tarifgemeinschaften*) but would deal with other questions apart from wages and work conditions. They could deal, for instance, with the regulation of production and prices, by sector. That 'state corporatism' (Bauer called it ('Italian') *Korporationensystem*) would kill social corporatism was a point explicitly made by Bauer. Since the Catholics held on to the anti-statist 'subsidiarity principle', he hoped they would agree with him. The specific question of a Corporative Chamber vs a Parliament of political parties was not discussed by Bauer in this series of articles.

Bauer pointed out the loss of strength by industrialists and bankers after the First World War in Austria to the benefit of aristocrats, bureaucrats and generals, but he felt (or at least he wrote, although this was in the autumn of 1933) that there was a *Gleichgewicht* between the workers and the capitalists. *Berufssständische Selbstverwaltung* was thus in no sense a 'road to socialism'. It was a 'left-wing' interpretation of *Quadragesimo Anno*, rooted in social-democratic theory. In a Spanish (or Italian) context, 'corporative auto-regulation' or 'self-administration', which Bauer used as a 'good' term, does not seem useful to legitimise social democratic (or Eurocommunist) neo-corporatist practice, but perhaps 'economic democracy' would be more useful, giving to it Bauer's definition and making it synonymous with 'neo-corporatism'. The need to move from a system of representation of citizens, associated with parliamentary democracy, to a functional system of social integration was proposed by Bauer* more or less at the same time as Manoïlescu's *Le*

---

*Articles in *Arbeiter-Zeitung*, 1933, in *Werkausgabe*, vol. 7, pp. 496–517; 'Klassenkampf und Ständeverfassung', *Der Kampf*, January 1934, in *Werkausgabe*, vol. 9, p. 341 f; see, in English, Gulick (1948).

siècle du corporatisme (1934). Bauer saw both systems as complementary, Manoïlescu wanted to substitute the second one for the first one.

The terms 'corporatist state', 'corporatist economy' and 'corporatism' were used in the international debate since the mid-1970s more as terms of abuse than of terms of praise. This was clear even in the initial academic contributions, and also in political usage not only from the left, but also from the right (at least in Britain). Perhaps the word is now losing this pejorative character. Thus an antipathetic review of a book by Tony Benn said against him: 'Of course post-war government depended on a corporatist consensus which has now broken down. That is a Thatcherite truism.' And a favourable review of Shonfield's *In Defense of the Mixed Economy* states that he 'was a corporatist, and that is nowadays not a very fashionable thing to be'.* But in the radical atmosphere of the late 1960s and early 1970s the word 'corporatism' was used by academics leaning to the left, despite (or perhaps because of) its connotations. In Schmitter's original typology, presented in a brilliant article, 'Still, the century of corporatism?' (1974), which included some consideration of 'the basic institutions of capitalism and the class structure of property and power engendered by it', the 'syndicalist' alternative seemed to imply a working-class victory led by the unions (as in Catalonia, in 1936). 'Syndicalism' was 'societal corporatism' without capitalists, and possibly with a much weakened state, that is with a different structure of property, and a more equal distribution of power and income.

In the second half of the 1970s the neo-liberal reaction was growing, and in some countries the increase in unemployment made it attractive to attempt to do without social pacts. Neo-liberals were certainly entitled to the derogatory use of the 'corporatist' tag, perhaps even more so than leftists, because the first time that the word 'corporatism' was used as a term of abuse after 1945, in the Keynesian social-democratic era in Europe, was probably by Hayek in 1960. (Mendès-France had felt obliged to include some pages in *La République moderne* (1962), explaining why his proposals for concerted planning could *not* be described as corporatism, probably in the French context looking over his shoulder to the Communists rather than to the right.) Hayek wrote that in countries where, because of the monopolistic behaviour of the unions, inflationary tendencies began to appear, there were increasing demands for an 'overall wage policy'. Wages were to be determined by some conception of 'justice' rather than by the forces of the market. This would of course force unions to choose

*See *Times Literary Supplement*, 11 September 1981; *Financial Times*, 25 February 1984.

between becoming the willing instrument of governmental policy, on the one hand, and being totally abolished, on the other. The former alternative is more likely to be chosen, since it would enable the existing union bureaucracy to retain their position and some of their personal power. But to the workers it would mean complete subjection to the control of a corporative state. (Hayek 1960: 282–3)

Free collective bargaining was here compared by Hayek to an 'overall wage policy' implemented by a corporative state with the agreement of the union leadership (and not of the rank-and-file, since Hayek thought that in a period of full employment they would not give permanent consent to a wage norm). The distinction between the two varieties of corporatism got lost in Hayek's polemics. 'Corporatism' was used as an insult, and Hayek is certainly an exception to Shonfield's rule, that 'the corporatist form of organization seems to be almost second nature to the Austrians' (Shonfield 1965: 193). In Hayek's view, 'corporatism' was a bad thing because it politicises the economy: the market should rule undisturbed. Corporatist proposals, such as those by Aubrey Jones in his book *The New Inflation* (1973) of a Corporative Chamber of Employers and Unions, certainly meant a politicisation of the economy; the subtitle of Aubrey Jones's book was 'The politics [not economics] of prices and incomes'. But neo-corporatist structures also assimilate politics to economics in the sense that macro-economic guidelines become the basis for social pacts: this is what we mean by the 'primacy of the economy'.

Nobody writing on Spain (or Austria, Portugal or Italy) would be under the impression, which perhaps prevailed during the 1970s in Britain, that corporatism was a feature of modern capitalism, born after 1945. Indeed the historical relevance of the concept of corporatism in order to understand the 'recasting' of bourgeois Europe, and especially of Germany after the First World War, was one of the topics of the debate on corporatism of the 1970s (Maier 1975). There is certainly a difference between the 'old' corporatism, compatible with fascism, and the 'new' corporatism, which is more or less compatible with parliamentary democracy.* The word 'corporatism', whether analytically useful or not, has been embarrassing not only to Spanish politicians, unionists and employers' leaders, but also to Spanish political analysts. Thus it has been said to be 'unfortunate that both forms of interest organization and control (both forms being the 'old' and the 'new'

*When writing in Spanish, Salvador Giner and Victor Pérez-Diaz use 'corporativismo' for the 'old' corporatism, and the neologism 'corporatismo' for the 'new' corporatism. Such things happen also in Italy; one wonders how they would translate the title of Schmitter's article, 'Still the century of corporatism?'.

corporatisms) go by the same name' (Giner and Sevilla 1984). Now, however, whether use of 'corporatism' in order to describe the 'new' corporatism, is considered to be fortunate or unfortunate depends on the outlook of author and reader. The distinction between descriptive and normative terms is difficult to make in political science, words are themselves part of the political contest (Connolly 1983).

We do not believe that Spanish neo-corporatism is to be explained by a specific 'Iberic-Latin' political culture (Wiarda 1974). Corporatist structures have grown after 1977 because the left (with the exception of the Basque County) had long made itself ready for a tame transition out of the Franco regime. The right came out of that regime politically weakened, but socially and ideologically on top. The language of Spanish corporatism is nowadays the language of macro-economics, in which the Socialists concur, and not that of Christian 'social harmony' or even Durkheimian 'organic solidarity'. Post-Franco corporatist structures have developed, without any of the social agents adopting an explicitly corporatist ideology. On the contrary, the word as used in this chapter is seen as an insult, especially by Socialist intellectuals.

References

Aglietta, Michel (1977) *A Theory of Capitalist Regulation: The US Experience*, London, New Left Books.

Aguilar, Salvador (1985), 'Burgueses sin burguesía? La trayectoria corporativa de la burguesía empresarial catalana', *Revista Española de Investigaciones Sociológicas*, **31**, 183–211.

Amsden, Jon (1971), *Collective Bargaining and Class Conflict in Spain*, London, Weidenfeld and Nicholson.

Anderson, Charles W. (1970), *The Political Economy of Modern Spain*, Madison, Wis., University of Wisconsin Press.

Aznar, Serverino (1946), *Estudios económico-sociales* (Preface, José Larraz), Madrid, Instituto de Estudios Políticos.

Burke, Edmund (1790), *Reflections on the Revolution in France* (Penguin edn).

Carrillo, Santiago (1975), 'Franco desaparecido. Las tareas del movimiento obrero para que el franquismo desaparezca también', *Nuestra Bandera*, **82**.

Clavera, J., Monés, A., Montserrat, A. and Ros Hombravella, J. (1973), *Capitalismo español: de la autarquia a la estabilización (1939–1959)*, Madrid, Edicusa.

Collier, R. B. and Collier, D. (1979), 'Inducements versus constraints: disaggregating corporatism', *American Political Science Review*, **73**(4), 967–86.

Connolly, W. (1983), *The Terms of Political Discourse* (2nd edn), Oxford, Martin Robertson.

Cuadrado, Juan R. and Villena, J. (1979), 'La política de rentas en España', *Cuadernos de Ciencias Económicas y Empresariales*, **5**; also in Espina *et al.*, 1987, 839–58.

Departamento de Investigaciónes Sociales de la Fundación FIES (1985), 'Representatividad y organización de Comisiones Obreras y UGT', *Papeles de Economía Española*, **22**, 235–43.

Duguit, Léon (1909), *La Transformación del Estado*, Madrid, Revista de Derecho Privado.

Durkheim, E. (1902), 'Preface' in *La División social del trabajo* (2nd edn), Madrid, Akal, 1982.

Espina, A. (1985), 'Políticas de rentas en España: 1977–86', *Papeles de Economía Española*, **22**, 343–60.

Espina, A., Fina, Ll. and Sáez, F. (eds) (1987), *Estudios de economía del trabajo en España. II, Salarios y política de rentas*, Madrid, Ministry of Labour.

Estradé, A. and Casado, J. A. (1979), 'El nuevo corporativismo: una salida capitalista ante la crisis', *Transición*, n.14.

Fina, Ll. (1983), 'Salaris i fiscalitat. El cas espanyol durant el periode 1965–75', *Recerques*, **13**; also in Espina *et al.*, 1987, 353–75.

Fishman, Robert (1984), El movimiento obrero en la transición: objetivos políticos y organizativos', *Revista Española de Investigaciones Sociológicas*, **26**, 61–112.

Frías, J. and Lorente, J. R. (1983), 'Seguridad social y deslizamiento salarial', *Información Comercial Española*, 1913; also in Espina *et al.*, 1987, 989–94.

Giner, S. and Sevilla, E. (1984), 'Spain: from corporatism to corporatism' in A. Williams (ed.), *Southern Europe Transformed*, London, Harper and Row.

Gulick, Charles (1948), *Austria: From Habsburg to Hitler*, Berkeley, Calif., University of California Press.

Hayek, F. A. von (1960), *The Constitution of Liberty*, London, Routledge and Kegan Paul.

Herrera Oria, A. (1933), 'Preface' in *Doctrina Social Católica de León XIII y Pio XI* (eds, A. Martín-Artajo and M. Cuervo), Barcelona, Labor.

Ibarra Güelli, P. (1987), *El Movimiento Obrero en Vizcaya: 1967–1977*, Bilbao, Servicio Editorial Universidad del País Vasco.

Inza, Carlos de (1952), 'Problemas del trabajo', *XII Semana Social*, Madrid.

Lang, W. (1981), 'Spanien nach Franco: vom autoritären zum liberalen Korporatismus?' in Ulrich von Alemann (ed.), *Neokorporatismus*, Frankfurt, Campus Verlag.

Linz, Juan (1964), 'An authoritarian regime: Spain' in E. Allardt and Y. Littunen (eds), *Cleavages, Ideologies and Party Systems*, Helsinki.

Linz, Juan (1981), 'A century of politics and interests in Spain' in S. Berger (ed.), *Organizing Interests in Western Europe*, Cambridge, Cambridge University Press.

Lorente, J. R. (1982), 'Notas criticas sobre las estadísticas salariales' in Ministerio de Economía y Comercio (ed.), *El Mercado de trabajo en España*, Madrid; also in Espina *et. al.*, 1987, 979–88.

Maier, Charles (1975), *Recasting Bourgeois Europe*, Princeton, NJ, Princeton University Press.

Malefakis, Edward E. (1970), *Agrarian Reform and Peasant Revolution in Spain: Origins of the Civil War*, New Haven, Conn. and London, Yale University Press.

Maravall, J. M. (1982), *La Política de la transición*, Madrid, Taurus.

Martinez-Alier, J. (1967), 'Un edificio capitalista con una fachada feudal? El latifundio en Andalucía y América Latina', *Cuadernos de Ruedo Ibérico*, **15**, 3–53.

Martinez-Alier, J. (1971), *Labourers and Landowners in Southern Spain*, London, Allen and Unwin.

Martinez-Alier, J. (1973), Review of Malefakis, E., *Agrarian Reform and Peasant Revolution in Spain : Origins of the Civil War, Journal of Peasant Studies*, **1**.

Martinez-Alier, J. (1975), 'Critica de la caracterización del franquismo como régimen "autoritario" de "pluralismo limitado"', *Cuadernos de Ruedo Ibérico*, 43–45, 67–75.

Martinez-Alier, J. (1977), 'El Pacto de la Moncloa. La lucha sindical y el nuevo corporativismo', *Cuadernos de Ruedo Ibérico*, 58–60, 32–51.

Martinez-Alier, J. (1978), 'Notas sobre el franquismo', *Papers Revista de Sociologia*, **8**, 27–51.

Martinez-Alier, J. (1981), 'El viejo y el nuevo corporativismo', *El País*, 5 December.

Martinez-Alier, J. (1985a), 'Velles ideologies i noves realitats corporativistes', *Papers Revista de Sociologia*, **24**, 25–51.

Martinez-Alier, J. (1985b), 'Viejas ideologías y nuevas realidades corporativistas', *Revista Española de Investigaciones Sociológicas*, **31**, 119–42.

Martinez-Alier, J. and Roca, J. (1986), 'El debate sobre neocorporativismo', *Pensamiento*

Iberoamericano. Revista de Economía Política, **8**. 492–502.

Molinero, C. and Ysàs, P. (1985), '*Patria, Justicia y Pan*'. *Nivell de vida i condicions de trebalil a Catalunya 1939–1959*, Barcelona, La Magrana.

Muñoz, Juan (1969), *El Poder de la banca en España*, Madrid, Zero.

Naredo, J. M. and Campos, P. (1980), 'Los balances energéticos de la agricultura española', *Agricultura y Sociedad*, **15**, 163–255.

Paine, Tom (1791), *The Rights of Man*, Harmondsworth, Penguin.

Pérez-Díaz, Victor (1979), 'Orientaciones políticas de los obreros españoles hoy', *Sistema*, 29–30, 159–79.

Pérez-Díaz, Victor (1987), 'Economic policies and social pacts in Spain during the transition' in Ilja Scholten (ed.), *Political Stability and Neo-Corporatism*, London, Sage, 216–46.

Poveda Anadón, R. (1974), 'El control de precios y rentas en España', *Boletín de Estudios Económicos*, **93**; also in Espina *et al.*, 1987, 817–38.

Preston, Paul (ed) (1976), *Spain in Crisis. The Evolution and Decline of the Franco Regime*, Hassocks, Harvester Press.

Roca, Jordi (1985), 'Neocorporativisme a l'estat espanyol postfranquista (1977–1983)', *Papers Revista de Sociologia*, **24**, 85–117.

Roca Jordi (1987), 'Neo-corporatism in post-Franco Spain' in Ilja Scholten (ed), *Political Stability and Neo-Corporatism*, London, Sage, 247–68.

Sáez Alba, A. (pseud.) (1974), *La Asociación Católica Nacional de Propagandistas*, Paris, Ruedo Ibérico.

Schmitter, P. C. (1974), 'Still the century of corporatism?' in P. C. Schmitter and G. Lehmbruch (eds), *Trends towards Corporatist Intermediation*, London, Sage, 1979, 7–52.

Serrano, A. and Malo de Molina, J. L. (1979), *Salarios y mercado de trabajo en España*, Madrid, Blume.

Shonfield, A. (1965), *Modern Capitalism*, Oxford, Oxford University Press.

Tierno Galván, E. (1981), *Cabos sueltos*, Barcelona, Bruguera.

Toharia, Luis (1981a), 'La tasa agregada de beneficios de la economía española 1965–79', *Revista Mensual*, **4**(9).

Toharia, Luis (1981b), 'Precios, costes y beneficios y la "tasa justificada de inflación" en la economía española (1965–79), *Investigaciones Económicas*, **16**; also in Espina *et al.*, 1987, 239–78.

Toharia, Luis (1986), 'Un fordismo inacabado, entre la transición política y la crisis económica: España' in R. Boyer (ed.), *La Flexibilidad del trabajo en Europa*, Madrid, Ministry of Labour.

Viñas, Miguel (pseud.) (1972), 'Franquismo y revolución burguesa' in *Horizonte Español 1972*, III, Ruedo Ibérico, Paris.

Wiarda, H. (1974), 'Corporatism and development in the Iberic-Latin World' in F. Pike and T. Stritch (eds), *The New Corporatism. Social Political Structures in the Iberian World*. Notre Dame University Press.

Zufiaur, J. L. (1985), 'El sindicalismo español en la transición y la crisis', *Papeles de Economía Española*, **22**, 202–34.

Note

1. The authors are grateful for the stimulus provided by invitations to a Summer School on Neocorporatism at the European University Institute in Florence, and to a Conference on Spain at the Center for European Studies of Harvard University in 1988. A first version of this chapter was published in the *International Journal of Political Economy*, **17** (4), 1987.

7 Corporatism in Sweden
Neil Elder

Sweden was described in 1975 as 'the real model of a corporate society'.[1] This was written in the wake of the miners' strike in Britain associated with the fall of the Heath government, at a time therefore when the Swedish case was apt to be viewed by liberal pluralists as approximating to the final perfect state of an advanced industrial society. Here, it seemed, was the answer to the problems of government 'overload', a preoccupation with which was much in evidence at that period: a self-regulating labour market insulated from governmental interference on the basis of a perceived common interest between the peak economic organisations on either side. 'From the state's viewpoint', as Elvander put it, 'the organizations, by virtue of their material strength, their sense of social responsibility and their self-discipline showed that they merited the trust placed in them by the state through the delegation, so to speak, of the right to determine incomes policy and other conditions of employment to the parties'[2] in the labour market. Various shadows have darkened this rosy vision in the past twelve years, and it will be a part of the task of this present survey to identify and seek to evaluate them. At the same time, it will be argued that the vision has not suffered total effacement.

Not every observer shared the vision, of course. In 1971, Roland Huntford, in his book, *The New Totalitarians*, had written, 'Like Fascist Italy, Sweden is today a corporate State.'[3] The argument was conducted at two levels in an extended polemic which, naturally enough, attracted more media attention in Sweden than any subsequent academic investigation into corporatism in that country. In the first place, the Social Democrats had been in power for thirty-nine years when the book was written, and their tenure appeared to be irreversible. Secondly, and more important, Swedish society was seen as being for historical reasons completely saturated by collectivist norms. 'You must belong to an organization', as one official put it, 'in order to have a framework of reference'.[4] The second part of the argument was congruent with the first. The Social Democrats thus appeared as the natural political expression of the Swedish psyche, and at the end of the road the author could only see an approximation to Aldous Huxley's *Brave New World*.

It is easy to say, with benefit of hindsight, that the Social Democrats lost power in 1976 for a six-year span in opposition. This circumstance certainly disposed of some of Huntford's arguments, but not the weightier ones. However, in the present context it is only relevant to go a little way down that particular road. What is relevant here is to note, in a systematic rather than impressionistic manner, the factors underlying the description of Sweden as 'the real model of a corporate society'.

Sweden has a highly developed participatory civic culture and a long-established and pervasive tradition of functional representation. The ground-plan for the country's system of corporatist concertation can be said to date from the Saltsjöbaden Agreement of 1938 between the Swedish Confederation of Trade Unions (LO–Landsorganisationen) and the Swedish Employers' Confederation (SAF-Svenska Arbetsgivare-föreningen). Even then, Sweden had moved into the top third of western industrialised countries in respect of the degree of unionisation of the workforce. During the 1961–76 period the Swedes came to occupy the top position in this particular league, with an average of 76 per cent unionised among those employed outside the agricultural sector.[5] By 1980 union membership density stood at 87.7 per cent.[6] Some 90 per cent of blue-collar workers belong to the 22 unions which are affiliated to LO and structured on an industrial rather than a craft basis. In addition, white-collar union mobilisation has proceeded apace in the years since the Second World War, with a score of unions banded together in a powerful peak organisation, the Central Organisation of Salaried Employees (TCO-Tjanstemännens Centralorganisationen). This has over 1 million members, as compared with LO's 2.3 million in 1986.[7] Well over a quarter of a million also belong to the Swedish Confederation of Professional Associations (SACO/SR – Sveriges Akademikers Centralorganisationen/Statistjänstemannens Riksförbund): these are professional people with university degrees or the equivalent.

The unions in Sweden are not divided by ideological, ethnic or religious cleavages. There is a syndicalist union, the Swedish Workers' Central Organisation, with some support among forestry workers and navvies, but only 20,000–30,000 members in all.[8] The largest single union is that of the municipal workers (well over half a million members), which perhaps gives a new twist to Ionescu's observation that Sweden is 'nearer to the image of "a more-administered-than-governed society" (in the Saint Simonian sense) than any other country in the contemporary world'.[9] However, not only does the union movement in Sweden enjoy a unique degree of comprehensiveness of coverage, and probably of homogeneity also, among advanced industrial societies, but it developed in addition a high degree of centralisation.

Historically this centralisation started as a defensive response to the appearance of a comprehensive and tightly knit peak organisation on the employers' side in the shape of SAF. The process began in 1902 with SAF's foundation, moved ahead swiftly until the general strike of 1909, then suffered a long period of abeyance until revived by the Saltsjöbaden Agreement of 1938. The years from 1909 to 1936 were years of conflict and bitterness in the Swedish labour market, symbolised by the shootings at Ådalen in 1931. A long strike in the building industry in 1933–4 caused LO to intervene and pressurise the union involved in order to head off the threat of emergency legislation. At the same time, SAF, alive to the possible implications of the fact that the Social Democrats had come to power in 1932 and were consolidating their hold upon it, moved towards proposing rules for the joint voluntary regulation of the labour market.[10] Saltsjöbaden marked the end of two years of negotiations and led directly to a revision of LO's constitution in 1941 which effectively centralised control of the strike weapon. The process was rounded off in 1956 when, on SAF's initiative, the first of many normative wage agreements was reached with LO at national level in order to provide a framework settlement for the largest part of the industrial sector. Therefore, by these stages LO took powers of control over its constituent unions to parallel the powers which SAF already possessed over its member firms. In 1986, it may be added, most private sector employers are affiliated to SAF, which covers some 42,000 firms with a workforce of over 1.2 million.

The Saltsjöbaden Agreement has been described as the symbol of a 'historical compromise' between capital and labour.[11] The essence of that compromise was that the unions were to cooperate with management as partners in an effort to rationalise and maximise production; production decisions were to be left to management in an industrial structure which was overwhelmingly in private ownership and control; and the state, while staying out of labour market negotiations, was to see to an equitable distribution of the product and, at the same time, use Keynesian, or quasi-Keynesian, means to counter unemployment. Moreover, the state would promote structural changes directed to the increase of economic efficiency.

This accord paved the way for three decades of industrial peace in Sweden, unbroken save for isolated major conflicts in 1945 (metalworkers), 1953 (foodstuffs industry) and 1966 (teachers and other public service professionals). For SAF, the conclusion of one- and two-year framework agreements – which were backed by a legal ban on strike action during their period of validity – brought with it a measure of background security for the taking of investment decisions. For LO, the trend towards centralisation maximised its resources in the pursuit of a 'solidaristic' wages policy. The intention here was twofold: to jack up wage levels at the bottom end of the scale; and, at the same time, to seek to ensure equal wages for equal work without regard to the capacity of a firm to pay.

For a Marxist observer, the Swedish model which began to emerge at Saltsjöbaden represented an inherently unstable equilibrium, a truce between warring interests brought about by a temporary equality of power. It represented the 'politics of necessary compromise', which 'seems to be an inescapable step in the maturation of capitalism'.[12] Thus a period of positive-sum class conflict was required in order to enable the fruits of capitalism to ripen; when the fruits were ready for picking, the socialist dynamic would reassert itself and transform the structures of Swedish industrial and economic life in the appropriate ideological direction. Until that time the power resources newly available to the Social Democratic Party would be used to maximise welfare provision and promote labour market policies designed to maintain full employment. Full employment, in turn, would increase the bargaining power of the union side of the labour movement both in the labour market and at the workplace.

Following this line of analysis, and writing in 1978, Korpi was of the opinion that the power balance between capital and labour had undergone a major shift in favour of labour since the days of Saltsjöbaden and equality. At one level this interpretation might appear paradoxical: the Social Democrats had lost office in 1976. The defeat was attributed in part to the negative political consequences for the party of pursuing compromise policies within a capitalist framework: regional imbalance, energy and environmental questions (especially the nuclear issue), and rapid urbanisation. In part also the deteriorating international economic situation was making welfare provision more difficult, and the non-socialist parties were able to indulge in competitive bidding in this sector of public policy.

LO responding, *inter alia*, to the New Left current flowing strongly at that time set up a Committee of Inquiry into industrial democracy in 1969. The initiative, as was commonly the case with reform proposals in the workers' interest, came from the Metalworkers' Union. The report was published in 1971. Since the measures envisaged could not be agreed between both sides of industry through the normal processes of collective bargaining, the unions looked to the Social Democratic government to pass the necessary legislation. From 1973 to 1976, however, Sweden had a hung Parliament in which the parties of the left had exactly the same representation (175 seats) as those on the 'bourgeois' side. Consequently the government needed support from some other quarter in order to carry out the later and more crucial stages of its programme, and this support it found in particular from the Liberals with their commitment to 'grassroots democracy' (*närdemokrati*).[13] It was a factor in this situation that the peak white-collar union organisation (TCO) aligned itself with LO on the issue, at least at the level of the leadership. This, in turn, encouraged the view on the radical left that a wage-earner front was beginning to appear, with the capacity and inclination to engage in a class struggle against the employers – and in the process revivify the socialist dynamic which had been in a state of suspended animation since the signing of the Saltsjöbaden Agreement.

From this perspective the two-pronged reform movement which emerged in the 1970s marked the end of the old bilateral corporatist balance and, at the same time, a significant stage in the reduction of capitalist power. The first prong involved making the prerogatives of management at the workplace subject to the processes of collective bargaining. The second prong involved the introduction of schemes for worker funds, later called (significantly) 'wage-earner funds' and, finally (equally significantly), 'security funds'. Both lines of reform could be regarded, initially at least, as manifestations of the 'functional socialism' of the Social Democratic ideologue, Gunnar Adler-Karlsson:

> Let us look upon our capitalists in the same way as we have looked upon our kings in Scandinavia ... According to our constitution the king still has equally as much formal power as a hundred years ago, but in reality we have undressed him of all his power functions so that today he is in fact powerless ... Let us ... divest our present capitalists one after another of their ownership functions ... After a few decades they will then remain, perhaps formally as kings but in reality as naked symbols of a passed and inferior stage of development.[14]

A series of statutes was put through the Swedish Parliament from 1971 onwards which certainly reflected a leftward shift in the balance between capital and labour. For example, it included the placement of employee representatives on company boards together with increased union access to a firm's documents, with safeguards for business secrets. The Åman Laws of 1974 made layoffs of workers illegal unless 'objectively justified' and required employers to give six months' notice whenever they proposed to shed labour. The process culminated in the Co-Determination Act (*Medbestämmandelagen*) of June 1976 – i.e. three months before the Social Democratic government was ousted from office.

This last statute has been described as marking 'the dissolution of the historical compromise . . . symbolised by the withdrawal of LO from the Saltsjöbaden Agreement'.[15] It made the direction and division of work within a firm or organisation a matter for collective bargaining; gave unions the right to strike in pursuit of a co-determination agreement; abolished the unilateral right of management to hire and fire labour; established a legal presumption in favour of the union view in disputes over the interpretation of co-determination agreements; and, with some reservations, extended beyond the private sector to cover also the public sector. It was essentially a framework statute, intended to guarantee that major changes in working operations occurred only after close consultation between both sides. A series of sectoral co-determination agreements have since been concluded, the first of these coming in the public sector some fourteen months after the passage of the enabling Act.

The second prong of reform appeared much more radical in its implications, not least to the 'bourgeois' parties, and sharply polarized the political scene along the left–right divide for a decade after 1976 when it first hit the headlines. Once again, the initiative on a scheme for worker funds came from the Metalworkers' Union in the shape of a motion at the 1971 LO Congress. The first blueprint was associated with the name of Rudolf Meidner, an economist working in the LO Secretariat – the powerhouse for a number of major reform projects in the years after the Second World War. This draft was enthusiastically endorsed by the LO Congress in June 1976 after extensive grassroots discussions – again, just three months before the Social Democratic government lost power after the general elections. The issue was in fact one element in the party's loss of power.[16] It opened up a temporary fissure between the union movement and the party, which was anxious to play for time and work out the implications of the scheme. It also united the Liberals, Centre Party and Moderates (Conservatives) in a common front of opposition, and helped them tide over their severe difficulties on the nuclear power question which at that time was also at the forefront of political controversy.

The funds issue was one of considerable complexity which went through a number of mutations before the Social Democrats eventually put a measure on the statute-book in December 1983, just fifteen months after their return to power. The party used the six years in opposition to mend its fences with the union movement, reaching agreement with LO on an outline scheme by June 1980: this was ratified in essentials by both partners at their respective congresses in September–October 1981 and formed the basis of the subsequent legislation. In the present context the focus will be narrowed to a few salient points of relevance to the theme of corporatism in Sweden.

The solidaristic wages policy pursued by LO contributed towards increasing profits in the more expansive sectors of the Swedish economy in the 1950s and 1960s: this was a period of industrial mergers and an increasing concentration of capital. In 1968 a Commission of Inquiry report drew public attention to this crystallisation of economic power in the hands of a relatively small number of companies – and of families.[17] It seemed plausible to argue that the maturation of capitalism had now taken place in Sweden: the hidden dynamics of the Saltsjöbaden settlement had produced a situation where the fruit had ripened and was now ready for the socialist harvest.

Again this background the original Meidner Plan, as approved by LO in 1976, could be seen as the first and crucial step towards the abolition of the mixed economy. The Plan envisaged that one-fifth of the profits of larger firms (those with 50 and more workers) would be transferred annually to a central fund run by the unions and their peak organisations in both the blue- and white-collar sectors. The yield was to be used to buy shares. This would result in a slow but steady growth of worker representatives at shareholders' meeting until eventually a workers' majority would be reached and a fundamental structural change would take place in the Swedish economy.

The Swedish system of corporatist concertation, as established at Saltsjöbaden, bore even less resemblance to the Schmitter model[18] than that in force in the neighbouring Scandinavian states. The state was far from assuming an 'incorporating' role *vis-à-vis* the peak labour market organisations in the pursuit of a rational and efficient economic policy directed by bureaucratic experts. It is true that the organisations effected a wage-freeze in response to government prompting during the inflationary period at the time of the Korean War, but from 1955 until the 1970s the government did not even intervene to the extent of suggesting a ceiling for collective bargaining settlements.[19] However, the situation changed under the impact of economic adversity in the 1970s – a theme which will be reverted to later in this chapter.

The worker funds scheme, as originally formulated, posed a threat to the foundations of the Swedish corporatist system and raised a question about the role of the state that was of quite a different order to those raised by Schmitter's analysis. Could state power be enlisted to bring about a socialist transformation of society? Of Sweden, less than any other western European state, was it true that the historical condition under which Social Democrats must act is that of minority status under majority rule: the party came back to power in 1982, for example, with three more seats than the 'bourgeois' parties combined, and 23 more if the Communist left is included in the reckoning. At the same time, the party had had to broaden its appeal beyond its traditional worker base:

a tension was inescapable, in Sweden as elsewhere, between its own involvement in pluralist competition and the class-oriented perspective of the union part of the labour movement. As Korpi, writing in 1977, put it,

> The Social Democratic Party is now at a crossroads. It can attempt to win back government power with a programme of welfare policies based on compromises with capital . . . The other alternative is to adhere to its distinctiveness . . . This latter alternative would imply that the party accepts the challenge of economic democracy.[20]

The enlistment of white-collar support for the worker funds campaign – restyled in consequence the campaign for 'wage-earner funds' – involved the formation of a common front for a socialist objective. Korpi concluded:

> The Swedish experience attests to the crucial role of organization among the wage-earners in changing the power structure of society . . . Where the competition among the wage-earners ceases, the foundation of capitalism has eroded.[21]

The funds issue certainly polarized Swedish political opinion on left–right lines and impassioned the Swedish political debate. Businessmen demonstrated in their thousands in the streets of Stockholm; trade unionists counter-demonstrated. Some distinguished Social Democrats distanced themselves from the party in their opposition to the scheme.[22] Yet Sifo (Swedish) public opinion polls in June and August 1982 showed that the funds question only ranked eighth out of ten priority issues in the consciousness of voters in the run-up period to the September general election. Unemployment came top, with youth unemployment then running at about 6 per cent, a figure which by Swedish standards was considered shockingly high. Another prominent question in the campaign was that of the maintenance of welfare provision in the face of economic adversity. The Social Democrats made four specific pledges on this front to ensure its salience, notably a promise not to cut the first three days of sickness benefit as the non-socialist parties if returned to power were threatening to do as an economy measure. Behind these later issues was the wider background question of whether the Social Democrats or their 'bourgeois' opponents were the better qualified to manage the economy. A SIFO poll in the spring of 1982 showed 37 per cent favouring the Social Democrats on this point, 27 per cent the Conservatives and 2 per cent the Centre Party and the Liberals respectively; 17 per cent didn't know, and 15 per cent didn't think it mattered who was in. The government at that time was a Centre–Liberal coalition.

The ideological threat to corporatist concertation in Sweden has dwindled steadily since the early days of the worker funds controversy. The arrival of economic hard times in the 1970s was accompanied by a change in emphasis. The funds were increasingly promoted as a means of encouraging wage restraint at a time when Swedish exports were facing tougher competition in world markets. They were also urged as a way to maximise the resources available for capital investment. In the final stages of the controversy a new thread appeared in the argument. In 1982 an inquiry set up by the Ministry of Economic Affairs reported that supplementary pensions contributions would need to rise from their current level of 7 per cent of pay to 17 per cent by the year 2000 if pensions were to maintain their value. Out-payments from the large supplementary pensions funds were beginning to exceed receipts. A linkage was thus established between the funds issue and the level of welfare provision. The funds – now increasingly restyled 'security funds' (*trygghetsfonder*) by the Social Democrats – were plugged into the pensions fund system in the final draft, which became law in December 1983. A one-off dividend tax of 20 per cent was put through by the party on its return to power to strengthen pensions funding, and the element of compulsory profit-sharing was much reduced in comparison with the original Meidner scheme. Finally, the percentage of shares that could be brought by fund administrators – union officials and public servants sympathetic to the Social Democratic cause since industrialists and the non-socialist parties boycotted the scheme – was restricted to 8 per cent in any one company for any one fund.

Summing up thus far, it may be said that the Social Democratic Party leadership under Olof Palme was content to legislate for increased instalments of 'industrial democracy' while leaving the Swedish economy's structures substantially unchanged. Palme's personal political style reflected his sensitivity to the radical currents that were running within the labour movement. However, the fact that the key position of Finance Minister was held throughout the later vicissitudes of the funds question by Kjell-Olof Feldt, a decidedly undoctrinaire figure, symbolised the party's continuing desire to do business with business. Here there is a parallel with the lengthy earlier incumbency of Gunnar Sträng in the same office, for he was also a man with whom business pre-eminently felt that business could be done. Legislation was needed by the party in office to achieve for the union movement what could not be obtained through the processes of collective bargaining, and this marked a break with the 1938 Saltsjöbaden Agreement. But the 'historical compromise' has, in effect, been recast at a new equilibrium point between capital and labour within the pluralist democratic framework.

The evidence suggests strongly that the Social Democrats regained power, in 1982, largely on the strength of their welfare commitment while, at the same time, distancing themselves from capital, and mobilising their more radical supporters, by means of the funds question; SIFO polls taken at intervals before the general election of that year showed between a third and a half of all respondents returning 'Don't know' answers when asked for their opinion of the funds scheme. The highest figure for Social Democratic voters in favour was 56 per cent; more often, less than half of them expressed support. Not surprisingly, a large majority of those 'bourgeois' party supporters with an opinion on the matter opposed the funds. In short, the funds issue was borne along in the large groundswell of support for the Social Democrats on the staple questions of Swedish politics. The general election of 1985 again centred on the staple questions – welfare and, in this instance, tax policies. The Liberals, under their charismatic new leader, Bengt Westerberg, prospered at the polls after a fierce attack upon the funds as a creeping threat to the market economy. But the Social Democrats emerged with qualified public approval for their conduct of affairs in office: a majority for the parties of the left over the 'bourgeois' parties, though no longer for the Social Democrats alone. The assassination of Olof Palme in February 1986 was followed by a renewed emphasis on continuity and conciliation: Ingvar Carlsson, the Deputy Premier, succeeded unopposed to the leadership and continued Kjell-Olof Feldt in office at the Finance Ministry, subsequently designating him as the new Deputy Premier.

The state is a leading partner in corporatist arrangements on what might be called the classical (Schmitter) view of corporatism. Plainly the fact that the Social Democrats have, to a degree unique among parties in western advanced industrial societies, become almost identified with the power of the state since their arrival in office in 1932 – their only significant spell in opposition being from 1976 to 1982 – has been of major significance for the evolution of corporatism in Sweden. At first, it allowed the emergence of a strong private system of government on the labour market. Later it opened up the possibility of systematic change in response to the resurfacing of socialist ideology. The modest scope of the change that has actually taken place recalls the trenchant conclusion of Przeworski's panoramic survey of social democracy: that the *capacity* of Social Democrats to regulate the economy depends upon the profits of capital, and that the basic compromise between social democracy and private capital is an expression of the structure of capitalist society.[23] On this analysis, an ideological threat to Swedish corporatism will always be an appearance rather than a reality. But it is also the case that Social Democratic policy is ambivalent, in Sweden as elsewhere, in reflection of the inner contradictions within the wider labour movement. Thus, on the one hand, business has been resumed with business by the Social Democrats since their return in 1982. Industrialists grumble freely about, for example, the new inflexibilities in the labour market resulting from the 1974 (Åman) laws on the security of employment; about the adverse effect of co-determination legislation on innovation;[24] and about amateurish investment decisions by the managers of the new funds. At the same time, the main economic indicators have improved markedly since 1982. On the other hand, for example, funds administrations were set up on a regional basis – to counter the charge of over-centralisation of power – in the statute of 1983; and in 1985 three of them pooled resources to buy 18 per cent of the shares in a single firm (any one fund, it will be recalled, has a limit of 8 per cent). It is this kind of operation that forms the background to the fears expressed by the opposition parties about the introduction of socialism by slow and stealthy steps. Nevertheless, the overall conclusion must remain, on present evidence, that the historical compromise, although re-jigged, survives in Sweden intact in essence.

The relatively brief tenure of office by the non-socialist parties (1976–82) raises the question of whether only the Social Democrats can manage corporatist concertation in Sweden. Elvander, writing in 1978, thought so, on the grounds that they alone, in his opinion, could command the necessary wage restraint from the union movement.[25] Several points may be briefly made in this connection. First, economic wealth generation has been aptly described as 'the silent third partner' in the bilateral agreement reached at Saltsjöbaden.[26] Steady and sustained economic growth had been a feature of the Swedish scene for over three decades before the arrival of hard times in the 1970.[27] Corporatist concertation had been a contributory factor as well as a beneficiary. Structural decline in the economy and the impact of high energy costs, in Sweden as elsewhere, brought recession in their wake in the 1970s. This, in turn, inevitably drew the state into what was in effect incomes policy formation, characteristically by manipulating tax policy, employers' contributions, etc. as part of an economic package in advance of collective bargaining rounds with the aim of securing wage restraint. So one might say that the state – whichever party was in power – increasingly emerged as the third partner in the process of concertation. If this brought Swedish arrangements into somewhat closer corresponence with the classical (Schmitter) model of corporatism, it also was an index of the greater difficulty of managing the system.

Secondly, it is true that the non-socialist parties fell from office four years after Elvander's prediction and that their fall was preceded by the worst outbreak of trouble on the Sweden labour market since the Second World War. The lockout and general strike which followed the breakdown of wage negotiations in May 1980 caused a severe ten-day social dislocation and a knock-on disruption to the country's economy. It can hardly be doubted that the non-socialist parties had less to offer than their rivals when it came to competitive bidding for union support: the indexation of tax scales as a hedge against inflation was, for example, unpopular with LO on egalitarian grounds and eventually was rescinded. Nevertheless, the conclusion that the 'bourgeois' parties were foredoomed to failure carries a worrying implication about the substance of Sweden pluralist democracy and does not have to be accepted. The non-socialist parties were unlucky. They inherited a drastic price/wage explosion which sprang ultimately from over-optimism about Sweden's ability to tide over recession, and they fell foul of the second rise in energy prices at the end of the 1970s. Increasingly they were also divided among themselves. Finally, they compounded their own difficulties by large-scale expenditure on industrial 'lame ducks' and by positively encouraging a fast expansion of the already swollen public sector of the economy: this doubled between 1970 and 1983 to account for 67 per cent of GNP, a record for a western advanced industrial society. Of course, it could be argued that the root cause of these later difficuties was an overzealous acceptance of the policies which their predecessors in office had supported.[28] At all events, it would give a misleading picture of Swedish political life to concentrate on the dominance of the Social Democrats in government, while ignoring the fineness of the electoral margin which has usually separated victory from defeat.

Thirdly, the management of corporatist concertation has become harder for all Swedish governments because of the growing scale and political clout of the tertiary sector of the economy, and because of increasing tensions between those who work in the public and in the private sectors. These difficulties have been compounded by economic recession, but they began to show themselves before the recession. For example, no sooner had public servants been given the right to strike than SACO – the peak union organisation for higher professional people – put it into effect, with some success, in 1966, partly in order to try to restore differentials held to have been eroded by LO's solidary wages policy. Another SACO/SR (higher civil servants) strike in 1971 led to the unprecedented use of legislation by the Social Democratic government in order to enforce a settlement, on the ground that vital national services were being endangered. More recently, in 1985–6, was a rash of public sector labour market conflicts in the effort to secure pay adjustments in line with developments in the private sector. Since these entailed strike action at different times by e.g. doctors, dentists and nurses, they caused even the Minister of Labour to comment on declining respect for the collective bargaining system, and many Swedes to wonder about whither their country was heading. An acrimonious attack was made by a leader of the Metalworkers' Union on public sector unions within LO for being 'cuckoos in the nest' – and this during the September 1986 LO Congress. Cooperation between the leaders of blue- and white-collar unions on the matter of wage-earner funds – Lennart Bodström, the leader of TCO, the main white-collar peak organisation, was made Foreign Minister for a time under Palme – did not extend to the processes of collective bargining when times became hard.

The hope expressed by the LO economist Anna Hedborg that the passage of the funds statute would encourage the moderation of wage claims has scarcely been realised in practice. The difficult economic situation encouraged the decentralisation of the collective bargaining round in 1983–4, for example, with the 22 LO unions negotiating separately with 37 SAF counterparts: SAF had pressed for this on the ground of the differential ability of firms to pay. In the event, the metalworkers came out best, which contributed to putting the Social Democratic government's inflation-pegging target into jeopardy. Pressure from white-collar and public sector unions for compensation for the perennial problem of wage-drift in industry has powerfully strengthened the ratchet tendency upwards. The government has countered with the usual anti-inflationary measures of price freezes, tax increases and credit restrictions. These, in turn, have caused fresh outbreaks of white-collar militancy and tensions between unions and government, while industrialists complain that price freezes entail their having to reach collective bargaining agreements without knowing whether they will be able to cover the costs. In short, Social Democratic tenure of office has certainly been latterly no guarantee of peace on the labour market, and government has become a central actor in the search for orderly labour market management. But this is as much as to say that the Swedish system has become less exceptional in character.

The original simplicity of the collective bargaining machinery in Sweden has been overtaken by events in the past two decades. The prototype model involved the hammering out of a centralised framework agreement between LO and SAF. The growth of the white-collar unions led to the appearance of a separate umbrella organisation (PTK) in 1973 to harmonise their negotiations with the private employers in

SAF. The increase in the public sector caused both LO and TCO unions there to group together in wages rounds with a specialised agency (OASEN) representing the employers. One result has been a marked tendency to jockey for position when it comes to the timing of negotiations, and occasionally (as in 1983) the government has requested public sector unions to inaugurate these in reversal of the usual procedure. At times, as in 1977–8 and again in 1985–86, LO and PTK have coordinated their bargaining efforts, but more often than not the problem of differentials has frustrated cooperative endeavours. On the other hand, the coherence of corporatist concertation has never been threatened by rank-and-file revolts within the union movement to the extent that had seemed likely at the time of the major wildcat strike of 1969–70 in the iron-ore mines of Arctic Sweden. A major cause of this strike had been the imposition of harsher working practices by an authoritarian management and the ineffectiveness of the local works councils. This provided another access of strength for the campaign for 'industrial democracy', and the Co-Determination Act of 1976, whatever its practical defects, seems likely to have been a factor in heading off further outbreaks of this type of discontent.

Quite apart from the labour market, Sweden has a long tradition of integrating the major interest organisations into the making and execution of public policy – whatever the government in power. In this respect, the norms of her political culture are consensual and corporatist. Of course, this holds true in some degree of all western advanced industrial societies, but the Swedish case has exceptional features. Representatives of the big interest organisations, for example, serve often on the Commissions of Inquiry which gestate reforms: 200 of these Commissions of Inquiry were operating in January 1984. Commission reports and draft Bills go to relevant organisations for comments which are then summarised in the final versions. Since the mid-1960s interest groups have been increasingly represented by 'lay members' on the administrative boards of the decentralised administrative system. A particularly significant example is that of the Labour Market Board (Arbetsmarknadsstyrelsen) with a majority of union/employer representatives and the disposal, within guidelines, of very large sums of money for unemployment relief, etc., but numerous other examples could be given. Forums for participation have been multiplying in the past two decades,[29] and this has caused a new anxiety to arise in connection with the public sector – in addition to the older and more familiar anxieties about responsibility and representativeness under this mode of government. The new worry is about possible conflicts between political democracy and workplace democracy as a result of direct union influence on public sector (including local government) management under the terms of the co-determination reform.[30]

The rapid growth in the public sector, powerfully stimulated, as mentioned earlier, by the non-socialist parties during their period of power links with the increase in white-collar militancy to compound the difficulties of corporatist concertation in Sweden. The 1980 general strike orginated in the public sector, and the question of what to do about the public sector has much exercised the Social Democratic Party.[31] It seems clear that those within the party who prioritise export effectiveness have had the edge since the party's return to power over those who are pessimistic about export-led growth and who consequently regard public sector expansion with equanimity.[32] Austerity policies have been continued, a matter of some friction between the government and LO, and the budgetary deficit has been reduced from 6 per cent of GNP in 1982 to 1 per cent early in 1986. At the same time, R and D expenditure has been high, and the Social Democrats have been at pains to represent themselves as cutting expenditure in a less socially divisive way than their 'bourgeois' opponents. A one-off tax on the assets of insurance companies, however, did not appear at all consensual to those opponents, even though the proceeds were earmarked as an additional resource for the pension funds. Despite this, or rather alongside, it, the Social Democrats have stayed in line with the long-standing tradition of concertation in the Swedish political culture.[33] Just as from 1949 to 1955 there were Thursday Club meetings between the government and representatives of the major interest organisations to discuss economic growth and the stimulation of exports, from 1959 to 1964 similar meetings at Harpsund, the Swedish Chequers – and from 1973 to 1975 more round-table discussions at Haga Castle, outside Stockholm, this time with the participation also of the Liberal and Centre parties – so now the government has promised consultations in connection with a proposed major overhaul of the country's tax system. The mushrooming of the public sector has had quite a lot to do with Sweden's uniquely high tax burden. However, tax questions have long been a political 'hot potato' – the Conservatives (or Moderates, as they call themselves in Sweden) left the tripartite non-socialist coalition in May 1981 on this issue – so political calculation no doubt enters into this scenario.

Swedish industry has extensive foreign operations in relation to the size of the country's economy.[34] A quarter of the GNP (a half of industrial production) is exported, and Swedish subsidiaries abroad account for some 40 per cent of total exports.[35] Against this background there is a premium on corporatist power-sharing mechanisms which tend to lower the level of distributive conflict. So *in this sense* to talk of a 'partnership' between capital and labour in Sweden is not political naïvety, nor on present evidence does the partnership appear to be dissolving.[36] What Finance Minister Feldt has called 'the third way' – in effect, the historical compromise recast – has, on the contrary, plenty going for it. A Eureka poll of leading Swedish industrialists taken in February 1986 showed 81 per cent having trust in Carlsson, the Prime Minister, and 93 per cent in Feldt. The main thrust of Social Democratic policy continues to be directed towards no conspicuous private affluence and no public squalor – modified Galbraith rather than Adler-Karlsson. So maybe Przeworski has the best of the argument after all?

Notes

1. G. Ionescu, *Centripetal Politics* (London, Hart-Davis, MacGibbon, London, 1975), p. 21.
2. N. Elvander, 'Organisationerna och staten på arbetsmarknaden i Sverige', *Tidskrift utgiven av Juridiska Föreningen i Finland* (Helsinki), 5 (1978), 447–7.
3. R. Huntford, *The New Totalitarians* (London, Allen Lane/The Penguin Press, 1971), p. 86.
4. *Ibid.*, p. 116.
5. W. Korpi, 'The historical compromise and its dissolution' in B. Rydén and V. Bergström, *Sweden: Choices for Economic and Social Policy in the 1980s* (London, Allen and Unwin, 1982), table 9.1, p. 134.
6. D. Anckar and V. Helander, 'Corporatism and representative government in the nordic countries' in R. Alapuro *et al.* (eds), *Small States in Comparative Perspective* (Norwegian Universities Press, 1985), table 1, p. 128.
7. Elvander records that in 1967 over 90 per cent of public sector employees and 70 per cent of private sector belonged to TCO-affiliated unions: *Intresseorganisationerna i dagens Sverige (Lund, Gleerup, 2nd rev. edn, 1969), p. 48.*
8. *Ibid.*, p. 45.
9. Ionescu, *op. cit.*, p. 21.
10. See e.g. A. Martin's survey of Sweden in P. Gourevitch *et. al.*, *Unions and Economic Crisis: Britain, West Germany and Sweden* (London, Allen and Unwin, 1984), pp. 197–9.
11. W. Korpi, *The Working Class in Welfare Capitalism* (London, Routledge and Kegan Paul, 1978), pp. 80–6.
12. Korpi, *op. cit.* pp. 319–321.
13. N. Elder, *Bipolarity or Indeterminancy in a Multi-Party System?*, Hull Papers in Politics No. 14, Department of Politics, University of Hull, October 1979, pp. 15–16.
14. G. Adler-Karlsson, *Functional Socialism* (Stockholm, Bokförlaget Prisma, 1967), pp. 101–2. The quotation is a little dated: the 1975 Constitution reduced the monarchy to symbolic importance only. A fuller version is given in R. Scase, *Social Democracy in Capitalist Society* (London, Croom Helm, 1977), p. 80.
15. Korpi, 'The historical compromise and its dissolution', *op. cit.*, p. 137.
16. O. Petersson, *Valundersökningar, Rapport 2: Väljarna och valet 1976* (Stockholm, Statistiska centralbyrån, 1977), section 5.
17. Statens Offentliga Utredningar (SOU), Ägande och inflytande i det privata narings-livet, Finansdepartementet, Stockholm, 1968.
18. P. Schmitter, 'Still the century of corporatism?' in F. Pike and T. Strich (eds), *The*

New Corporatism (Notre Dame, Ind., University of Notre Dame Press, 1974), pp. 85–131.

19. Elvander, Organisationerna och staten på arbetsmarknaden i Sverige', *op. cit.*, p. 447.
20. Korpi, *The Working Class in Welfare Capitalism*, *op. cit.*, pp. 334–5.
21. *Ibid.*, p. 335.
22. Notably in Elvander *et al.*, *Sju socialdemokrater om löntagarfonderna* (Stockholm, Tidens förlag, 1979).
23. A Przeworski, 'Social democracy as a historical phenomenon', *New Left Review*, 122 (July–August 1980), pp. 27–58.
24. For example, L. Nabseth and J. Wallander, 'Can Sweden remain a leading industrial nation?' in Rydén and Bergström, *op. cit.*, pp. 72–92.
25. Elvander, 'Organisationerna och staten på arbetsmarknaden i Sverige', *op. cit.*, p. 449.
26. P. Benetazzo, in *Christian Science Monitor*, 11 October 1982.
27. The causes are analysed in A. Lindbeck, *Swedish Economic Policy* (London, Macmillan, 1975), chapter 1.
28. For a more extended analysis of some of these points, see N. Elder, 'Continuity and innovation in Sweden in the 1970s' in A. Cox (ed.), *Politics, Policy and the European Recession* (London, Macmillan, 1982), pp. 65–86.
29. O. Ruin, 'Towards a corporate society? Participatory democracy and corporativism: the case of Sweden', *Scandinavian Political Studies*, 9 (1974), 171–84.
30. For example, J. Westerståhl, 'What will happen to democracy in the 1980s?' in Rydén and Bergström, *op. cit.*, pp. 51–63.
31. P. Walters, 'Sweden's public sector crisis, before and after the 1982 elections', *Government and Opposition*, 18 (1) (Winter 1983), 23–39.
32. Cf. P. Walters, 'The legacy of Olof Palme', *Government and Opposition*, 22 (1) (Winter 1987), 64–77.
33. Some reflections on this will be found in N. Elder, A. H. Thomas and D. Arter, *The Consensual Democracies? The Government and Politics of the Scandinavian States* (Oxford, Basil Blackwell, 2nd rev. edn, 1988).
34. J.-E. Vahlne, *International Enterprise in Swedish Industry*, Current Sweden No. 343, Swedish Institute, Stockholm, December 1985.
35. G. Borg and B.-A. Vedin, 'Knowledge – the basis for industrial success' in Rydén and Bergström, *op. cit.*, pp. 93–107.
36. M. W. Childs, *Sweden: The Middle Way on Trial* (New Haven, Conn. and London, Yale University Press, 1980).

8 Some historical problems of corporatist development in the Netherlands

M. L. Smith

Describing the accommodation of interests between élites which he believed to characterise the politics of the Netherlands up to the late 1960s, Arend Lijphart claimed that 'the crown on this intricate system is the Social and Economic Council' (SER), the tripartite board established by the Industrial Organisation Act 1950. This council, embodying permanent formal collaboration between business, labour and experts, and with its wide constituted powers, Lijphart viewed as the pinnacle of an institutionalised practice of consensual politics. As such it stood as 'the end product of a slow incremental process starting shortly after 1917'.[1] In both its form and its continuity, the SER provided the key to understanding the apparent paradox of the lengthy survival of stable democracy in a nation whose degree of social and religious cleavage would lead the social scientist otherwise to predict dissension, ideological tension and 'governmental immobilism alternating with revolutionary upsets rather than evolutionary change'.[2] Instead the will to have created and carried through such 'summit organisations', of which the SER was the jewel, enabled the potentially isolated and mutually antagonistic *zuilen* (pillars') that formed Dutch society to resolve the danger of disputes between them. The SER typified the arrangement whereby the élites in the Netherlands had over half a century collaborated together in the depoliticising of potentially damaging major issues and, as a consequence, sustained harmony and validated their own power.

Whatever the merits of general extrapolation to other societies from this 'consociational democracy' model, its focus on the particular institution of the confederal or overarching summit organisation as most represented by a body such as the SER, rests on the uncontentious observation that this type of public body has been found in the Netherlands to a greater degree – and certainly over a longer period of time – than almost anywhere else in Europe. In the five years after the end of the Second World War alone, the Netherlands produced a virtual explosion of corporatist legislation: it was in these years that there appeared the SER itself, the Raad van Vakcentrales (Central Union Council), and immediately after the end of the war, the Stichting van Arbeid (Foundation of Labour), the consultative body composed of employers and employees and responsible for wage conciliation. The whole structure of the councils was held together within the framework of the PBO (Industrial Organisation under Public Law) by means of which binding decisions on socio-economic matters would be made for all who worked within a certain sector or group of enterprises ranging from heavy industry to agriculture. While this general legal framework was a specific creation of these years, it should not be thought that the public bodies which acted within it were a phenomenon purely of the postwar period. On the contrary, it appeared self-consciously to complete a network of legislation enacted in the interwar years. All parties to the legislation made in the 1940s looked back to the practices of the interwar period and even earlier: to the Kamers van Arbeid (Chambers of Labour), proposed as far back as 1897, and in which representatives of each side of a business concern could enforce social legislation to the *collectieve arbeidsovereenkomst* (collective work agreements) of 1907; or to the tripartite bodies of which the Hoge Raad van Arbeid (Supreme Labour Council) of 1919, those created by the *Arbeidsgeschillenwet* (Labour Dispute Act) of 1923, the Economische Raad (Economic Council) of 1932 and the Bedrijfsraden (Industrial Councils) of 1933 were the most noteworthy.

The Netherlands, then, has provided an extended case study of the willingness of organised interests to cooperate with the public power in the creation of corporatist intermediary structures. Moreover, the long development represented by the formation of the institutions listed above is argued as evidence of the predisposition of the élites in Dutch society to confer not only with government but, more crucially, among themselves in pursuit of conflict management. At the heart of the consociational analysis lies the argument that the summit organisations have been the form in which the élites have chosen to express their collaboration in the potentially divisive areas of the economic and social sphere; élite accommodation has therefore been the mainspring driving the formation of confederal bodies. So, too, it is these bodies with their heterogeneous class composition that have provided the necessary evidence to support the cognate theory of 'liberal corporatism' advanced by Lehmbruch and which similarly sees the process of bargaining between élites as having been channelled through and within the confederal institutions.[3]

What is clear is that these explanations of the corporatist forms that are seen as having dominated the Dutch experience are thoroughly historicist. This is so at two levels. First they operate at the level of looking back to a relatively recent but, essentially, completed and determining period of history. Thus they regard the bringing into being of the formal structure of bargaining and agreement as having come to fruition within a chronologically discrete 'golden age' whose most intense moment was from 1945 to 1950 but which continued either until the end of the 1950s, when the political coalition of the postwar period disintegrated, or as late as the end of the 1960s, when parties with new bases began to challenge on the political scene. The second edition of Lijphart's study devoted a new section to an analysis of the processes that were undermining accommodation; their triumph was underlined later by the rewriting of the last (1979) Dutch edition entirely in the past tense.[4] Lehmbruch also has tended to withdraw the Netherlands from still being considered as an active exemplar of liberal corporatism by recognising that those forces that once made the concept operational have largely ceased to apply.[5]

Secondly, and most crucially, the analysis of corporatist structures is historical, in that it depends on the view that Dutch politics progressed for almost exactly half a century along the lines determined by an arrangement made towards the end of the First World War. Briefly, the founding premiss is that there occurred around 1917 a 'big bang' (the 'Great Pacification') in Dutch political society – a compromise whereby the élites of the Confessional and secular blocs agreed to settle the three potentially destructive issues of the state funding of religious education, suffrage extension and the social and trade union questions. The Great Pacification is placed as a historical crux, in that it was this compromise that provided the first example of overarching cooperation and self-denial of purely segmental interests as well as being the starting-point for such agreements between the blocs to be continued in future. It was this package of agreements that produced the recognised pattern of the institutionalisation of negotiations over economic and social matters in the future. The Great Pacification therefore created, as much as it reflected, a particular pattern of prudent élite behaviour which was to guide the Netherlands safely through the difficult years of the coming century.[6] And even if the qualification is accepted that the Dutch élites had been master practitioners of negotiation among themselves for many years prior to 1917,[7] the case is still made that the three great issues that surfaced in the early twentieth century presented a special threat to stability and, as a consequence, called up the distinct and far-reaching solution of the development of formal confederal arrangements.

The importance of recognising these two historicist underpinnings is that they push to centre-stage the means by which the élites are said to have managed the depoliticisation of contentious issues. The idea that a 'golden age' of stability was dependent on the formal institutional development of cross-pillar and publicly sanctioned bodies has itself depended on the teleological perspective that such bodies have represented the long-drawn-out, but always conscious and purposeful, perfection of a will towards accommodation. It follows that the structure of Dutch politics has been largely understood as the gradual unwinding of a trail that was, in essence, conceived in 1917. This is a teleology that unites many of the analyses of politics in the Netherlands. Lijphart himself, as already noted, has from the start argued that the tripartite councils have been the typical devices of consociationalism as it has been practised.[8] And it has become commonplace to ascribe the success of the Dutch in carrying out reconstruction after the Second World War to the creation of the network of confederal bodies, which themselves grew from the 'precursors' of the interwar period. Gerard Scholten's study of the operation of the SER through the 1950s takes care to identify the experience of formal and frequent contact between worker representatives, employers and experts in the Supreme Labour Council of the 1920s as having provided the necessary preconditions for the transition to accept the wider powers of the later body.[9] Others, such as P. W. Klein or Roel Fernhout, have also stressed that the development of the regulatory bodies found in the Netherlands in the 1920s and 1930s directly heralded – and directly provided – the institutional form for conflict resolution that emerged so successfully after the Second World War.[10]

In short there has, in the area of corporatism, been a considerable propensity to read backwards in Dutch history the better to derive lessons for the present. This desire to intrude a teleology has created a particular picture of Dutch political behaviour. In the first place, the proposition that the events of 1917 demonstrated a conscious change of direction and practice in the relation between the élites has provided a pedigree to the actors who are taken to be at the heart of the *modus operandi* of accommodation: the *zuilen*, or 'pillars'. By making the Great Pacification bear such determining and far-reaching consequences consociationalism has had to assert the prior existence of four individual blocs – Catholics, Calvinists, Liberals and Socialists – each of which was already sufficiently extensive in its socio-economic structures to be accepted as an equal or, at any rate, to have an equal claim to a role in the accommodation play that was being initiated. In short, the question of proportionality – the willingness of each of the bloc élites to legitimise the claims the others – on which the institutional direction of the next 50 years was to depend, is taken to have been agreed in the process of the 1917 settlement.

It follows that the explanation of the development of consociationalism has rested on the claim that it was a necessary response to the extent of *verzuiling* ('pillarisation') – i.e. the crystallisation of parallel socio-economic structures charged with similar functions within each of the blocs. As Ilja Scholten has pointed out, the theory supposes that the entrenchment of the pillars at once indicated the degree of cleavage that there was in Dutch society and, by fostering a cross-cutting tension between religious and class loyalty, threatened to spill over into the arena of political values. The origins of the self-denying agreement of 1917 as well as its subsequent extensions are seen, then, as the method by which the élites sought to diminish the consequences of this entrenchment. In sum, it was the centrifugality of relations within the pillars following the growth of *verzuiling* that pushed the élites first to pursue formal accommodation. The settlement, at one stroke, of all the really dangerous issues left the way open for the blocs to respect each other's integrity, to encourage party development linked to the pillars and, on these bases, at one and the same time to extend the power of the separate blocs and to resolve conflicts between them in the agreed neutral bodies on which the whole was sustained.[11]

Lastly, the idea that the institutional form in which relations between the pillars were regulated exhibited an untroubled evolutionary path has played down the significance of economic conjuncture and its effect on class relations. By taking 1917 not just as a starting-point, but more as a determinant event, it is proposed that over a period which spanned, *inter alia*, the impact of two world wars, an economic depression of hitherto unimagined severity and the devastation of the country by a ruthless foreign occupier, the form of élite cooperation that had been arrived at to settle the major remaining problems of the nineteenth century, proved sufficient at each of these given moments and, equally, provided the model for the further adaptations that culminated in the SER. Specifically, if the confederal organisations were important precisely because they had the job of counteracting (and intentionally so) the centrifugal dangers of *verzuiling*, and that centrifugality was itself the result of the tension between class and pillar affiliation, the inevitable suggestion behind the theory is that the bases of class conflict diminished – or were successfully diverted – over the whole period notwithstanding changes in external economic factors.[12]

Before proposing a different approach to the history and function of the development of corporatist forms in the Netherlands, it is necessary to summarise some basic objections that can be made to the consociational case in the area that makes up its core: the supposed agreement between the pillars on which the creation of intermediary bodies depended. Central to the accommodation argument is its assertion of the proportionality that followed the mutual acceptance of each pillar's right to participate fully in policy formation. Yet this edifice meets the immediate objection that during all but a few months of the interwar period one of the pillars – the Socialist both in the form of the SDAP (Sociaal Democratische Arbeiders Partij) and of its trade union, the NVV (Nederlands Verbond van Vakvereningen) – was in fact excluded from the process, and this despite being the second largest party in the Lower Chamber. Not until 10 August 1939, when Europe had already entered the crisis of the Second World War, were Socialists invited for the first time to participate in government. Nor was the absence of Socialist representatives in the Cabinet up to this point anything, as will be shown below, but the consequence of an intention by the Confessional pillars that they should be excluded.

Such a twenty-year hiatus before the practice of élite accommodation came on-stream truncates the teleology by which the interwar years are interpreted as the necessary long maturation for the new world of 1945. It raises at least a suspicion that the theory may be near to stating only the tautology that corporatist structures operated successfully when (as between 1945 and 1952) there was cooperation between the Confessionals and the Socialists together with their associated trade unions. In any case, so far from 1917 marking the date at which the élites had settled the major divisive issues, it would be more accurate to see it as having ushered in a period of overt conflict between, in particular, two of the pillars (with Catholics taking the initiative among the Confessionals) expressed in a determination to keep the Socialists out of the system. In this context, it is revealing that towards the end of each period in question there occurred an issue ready-made for the Confessionals to hang the doubt that Socialists could ever be trusted to conform to the rules of the political game. First, in November 1918, in the aftermath of the Russian revolutions and the fall of the Prussian Reich, both of which events had inevitably found sympathetic echoes in the Netherlands, the Socialist leader Troelstra had appeared to advocate the revolutionary overthrow of the bourgeoisie and the creation of a socialist republic. Secondly, in 1933 a mutiny broke out in the warship, *De Zeven Provinciën*, sailing off the East Indies. The subsequent inquiry (somewhat reminiscent in the level of public partisanship it aroused of a Dutch Dreyfus Affair) failed to draw a condemnation of the mutineers from the Socialist Party. Each of these events provided the occasion to equate socialism with the undermining of national solidarity and consensus. They provided the bass line, as it were, to a melody consistently orchestrated in the interwar period to the effect that the Socialists should not be considered fit to be part of a natural government coalition.

For the Catholic pillar, above all, the events of 1918 and 1933 justified and maintained in being the commitment to avoid cooperation with the Socialists. This in fact received its formal expression in the principle, articulated first in 1922 by the leader of the RKSP (Roomsch-Katholieke Staatspartij), Nolens, that a coalition exclusively with the SDAP was to be entertained only *in extremis* – the principle of *uiterste noodzaak* ('grave necessity'). The shift of this formula to extend to any cooperation at governmental level – a position clearly enunciated by Nolens in 1925 and again by his successor, Aalberse, in 1933 and 1935 – is solid evidence of the true disposition of Catholic circles against any such notion as that the system would best function by an agreement to disagree. On the contrary, the refrain of needing to push the Socialists away from the possibility of influencing policy indicated that for the Catholic élite the gulf in values was considered to be too dangerous.[13] How strong this protective feeling in the Catholic pillar was during the interwar period is suggested in the fact that the principle of 'grave necessity' was abandoned only when the RKSP changed to the more broadly based KVP (Katholieke Volkspartij), thereby meeting half-way the similarly extended PvDA (Partij van de Arbeid) in the 'Roman-Red' coalition after 1945 – a coalition which itself equally suggests a considerable discontinuity in politics between the two periods.

From what has been indicated, it is hard to argue otherwise than that the direction of Dutch politics between the wars conform in few, if any, respects to the 'rules' of accommodation that 1917 is supposed to have set up.[14] Part of the explanation is that the universal suffrage that the Great Pacification introduced made the SDAP a substantial party in parliamentary terms, thereby creating a new and differently expressed cleavage between it and the non-socialist pillars. The elections of 1918, by giving the SDAP nearly a quarter of the available seats largely at the expense of the Liberals, brought into being a strongly divided Chamber in which policy agreement because of the presence of a class-based party was bound to be more problematic than it had been before the war. The emergence of the SDAP, however its adversaries might have tried to undermine its claims, put them on the spot. For the pacification of this newly arrived pretender by the hallowed device of admitting it to the coalition-forming process held the real danger to the Confessionals of diminishing the differences between the two groups and, in this way, setting up further inroads into their electoral support. Worse, the growth of support for the Socialists could only come from the Confessionals' working-class constituency. Faced with this danger, the Confessional élites chose to pursue the control over their members' allegiance not, as the accommodation case asserts by fudging or hiding substantive disagreements with the Socialist pillar, but on the contrary by acting publicly as if these were an insuperable danger.

Perhaps the clearest proof that such was the strategy is furnished by the reaction of the Confessional élites to the real threat brought about by the world depression. Unemployment and the government's evident inability, not to say unwillingness, to tackle its effects produced not just the rise of a Nazi-imitating, anti-system party (the Nationaal Socialistische Beweging – NSB), but a more general alienation from the stagnation of the pillarised parliamentary arrangements. Were the principles of accommodation to have operated at this time of acute division, the Netherlands ought to have seen a move either to an all-party Cabinet or, as elsewhere in Europe, a Popular Front in which a truce operated with the aim of solving, or at least mitigating, the crisis that was threatening the parliamentary system itself.

In sum, once it is accepted that the reality of relations between the pillars in the interwar period was, in large part, a coalition that sought to *prevent* the achievement of legitimacy by the Socialist pillar, then it is difficult to sustain the concept of self-denying élite behaviour as the key to understanding developments at the economic and social level. The consociational argument relies on the belief that accommodation was the device by which élites maintained political stability *in spite of* the spread of *verzuiling*.It would, as has been recently argued by I. Scholten, seem more appropriate to take the contrary as the case. *Verzuiling* so far from representing a difficulty to be overcome (that is the potential source of instability in itself), was encouraged and created by the need to keep the Socialists from sharing power.[15] Furthermore, the apartheid of a one-dimensional (in the sense of one class) Socialist pillar was necessary to preserve the essentially very different structures of the Confessionals, since it helped make unattractive a drift away of working-class members. This drift the élites tried to prevent not simply by reiterating the godless separateness of the Socialists (a warning backed up, in the case of the Catholics, by *ex cathedra* prohibitions), or by weakening the potential effectiveness of the Socialist unions by encouraging and subsidising Confessional competitors, but above all by vigorously pursuing *verzuiling*. For only the extension of *verzuiling* could provide the space in which the ruling coalition could protect its most fundamental interests.

What is taken as prudent accommodation is better seen as the recognition that the greatest threat to the traditional pillar élites would come from acknowledging that class conflict was a valid basis for constructing intermediary bodies in economic and social life. Agreement on this point sustained both the scepticism as to the role of unions in the liberal pillar and the development of ideologically quite distinct ones on the Confessional side. Moreover, it led in practice to the rigid separation between these latter and their Socialist counterpart. At no time during the period after the First World War were the Catholic and Protestant unions permitted to consider making federal arrangements with the Socialist NVV. *Verzuiling* was thoroughly enforced and provided the cover for keeping the working class divided.[16]

From the broad objections sketched above, it would seem that consociational theory's attempt to press a simple continuous link between the creation of corporatist forms in the Netherlands and the practice of élite accommodation is, at best, flawed. Nevertheless, if the development of summit organisations which characterised the interwar period was not linked (and perhaps even the contrary) to a commitment to proportionality among the élites, we are still faced with the problem of accounting for the phenomenon. For it is the clear case that the arguments and plans for managing economic and social change during this period *were* couched predominantly in corporatist terms, that is, the recognition of the right of all important interest groups in Dutch society to be represented in institutions of state specifically constituted for that purpose. What is more, this was so across the political and ideological spectrum. As J. van Doorn has expressed it describing the overwhelming vogue for corporatist solutions that characterised the long crisis of the late 1920s and 1930s in the Netherlands, 'Social-Democrats, Christian Socialists, Calvinists, Catholics, progressive Liberals and, it should be remembered, Fascists united without difficulty, despite their deep ideological differences, in a conviction that the period of unbridled individualism and capitalism was over and that values such as community, solidarity and social responsibility would determine the future'.[17] And even if we attribute much of this willingness to talk the language of corporatism to the fashion for a 'third way' between unrestrained free market capitalism and Soviet-style collectivism which reached its height in the 1930s its prevalence, long pedigree and, above all, institutional realisation in the Netherlands requires analysis in terms of the particular impetus of the proposals advanced over the whole period.

How, then, are the origins of corporatist proposals in the interwar period to be interpreted? It must be admitted that the case for accommodation marked by a steady evolution is attractive, in that the foundation of the most characteristic edifice of corporatism in the shape of tripartite boards on which sat representatives of employers, labour and Crown-appointed experts was erected in two complementary phrases of legislation a decade apart. The first phase, between 1918 and 1920, dealt with the regulation of social policy and centred on the creation of the Supreme Labour Council. The second, from 1931 to 1933, tackled advice to the government on economic policy through the institution of the Economic Council and the regulation of production through specific Industrial Boards. So, too, in all these structures the principle of proportionality was practised in so far as representation was by *zuil* affiliation.

Before looking more critically at this evolution, two observations need to be made. First, that the two periods of legislative activity coincided with Catholic-led Cabinets, namely the first and third administrations of Ruijs de Beerenbrouck. It should also be noted that, if as Schöffer has argued, the interwar period was the 'period of the Confessionals'[18] this is especially true as a description of the Catholic domination of the Confessional alliance. The Catholic Party not only participated in every Cabinet (bar the short-lived last Colijn administration just before the Second World War) between 1918 and 1939, also to it fell, in general, the key portfolios of economic and social affairs – the exceptions being de Geer's first Cabinet of 1926–9; two months in 1934 under Colijn; and two-and-a half weeks in 1939 also under Colijn's premiership. Secondly, it was specifically from these Cabinet posts that the proposals for corporatist institutions originated. Moreover, the drive to create corporatist structures coincided with, and was the outcome of, a reorganisation and redefinition of the portfolios for the purpose. This process is clearly on view when de Beerenbrouck's first Cabinet of September 1918 established the quite new portfolio of Minister of Labour whose first occupant, P. J. M. Aalberse, then carried through the legislation for the Supreme Labour Council (1919) of which he himself was the first chairman. So also, subsequently, in the third de Beerenbrouck Cabinet of 1929 to 1933 it was after redefining the post of Labour Affairs to the new, enlarged, Economic Affairs (a change effected symbolically on 1 May 1932) that the minister, T. J. Verschuur, set in motion the law for an Economic Council followed a year later by that on Industrial Boards.

It would seem plain that the creation of what was, in effect, a new ministry to promote each of the two major pieces of corporatist legislation in the interwar years, together with the highly concentrated timespan in which the new institutions were put on the statute-book, represented a Catholic initiative made under some pressure. The problem is to determine of what this consisted. Because the obvious answer that the legislation and the particular form of its expression was the conciliatory response to a threatening economic conjuncture does not easily survive the fact that the two periods were as dissimilar as they could be. The year 1919 stood in the middle of an intense, if short-lived, boom caused by the release of demand pent up by the effects of the First World War; 1932 was firmly in the middle of the depression which had already forced the de Beerenbrouck coalition to make large-scale public sector economies.

Yet if it is accepted that the corporatist initiative, taken in its two stages, was not crisis legislation in the sense of being the direct response to fears of imminent economic collapse, then this is not to say that it should not be seen as part of a reaction to a more general debate about the operation of liberal capitalism that was conducted in the Netherlands with some intensity from the end of the First World War. It is by reference to the lines of this debate that both the explanation of the predominant Catholic interest and (as will be discussed below) the timing of the response may begin to be understood. Of course, a concern with the non-revolutionary possibility of achieving social justice was of renewed interest after 1917 throughout Europe. But in the Netherlands the question of the necessary development of class antagonism and the possibility of an alternative development had a specific relevance. In part, this followed the 'Pacification' in which the recognition of the right of secular trade union activity and the extension of the suffrage so as to make inevitable a growth in support for a Socialist parliamentary party raised the issue of class conflict and its management as central. Equally, the Netherlands which had hitherto been relatively backward economically had, during the war and immediately after, begun a rapid industrialisation which, by being located largely in the Catholic south, juxtaposed strongly divergent views of class relations. Not surprisingly, while the debate about social and economic affairs was one engaged across Dutch political life, it was conducted with most urgency within the Catholic and Social Democrat movements. That this should be so additionally reflected the long relationship – found everywhere in Europe where there was a significant Catholic politics – between the Socialist critique of class conflict in industrialised society and the response in terms of the class-conciliation doctrines of Social Catholicism that had coalesced round the papal encyclical *Rerum Novarum* since the end of the nineteenth century. Against this background, in the special conjunction of Dutch postwar industrial modernisation with previous patterns of religious allegiance, it was inevitable that Catholics and Socialists, competing for the same working-class constituency, should have set the terms of the discussions of economic and social change since it was these that provided the arena in which each side could (indeed, had to) stake out its claim for legitimacy. Finally, and above all, the location and the vigour of the debate reflected the particular complication of a profound reorientation occurring separately within each of the movements. For Dutch Socialists, the internal rethinking centred on the question of the basis on which a policy that was sufficiently attractive electorally to lead to governmental power could be reconstructed after the debâcle of November 1918. For Catholics, the problem was what defence could be made to the encroachment of the secular state that had, in part, been encouraged by the 'Pacification' agreements and which threatened Catholic politics. What united both these internal debates was that they were conducted in terms of a redefinition of the question of socialisation. It was this interest, by means of which Catholics and Socialists faced and reacted to each other, that provided the mainspring for the legislative drive of the interwar years in the economic and social spheres as well as its particular corporatist direction.

For the SDAP before the First World War there had been no real dispute over the strategy by which socialism would be achieved in the Netherlands: a parliamentary majority would create the conditions for the use of state power in a programme of nationalisations and, in conjunction with the unions, of industrial reform. However, the failure of the 1918 'revolution', by increasing the power of the opposition ranged against both the party and the Socialist unions, made necessary the reconsideration if not of the ultimate goal, then of the intermediate stages in its realisation. In this process, the definition of socialisation as it would be practised was crucial. To this end, the SDAP Congress of Easter 1919 charged a Study Commission with the task of re-examining this question entirely. Their report which appeared in 1920, *De Sociaalvraagstuk* (*The Socialisation Question*), initiated a radical change of view that was to resonate in Dutch socialism for the next twenty-five years. Part of the report was conventional enough in its concentration on industrial reform and its recommendations for nationalisations and state-directed rationalisation of production. But what was new – and would cause a stir within the SDAP as much as among its political opponents – was the central discussion of the role of the state in the socialisation process. On the premiss that it was the task of a Socialist administration to ensure that production would be in the interests of society, the report proposed the creation of regulatory Industrial Boards which would have a public legal persona – the *Publiekrechtelijke Bedrijfsorganisatie* (PBO). These Boards would be composed of representatives of workers, consumers, technical experts and 'the community' and would be responsible for setting labour and production

conditions. The whole system of Boards, both within a particular industry and in relation to others, would be coordinated, especially in the
crucial area of wages and price policy, by a General Economic Council,
which would therefore in some respects (though these remained as yet
indistinctly defined in the report) supersede parliamentary responsibility
for the conduct of economic policy.[19]

The idea of a public legal structure for industrial relations was further
worked out in a second report, *Bedrijfsorganisatie en Medezeggenschap*
(*Industrial Organisation and Co-direction*), which the SDAP and NVV
produced jointly in 1923. In this document, while attention was again
given to the necessity of a programme of nationalisations, it was argued
that this would not of itself create socialisation. The essential precondition to achieve that lay, as the earlier report had proposed, in the
competence of the envisaged Industrial Boards. But here the key
development was made in the concept of 'functional decentralisation'
(an idea that was to continue to dominate discussion in the party for
the next decade) according to which the Boards, while formally 'state
organs', would none the less have their own powers that could be
executed independently of the central government. As with the report
on socialisation, the precise relationship between these new, widely
competent Boards and central authority remained to be worked out.
But there was little doubt within the Socialist movement that the proposals of the two reports together signified a revision, first, of the view
of the state and of class relations that veered, as many were quick to
point out, towards the dangers of syndicalism, and secondly, in the
authority that was to be granted in the PBO system to representatives of
functionally defined organised interests, a sharp move towards a corporatist strategy.[20]

It was this considerable shift of ground within the Socialist movement
made during the first years after the war that most threatened Catholics.
Notwithstanding the overall commitment in the two reports to the
pursuit of nationalisations and state monopolies, the major focus was on
the creation of intermediate organs that were seen as the vehicles to
reconcile opposed interests in society. However, this focus cut closely
into parallel developments within Dutch Catholic thinking. Since the
late nineteenth century, but most immediately towards the end of the
First World War, Catholics had themselves begun to formulate concrete
proposals on the need for institutions that would mediate between state
and society. The main motivation was the desire to slow down – or
better, to halt – the process of secularisation that was seen as having
remorselessly accompanied the growth in the extent and functions of
state power. The decision of the first postwar Catholic administration in

1918 to create the new Ministry of Labour was, in part, a strategy to promote a Confessional approach to social policy and thereby contain and compete with the increasing influence of the Socialist unions with their emphasis on state intervention; it also reflected a pressure in Catholic circles in favour of establishing a structure of their own which would make possible the conditions in which conflicts between capital and labour would be largely self-regulatory. In practice, this desire had a long pedigree of expression in corporatist formulations, associated especially with the attempts of A. S. Talma in the early part of the century to set up a network of Boards of Labour legally competent to enforce agreements on labour conditions.[21] During the First World War his views were extended by J. A. Veraart who, on the basis of a single successful mediation in the printing trade, began to argue the general case for introducing a system of tripartite-based Industrial Boards in which representatives of labour and employers under the beneficent eye of appointed representatives of the administration would be able to work out harmonious relations as well as the conformity of their interests with those of the community as a whole.[22]

What happened from 1918 until the early 1920s was that this corporatist current became a flood. In great measure the appointment of Aalbarse was a consequence of his own past as a supporter of corporatism. Temporarily, however, the initiative belonged to Veraart. By April 1919 he had secured an agreement from the four major Catholic *stand* organisations to issue a so-called *Paaschmanifest* (*Easter Manifesto*), which agreed to the setting up as soon as possible of a system of legally competent councils within each branch of industry composed of an equal representation between employers and workers, the whole to be coordinated in a Central Industrial Council whose care of the public interest would be ensured by the presence of experts.[23]

The acceptance of such an ambitious scheme – confined through it was to Catholic organisations – was without doubt prompted by the increased bargaining power of the labour unions at a time of great industrial expansion. Therefore, it could not easily survive the sharp economic down-swing that began to bite at the beginning of the 1920s when employers' groups, always reluctant to concede that the community had a legitimate role in their affairs, were only too ready to draw back. None the less, Veraart's vision (and near realisation) of a structure that expressed a relationship between *stand* groups and the public interest without going further down the path of state power provided the means of returning the political initiative to Catholic hands. The predisposition within the *zuil* as a whole (as demonstrated by the manifesto) to experiment with corporatism allowed Aalberse to embark on a legislative programme designed to counter the proposals that were beginning to cohere within the Socialist movement. The basis of his legislation was true to the Catholic principle of subsidiarity, which by granting to the state only a limited right to intervene in decisions that were regarded as better made at a lower level, refused to allow economic and social policy to be tackled as a whole. But this separation (which was to be upheld by his Catholic successors for the next thirty years) opened the way for a challenge to the secular unions, and hence the Socialist movement as a whole, in the area of labour relations that was their strength. The creation of the Supreme Labour Council, with its equal tripartite representation and its constituted role of advising the government across the range of social policy, including wages and insurance, affirmed a renewed Catholic interest in the formal realisation of conditions of social justice. That this was so was confirmed by the subsequent reform – against the objections of many of the employers' organisations – of the old Labour Boards in the *Arbeidsgeschillenwet* (Labour Disputes Act) of 1923 by which state mediators (*Rijksbemiddelaars*) were empowered to intervene with mandatory recommendations in the case of serious labour conflicts and also to establish permanent boards to mediate on questions of labour relations.[24]

By the mid-1920s both Catholics and Socialists had made large strides in the direction of corporatism. Naturally the concepts that sustained the debate on each side were quite different; but so, too, was the purpose envisaged for these developments. The turn to corporatist forms was not regarded as the means of defusing rivalry between the *zuilen*, rather it expressed and continued a competitive relation. If Socialists had moved to formulate the structure of corporatist functional decentralisation, it was because they believed that this would broaden the appeal of the party to the extent that it would attain power. For Catholics, who stood to lose most from such a change in allegiance, the corporatist legislation that as the major governmental party they had been able to impose was defensively designed to hold a Catholic politics together. Although the exploration of a corporatist solution to social problems had (certainly for Catholics) substantial roots, its course was dictated by the interaction between the two movements. Therefore, in so far as each saw the extension of corporatist institutions as providing the most effective challenge to the other, it is not suprising that as conditions worsened into depression and subsequently the ravages of the Nazi occupation, debate should have focused ever more intensely in this area.

The full range of the debates within the Socialist movement in the 1930s has been the subject of two recent surveys.[25] It will be sufficient, then, for the purpose of the present discussion to point to what were, in many ways, the apotheoses of the earlier SDAP and NVV reports: the joint document *Nieuwe Organen* (*New Organs*), which was published after five years' preparation in 1931; and the subsequent *Plan van de Arbeid* ('Labour Plan') of 1935, under which the party fought the general election campaign of 1937.[26]

Both documents extended the earlier premiss that since the achievement of socialism by parliamentary means alone would take too long and meet too great opposition, there was a need to develop a parallel strategy of economic reform that, equally, went beyond a simple commitment to nationalisation. The broad direction of such a reform had already been sketched out as functional decentralisation. What *Nieuwe Organen* did was to specify more precisely the form that this would take. Thus it was proposed that economic decisions should devolve largely to new Councils which were to be organised along both functional industrial lines (electrical goods, textiles, etc.) and territorially, by region. Each of these *schappen*, as the Councils were to be called, would have a tripartite structure of workers, management and technical (government-appointed experts) representation and would enjoy an autonomous legislative competence in most areas of labour relations and productive decisions. They would, however, contribute to the membership of, and be guided and coordinated by, a national Economic Parliament.[27] How exactly the separate competencies were to be reconciled was not made clear. In this and other respects, the scheme showed its obvious debt to the ideas expressed in Walter Rathenau's book *Neue Wirtschaft*, which had been much read by Dutch Socialists. There, too, was to be found the notion of a hierarchically related union of professional Councils with their own Parliament and legislative authority.[28] But these borrowings served only to emphasise how deep-seated the commitment to corporatist revisions had become as a conclusion to explorations begun ten year earlier.

Not surprisingly, the proposals in *Nieuwe Organen* caused a sharp criticism of the danger to the primacy of politics that the realisation of such a scheme would represent. In answer, a supplementary report, *Het Staatskundig Stelsel der Sociaal – Democratie* (*The Political System of Social Democracy*), published in 1935, took care to reiterate the commitment to parliamentary democracy and squashed the idea of a separate Economic Parliament. None the less, it too argued that the future development of a social democratic economy must rest on a corporatist base and, consequently, it decisively supported the formation of *schappen* as authorities that should have a key regulatory function.[29] This renewed evidence of how far the SDAP and NVV had travelled towards modifying the Socialist concept of the state was confirmed finally by the Labour Plan. It must be understood that the Plan was put forward as the centre-piece of a strategy to combat the depression. Therefore, its explicit position as an anti-Communist and anti-revolutionary vehicle to reform the capitalist economy was intended to help marshal as broad a band of forces as possible to revitalise production and, in this way, to counter the attraction of fascism which fed on the failure of the liberal state to provide work. Yet underlying this strategy was another that had far deeper roots: the aim of at last encouraging a change in electoral support that would lead to the creation of an enlarged, and no longer class-based, Socialist Party. Dutch Socialists were, then, in the hopes that they placed in the efficacy of *planisme* to cause a political break-through, the first and most convinced exponents of de Man's revision of Marxism. Reflecting this, the Plan clearly abandoned (as it had to if it was to succeed in being the instrument of forging a broad coalition) the idea of the class struggle. Further, and most crucially, it recognised that the means of creating the breakthrough must be by incorporating those economic interests which had hitherto been frightened away from cooperating with the Socialists. The Plan still envisaged that overall direction of economic policy would be safeguarded by the creation of a national Central Bank to control credit and a Conjuncture Office which would monitor the performance of the economy as a whole and advise on appropriate intervention. But at the very centre of the whole struc-ture stood the proposal for the further creation of *productschappen* which, following the institutional recommendations of *Nieuwe Organen*, were to have a pre-eminent role in the new General Economic Council that was to suggest and advise on the shape of economic policy, a role whose importance was underpinned by the primary responsibility and wide powers that the individual Councils were to enjoy for initiating a revived production.[30]

With the Labour Plan, the SDAP may be said to have completed its conversion to corporatism. This, and the related attempt to broaden its base to a *volkspartij*, struck deep into Catholic political territory. Catho-lics, then, had little option but to respond by trying themselves to occupy the same ground. For although the Commission which produced *Nieuwe Organen* had been set up at a time of relative economic stability, by the time the report was debated in public its recommendations appeared, because of the effects of the depression, to have an urgency which, in its turn, led inexorably to the concept of the Plan. Moreover, the Socialists' evident will to tackle the shortcomings in the conduct of the economy and the proposals from 1931 to create a corporate struc-ture were associated. It was this combination that effectively established that the agenda for a counter-move by the Catholics (already vulnerable by reason of their governmental responsibility) would likewise have to explore and extend the corporatist theme. For the Socialist appropriation of industrial Councils acting in conjunction with the state as the most relevant form of crisis management hit at the heart of the Catholic insistence, on which the cohesion of the *zuil* depended, that corporatist institutions could have no authority in economic policy. The pressure on Catholics to redefine their position was considerable. It was in line, too, with a larger debate in so far as the papal encyclical *Quadragesimo Anno* of May 1931 had expressed fears of the disintegrative effects of the economic crisis on faith and social harmony and urged Catholics to consider extending the forms of socio-economic corporatism.[31]

It is against this pressure that Verschuur's legislation of 1932–3 and the new RKSP programme of 1936 can be understood as a defensive reaction that took Catholics across a boundary hitherto absolute. The decision to create an Economic Council was an obvious response to Socialist proposals. But in taking up the challenge Verschuur had to make a substantial break with the past. The Council, instituted by the state, at once moved Catholics beyond Aalberse's policy with regard to the earlier *Nijverheidsraad* (Industrial Council) that such a body was a privately agreed initiative merely recognised by the state. Further, its formal constitution breached – as was pointed out in the parliamentary debates on the Bill – the principle of the state's incompetence in the sphere of economic relations. So too following this, the law establishing Economic Councils (*Bedrijfsradenwet*) from 'on high', as its critics complained, conceded that the state did have an interest in promoting and defining the form in which industry would best run its affairs. Here the Explanatory Memorandum that justified the proposed law is of interest. Verschuur insisted that the new Councils were required precisely because organised labour and management were increasingly in conflict, producing an inevitably disastrous effect on national economic life.[32] In the event, the *Bedrijfsradenwet* stopped short of yielding to the bodies it established the autonomous competence that the rival Socialist *Nieuwe Organen* envisaged. The subsidiarity principle remained alive. Indeed its restatement in the formal limitations that the law placed on the Councils – they could not make agreements that were legally binding – was necessary to continue to distinguish the Catholic position that prevented cooperation with the Socialists at government level. But as the Memorandum had revealed, the impetus to make new legislation was prompted in great part by the perception that relations within the Catholic *zuil* were in danger of breaking down and, with them, a separate Catholic politics. As the crisis decade of the 1930s drew to an end it was clear that the Catholics had been forced to move a long way from their position of 1918 – the revised Constitution of 1938 in fact provided for the extension of the legal powers of the Industrial Council. It also seems clear that the corporatist framework that had come into being owed as much to the challenge of a revised Dutch socialism as it did to Catholic social doctrine. In any case, so far from being the product of cooperation and agreement, its basis is more accurately seen as competetive and motivated by the need to exclude an increasingly dangerous political force.

If the corporatist developments of the interwar period can be read largely as the means by which Catholics and Socialists in the Netherlands expressed their competition, it also follows that the context was not one in which their approach to *verzuiling* was the same. Rather, while it is fair to argue that Catholics had an interest in extending *verzuiling* as part of a strategy of self-preservation through sharpening the boundaries of their own *zuil*, the Socialists moved, as they had to, in the opposite direction. The *productschappen* and the Plan Office that would draw in representatives of widely different affiliations, united simply by their determination to tackle the crisis, were developments that aimed to break through (hence their danger to the Confessionals) the protective *zuil* barriers. In this case, the relation between *verzuiling* and corporatism was a negative one, in that corporatist schemes were the reaction to, and consequence of, incomplete *verzuiling*. New versions of economic interest reconciliation and of socialisation found the space to be expressed (and to a degree put into practice) because the political map remained imprecisely fixed, and certainly in the opinion of the Socialists, capable of being changed. Above all, the evidence of the interwar period would suggest that corporatism was functional to the maintenance of an unequal access to the power structure. Socialists chose to propose a corporatist system that would work within and alongside central state initiatives because they believed that this would break the exclusion of *verzuiling*. Catholics, who had a natural propensity to think in corporatist terms, widened their interest into legislative action partly out of fear of losing the argument, but also because once pushed in this direction, to sanction a form of corporatism in which the state has as small an influence as possible was, in itself, to express the reality that defined the *zuil* and legitimised its pre-eminent position in government.

On the basis of this historical analysis the question remains whether the development of corporatism after 1945 into the finished system of the PBO and its pivotal summit organ, the SER, marked a change in pattern: whether, as the consociational model demands, there occurred the necessary shift of relationship between the élites towards accommodation? At first sight, the question may appear to have a self-evident answer, in that the postwar saw the Socialists admitted for the first time as a major and regular governmental party. Their acceptance into the coalition system – a change that occurred, it must be stressed, *before* the first elections – seems itself to provide the proof that the position and weight of the political parties had decisively altered as a result of the war. Moreover, the subsequent erection of a corporatist structure would thus appear to indicate that Socialists after 1945 did not just participate in *verzuiling*, but that they themselves now accepted the boundaries inherent in its operation. The will to create the summit organisations, then, may be said to have reflected the completion of *verzuiling*, since only if that was the case, did there arise the need for their function of depoliticising the potential abrasions between the *zuilen* as the means of agreeing to the system itself.

This is a persuasive case given, especially, the fact of the increased weight of the Socialists as evidenced by their postwar electoral performances: the near-matching of the Catholic vote setting up the conditions for an end to their isolation from government. But if it is to be assumed that this created a predisposition to formalise *verzuiling*, of which the progress of corporatist legislation was the sign, it is necessary to discount two major characteristics of postwar relations which worked against accommodation. First, the fact that the immediate postwar years saw an attack led by the Socialists (but which also found widespread resonance among Confessionals) on the validity of separate pillar-based parties – an attack therefore on the very existence of *verzuiling*. Secondly, that so far from there being even broad agreement on the scope and function of a corporatist approach to economic and social affairs, there was increased competition between Catholics and Socialists, with each promoting solutions that were more a continuation of their prewar positions than representative of a new spirit of cooperation.

The foremost concern at the Liberation was to harness the national effort towards the reconstruction of economic and social life. This was the charge given to the first, interim, government appointed by the Queen. What must be noted is the relation between this commission and the composition of the administration appointed to achieve it. For the 'old' parties were joined by ministers from the *Nederlandse Volksbeweging* (NVB), a new movement created out of a commitment to *doorbraak* ('breakthrough') of what its leaders regarded as the straitjacket of the prewar pillarised politics.[33] The inclusion of five members of the NVB out of the total of fifteen ministers in the reconstruction Cabinet was a measure of how strong a current there was in favour of 'renewal' at the

Liberation. Of course, this spirit had thoroughly pervaded SDAP thinking in the 1930s. But so, too, the view that the political vitality of the
Netherlands suffered from an artificial, enervating spirit of compart-
mentalisation (*hokjesgeest*) had become increasingly articulated in
young Confessional circles. Their somewhat isolated demand for new
issue parties had found a wider opportunity for expression during the
war when the absence of the old political leaders, together with a
national desire for solidarity in the face of the German occupation and
the threat posed by their client Dutch National Socialists, had encouraged the emergence of a new movement, the Nederlandse Unie
(Netherlands Union) in July 1940. The strength of the demand for
change may be gauged by the fact that the Unie attracted over 800,000
members (about one in six of the adult population) before the end of the
year.[34] Although as a political force the Unie was tainted with its origins
under Nazi occupation, the desire for *doorbraak* at the end of the war
was, if anything, intensified. From the Unie's leading cadres, and pre-
eminently from the group of political figures from all backgrounds who
had been interned together as hostages during the latter part of the
occupation, there arose a legitimate successor in the shape of the NVB.
It was this movement, within which were drawn together and concentrated those critiques of the segmented political system voiced in the
past decade, that provided the motor-force for the policies of the
Schermerhorn-Drees Cabinet that governed until July 1946.

The greatest resonance and political utility of the call for *doorbraak*
was in the old SDAP. Its prewar attempt to broaden its appeal and, on
that basis, push through centrally led economic reform, had foundered
on the continuing cohesion of the Catholic *zuil*. However, in the enthusiasm of the Liberation the solidarity of the Catholics showed some sign
of cracking. The greatest support for the Unie had been in the Catholic
south. Following this, throughout 1945 a number of Catholic intellectuals, centred on the ex-resistance group, Christofoor, and much
influenced by personalist socialism, argued against the idea of a revived
Catholic Party and, equally, of a Marxist Social Democratic Party. It
was they who, together with other smaller Christian Democrat groups,
pushed to realise *doorbraak* by choosing to unite with the former SDAP
and help found the new Labour Party (PvdA) in February 1946. Most
indicative of the new spirit was the creation within the PvdA of a
Catholic section whose rejection of Confessional politics was
emphasised by the title of their monthly journal, *De Katholiek in de
Partij van de Arbeid*.

This 'defection' which was interpreted as proof that the tide was
running inexorably for *doorbraak* reinforced the belief among the

Socialists that the level of potential support for a new politics would be secured by putting into practice many of the proposals that had been worked out in the 1930s. Bolstered by their control of the Cabinet portfolios responsible for economic and social matters, and freed for nearly six months from the constraints of parliamentary debate, they began to outline extensive legislation. As early as June 1945, Schermerhorn indicated that the government would introduce a general social-economic-financial plan for which nationalisations and a public-legal structure of industrial organisation were preconditions. Although the government brought in immediate legislation on wage levels, which in the eventual *Buitengewoon Besluit Arbeidsverhoudingen* ('Extraordinary Order on Labour Relations') of October 1945 extended the powers of the Board of Conciliators to make binding orders, it was made plain that this was just one step towards the articulation of a coordinated social and economic policy. To this purpose, the Minister of Trade, H. Vos, announced in September 1945 the establishment of a Central Plan Bureau to be under the chairmanship of the economist J. Tinbergen, who, like Vos, had been responsible for much of the detail of the prewar Labour Plan. The link with the prewar period was made even more explicit when Vos published, in December 1945, his *Voorontwerp* (Green Paper) on the creation of a PBO in which, reminiscent of the proposals made in *Nieuwe Organen* in 1931, there was envisaged a system of vertically linked tripartite Industrial Boards with wide competence in determining production and wage questions. Central coordination would be ensured by means of formal government-supervised horizontal links betwen enterprises engaged in related areas, and overall by a General Economic Council.[35]

The commitment to introduce a corporatist structure to underpin the Central Plan represented the Labour Party's inheritance from the prewar period. The creation of the PBO system was still seen, precisely as it had been in the 1930s, as necessary to ensure the moulding of that broad support that would sweep the party to power at the forthcoming general election. Moreover, as the general statement of intent which the Schermerhorn-Drees government put to the returning Parliament in late 1945 suggested, this was to be *doorbraak* in practice: an active state responsibility for planning, monitoring and carrying through economic and social policy was the precondition for reconstruction; and an enlarged role for the community and for the practice of functional representation was the guarantee of its success.[36] What was being argued was that corporatism was necessary if *doorbraak* was to be realised. The intention of the PvdA remained the same as it had been for the SDAP before the war: to provide the form that would cut through Confessional politics and break the structure of *verzuiling* sustained by them. In this case, while we may say that there was an accommodative urge intrinsic to the proposals made during the first year of peace, there is no basis to regard this as the result of a compromise reached between political élites. On the contrary, the PvdA strategy, by seeking to remove the justification for the existence of Confessional parties, represented an aggressive attempt to alter the ground on which accommodation in Dutch politics was required – as well therefore as the political system itself. That it was seen in this light by the Catholic *zuil* is evident from the very rapid rejection of *doorbraak* by party and religious leaders: even before the end of the war, the bishops in the newly liberated dioceses of Breda and den Bosch had called for the immediate reconstitution of all prewar Catholic economic, social and cultural organisations.[37]

In the event, the combination of episcopal intervention, the poor economic situation of the south and, ultimately, the defensive solidarity engendered within the Catholic *zuil* by the postwar talk of the end of its political voice, helped the new Catholic Party to emerge victorious from the 1946 elections. Yet, if *doorbraak* was checked, its full defeat demanded the diversion of its associated corporatist structures. Nowhere is the essential link between *doorbraak* and the corporatism urged by the PvdA more clearly demonstrated than in the immediate efforts of the Catholic-led government to dismantle the legislative proposals of its predecessor in this area. Secure in its repossession of the key economic and social portfolios, the Beel Cabinet was able to distance itself rapidly from ideas of central planning and government supervised associations of *productschappen* and move, in its turn, to restate a prewar position in which the state's role was limited as far as possible to providing a framework to enable conflicts between opposed interests to be reconciled. Already, before the election, the Catholic Centrum voor Staatkundige Vorming (Centre for Political Education) had produced in reply to Vos's Green Paper its own counter *Proeve* ('Specimen') of a Law on Industrial Councils and a Social-Economic Council, where the central recommendation was to leave the development of the particular Boards as a matter of independent organisation under the umbrella of the recently formed private Stichting van de Arbeid (Labour Foundation). It was this recommendation that provided the basis for the new Catholic Minister of Economic Affairs, Huysmans, to establish a commission to write its own *Voorontwerp* to replace that of Vos.[38]

Yet behind the confident counterattack was an uncertainty as to the consequences of a return to the past on the preservation of the Catholic *zuil.* Between 1947 and 1950 the Catholics had to move their ground. The whole progress of memoranda and provisional reports brought before Parliament during this period, and out of which was finalised the eventual agreement on the PBO and the role of the SER, conceded most of what Verschuur had been reluctant to do. In fact at the end of the war, Catholic hopes centred on developing the Labour Foundation as the main institution intervening in wage control and labour relations. For the Foundation, the product in 1945 of the secret agreements between representatives of the old labour and employers organisations, exemplified the principles essential to the Catholic view by virtue of its private status, its assumption of the possibility of harmony between management and labour through mutual contact and, above all, the limitations of its field of action. That the Foundation proved not to be the form that would link the pre- and postwar world for the Catholics testified to the pressures which the *zuil* faced from the 'renewers' within its own ranks. The creation in December 1945 of a new party, the Katholieke Volkspartij (KVP), had itself been to admit that if Catholics retreated to a pure Confessionalism, then they risked the haemorrhage of the more radical wing of the old RKSP. Worse, and more serious, the strengthening of the type of progressive party that indeed was shortly to emerge as the Labour Party that this desertion would ensure threatened to be of a sufficient attraction to the Catholic working class as further to weaken the claims of a separate Catholic politics. The experience of the interest in the Comités van Maatschappelijke Wederopbouw (Committees for Social Reconstruction) that had sprung up in the Catholic southern provinces at the time of the Liberation already provided an illustrative warning.[39] It was for this reason that the KVP not only came into being, but had to show its own progressive credentials from the start. The new party, particularly after it had achieved its first aim of at least maintaining the level of prewar electoral support, could not then stand aloof from the social and economic debates that the war and the climate of a desire for a new start had brought to the fore, and which the KVP had endorsed in its own 'emergency' programme. As it was, the necessity of cooperating with the Socialists succeeded in alienating the conservative and (in respect of the colonial problem) nationalist wing of the KVP, so that by 1948 it broke away to form its own rival Katholieke Nationale Partij. More troublesome still was the coalescing of a faction which decided to stay within the KVP and which fought against what it regarded as the drift to collectivism that followed coalition with the Socialists.[40]

The results of the 1946 election, and especially those of 1948 when the PvdA lost two seats, confirmed that *doorbraak* was not to be realised.

But if the setback for the PvdA could be read as a repeat of the failure of the SDAP strategy in 1937 when the attempt to forge a wide electoral coalition had foundered on the apparent irreducibility of the Confessional vote, the postwar results were also a victory, in that they established the permanent presence of the party in the formation of governments. The dream of *doorbraak* may have been in ruins, but there was no prospect of a return to a Confessional era. The coalition that formed after 1948 was, then, founded on the necessity of recognising a quite new reality. This was not simply because the two major parties appeared to have reached a position of stasis, but as much because of the result of arguments internal to each. We have already suggested that the KVP was squeezed between the imperative of maintaining its Confessionalism and the need to push the boundaries of its appeal outwards so as to head off the danger of encroachment from the PvdA which threatened the basis of the *zuil* itself. These contrary pulls also affected its adversary. The PvdA, by virtue of the context which had given it birth, had to be heterogeneous in its ideological orientation. But the failure of *doorbraak* increased the current, which had been present in the party since the Plan debates of the 1930s, in favour of the re-creation of a purer Socialist Party. This tendency, fuelled by the unprecedented electoral success of the hitherto marginal Communist Party, found its most influential voice in the Sociaal-Democratisch Centrum (SDC) whose arguments, in which were restated the theory of class conflict and of the need for socialisation, gained sufficient support to shift the PvdA programme of 1947 to a platform of increased nationalisations[41] This internal debate raised similar problems to those experienced in the KVP. For taken to its conclusion, the reorientation of the PvdA would – as its leadership was aware – make almost certain the defection of those voters attracted precisely because of the breadth of the postwar party and their subsequent return to former allegiances.

From the working through of these positions, it was inevitable that the KVP and PvdA leaderships should have promoted the compromise corporatist system that came into being in 1950. It is perfectly accurate to make the case that the Industrial Organisation Act of that year drew on proposals that had a long pedigree in each of the parties and struck a balance between them. Thus, if the Catholics abandoned their adhesion to a purely organic corporatism and recognised the claim of a nationally coordinated and enforceable economic and social policy, the PvdA gave up, particularly in the form of the Product and Industrial Councils that the Act created, both the idea of the class struggle and the belief that they were setting up the first stage of socialisation.

It is another matter to propose that the system was the result, let alone the perfection, of a long process of agreement. It has been the contention of the argument above that we would do better to see the achievement of the structure sustaining the SER as the first recognition of the need to provide a form in which further bargaining would take place. That need arose because, for the first time, all parties had accepted the basis of *verzuiling*. Most of all, the Socialists – always outside the system – had by 1948 in the shape of the PvdA conceded that their future lay in a *verzuild* politics. Corporatism, as it was finally put into practice, was not a solution made urgent by the disintegrative pressure of *verzuiling* but, on the contrary, opened the way for its completion. It is not surprising to find that it was after 1950 that *verzuiling* spread into virtually every area of Dutch social and cultural life.[42]

It is this rapid and thorough *verzuiling* which provided the basis for the accommodation arguments analysed at the beginning of this chapter. But it must be questioned, finally, whether the SER represented anything more than that the SDAP had moved to the centre. The agreement to run a welfare state within a free market economy was not, as the consociational case would have us believe, the fruit of the mediating form of the summit organisation. Rather corporatism in the postwar Netherlands expressed the fact that there was, by 1950, not anything fundamental to disagree about, nor in any case the means to carry disagreement into change.

Notes

1. A. Lijphart, *The Politics of Accommodation: Pluralism and Democracy in the Netherlands* (Berkeley, Calif., University of California, 1968), pp. 113–4.
2. *Ibid.*, pp. 1–2.
3. G. Lehmbruch, 'Consociational democracy, class conflict and the new corporatism' in P. C. Schmitter and G. Lehmbruch (eds), *Trends toward Corporatist Intermediation* (London, Sage, 1979), pp. 53–9, and 'Liberal corporatism and party Government' in *ibid.*, p. 150.
4. M. P. C. M. van Schendelen, 'The views of Lijphart and collected criticisms', *Acta Politica*, XIX (1) (1984), 25.
5. Lehmbruch, 'Consociational democracy', *op. cit.*, p. 61.
6. Lijphart, *The Politics of Accommodation*, *op. cit.*, pp. 104–18.
7. H. Daalder, 'The consociational democracy theme', *World Politics*, 26 (4) (1974), 616.
8. A. Lijphart, 'Consociational democracy', *World Politics*, 21 (4) (1969), 213–4.
9. G. H. Scholten, *De Sociaal-Economische Raad en de ministeriele verantwoordelijkheid* (Meppel, Boom, 1968), pp. 54–6.
10. P. W. Klein, 'Wegen naar economisch herstel 1945–1959', *Bijdragen en Mededelingen betreffende de Geschiedenis der Nederlanden*, 96 (1981), 269; R. Fernhout, 'Incorporatie van belangengroeperingen in de sociale en economische wetgeving' in H. Verhallen (ed.), *Corporatisme in Nederland* (Alphen-aan-den-Rijn, Samson,

1984), p.126ff.; G. J. van Oenen (ed.), *Staat en klassen in Nederland. De arbeidersbeweging in een periode van aanpassing en ordening in Nederland 1918–1940* (Amsterdam, Universiteit van Amsterdam, 1982), pp.645–50.

11. For a fuller discussion, to which I am indebted, see: I. Scholten, 'Does consociationalism exist? A critique of the Dutch experience' in R. Rose (ed.), *Electoral Participation: A Comparative Analysis* (London, Sage 1980), pp.329–51.

12. The features of the consociational case identified above have been extensively discussed in the pages of the main Dutch political science journal. See especially M. Fennema, 'Professor Lijphart en de Nederlandse politiek', *Acta Politica*, XI (1) (1976), 54–77; the survey by van Schendelen, *op. cit.*, in the special issue devoted to Lijphart: 'Consociationalism, pillarisation and conflict management in the Low Countries', *Acta Politica*, XIX (1) (1984); and a recent return to the topic, A. Lijphart, 'De pacificatietheorie en haar critici', *Acta Politica*, XXII (2) (1987), 190–204.

13. J. Th. J. van de Berg, 'Hervormingen, machtsverhoudingen en coalitievorming in Nederland', *Acta Politica*, XXI (3) (1986), 279–81; J. Bosmans, 'Historische twijfel aan de "uiterste noodzaak": de onzin van Daudt', *Acta Politica*, XXII (1) (1987), 227–33.

14. Lijphart, *Politics of Accommodation*, *op. cit.*, pp.123–31.

15. I. Scholten, *op. cit.*, pp.341–2.

16. By contrast, on the employers' side what were in origin pillar organisations rapidly moved after the war to taking on a cross-pillar affiliation. By 1921 the separate Liberal, Catholic and Protestant employers' groups had agreed to form a permanent federal committee, the Kring van Werkgevercentralen: I. Scholten, *op. cit.*, p.338; J. H. H. J. Eikema and J. M. de Jong, 'Struktuur, organisatie en aktiviteiten van de kapitalistische klasse in het Interbellum' in van Oenen, *op. cit.*, pp.125–93.

17. J. A. A. van Doorn, 'Anatomie van de interventiestaat' in J. W. de Beus and J. A. A. van Doorn (eds), *De Interventiestaat. Tradities-ervaringen-reacties* (Meppel, Boom, 1984), p.16.

18. I. Schoffer, 'De Nederlandse confessionele partijen 1918–1939' in L. W. G. Scholten *et al.* (eds), *De confessionelen. Ontstaan en ontwikkeling van de christelijke partijen* (Utrecht, Ambo, 1968).

19. *Het Socialisatie-vraagstuk. Rapport uitgebracht door de commissie aangewezen uit de SDAP* (Amsterdam SDAP, 1920).

20. Percy B. Lehning, 'Socialisten tussen plan en macht' in de Beus and van Doorn, *op. cit.*, pp.56–7.

21. T. de Ruiter, *Minister A. S. Talma* (Franeker, Wever, 1946), pp.95–156.

22. E. H. Kossman, *The Low Countries, 1780–1940* (Oxford, Clarendon Press, 1978), p.97.

23. F. J. H. M. van der Ven, *Economische en sociale opvattingen in Nederland* (Antwerp, Spectrum, 1952), pp.25–9.

24. *Ibid.*, pp.42–59; J. J. Woldendorp and M. Grunell, 'Sociale politiek in het interbellum' in van Oenen, *op. cit.*, pp.332–6; see also T. J. Verschuur *et al.* (eds), *Tien jaren Raden van Arbeid* (Haarlem, Tjeenk Willink, 1930).

25. Lehning, *op. cit.*, pp.53–72; P. J. Knegtmans and J. J. Woldendorp, 'Tussen ordening en revolutie. Over CPN en SDAP van 1918 tot 1940; in van Oenen (ed.), *op. cit.*, pp.543–76.

26. *Nieuwe Organen. Rapport tot de nadere uitwerking der artikelen 78 en 194 der Grondwet uitgebracht door de Commissie ingesteld door de SDAP* (Amsterdam, Arbeiderspers, 1931); *Het Plan van de arbeid. Rapport van de commissie uit NVV en SDAP* (Amsterdam, Arbeiderspers, 1935).

27. *Nieuwe Organen*, *op. cit.*, pp.12–60, 89–97.

28. J. van der Linden, 'De bedrihfsorganisatie: een discussie over de verhouding van staat en maatschappij' in Verhallen, *op. cit.*, pp.232–3.

29. Lehning, *op. cit.*, pp.59–60.

30. *Plan van de Arbeid*, *op. cit.*, pp.9–131; on the new approach to the *middenstand*

evolved in the Plan, see *ibid.*, pp. 200–22; H. Vos, 'Het Plan van de arbeid', *Socialistische Gids*, XX (6) (1935), 381–95; R. Abma, 'Het Plan van de arbeid en de SDAP', *Bijdragen en Mededelingen betreffende de Geschiedenis der Nederlanden*, 92 (1976), 37–68.

31. 'Quadragesimo Anno' in C. Carlen (ed.), *The Papal Encyclicals 1903–1939* (Raleigh, McGrath, 1981), pp. 431–7.

32. van der Ven, *op. cit.*, pp. 74–5.

33. *Program en toelichting van de Nederlandse Volksbeweging* (Amsterdam, NVB, 1945), pp. 1–4, 18–30; A. F. Manning, 'Het bevrijde zuiden': kanttekeningen bij het historisch onderzoek', *Bijdragen en Mededelingen betreffende de Geschiedenis der Nederlanden*, 96 (1981), 184–203.

34. M. L. Smith, 'Neither resistance nor collaboration: historians and the problem of the *Nederlandse Unie*', *History*, 235 (1987), 256–8.

35. Lehning, *op. cit.*, p. 68.

36. van der Linden, *op. cit.*, pp. 245–6.

37. A. F. Manning, 'Geen doorbraak van de oude structuren' in L. Scholten, *op. cit.*, pp. 70–4.

38. van der Linden, *op. cit.*, pp. 249–51.

39. J. L. G. van Oudsheusden and J. A. M. Verboom, *Herstel-en Vernieuwingsbeweging in het bevrijde zuiden. Eindhoven, 's-Hertogenbosch en Waalwijk 1944-1945* (Tilburg, Stichting Zuidelijk Historisch Contact, 1977), pp. 14–5, 117–22, 239–59.

40. J. Beaufays, *Les Partis Catholiques en Belgique et au Pays-Bas, 1918–1958* (Brussels, Emile Bruylant, 1973), pp. 603–4.

41. J. Bosmans, '"Beide er in en geen van beide er uit". De rooms-rode samenwerking 1945–1952', *Bijdragen en Mededelingen betreffende de Geschiedenis der Nederlanden*, 96 (1981), pp. 213–15.

42. J. P. Kruit and W. Goddijn, 'Verzuiling en ontzuiling als sociologisch proces' in A. N. J. den Hollander *et al.*, (eds), *Drift en koers: een halve eeuw sociale verandering in Nederland* (Assen, van Gorcum, 1968) pp. 244–5.

9 The failure of corporatist state forms and policies in postwar Britain

Andrew Cox

This chapter contends that a pluralist state form with a Keynesian policy bias was created in Britian in the period between 1945 and 1960. Since the early 1960s this pluralist form persisted, but with experiments in corporatist institutional forms and policies. These experiments lasted until the mid to late 1970s but were never able to replace successfully the pluralist form they challenged. Since 1979, however, this pluralist state form with a Keynesian policy bias has been challenged by a new-found faith in nineteenth-century neo-liberal state forms and policies. While this conflict has not been successfully resolved as yet, this postwar history demonstrates that, at the macro level of policy-making, corporatism was not, and is never likely to be, successfully constructed in Britain.

Before describing the postwar history of state-society relationships in Britain, it is perhaps necessary to outline briefly the main features of the state forms to be discussed here. The corporatist form is straightforward. It involves the state in creating a privileged policy-making role for key interest groups at the expense of the legislature and individual representation on a territorial basis. The state licenses and controls the forms of representation and works through, and with, the key groups in society to implement agreed policy objectives. The state must be undertaking a controlling and, if necessary, an extended interventionist and ownership role in society and the economy.

The pluralist state form, with a Keynesian policy bias, operates through a political form of representation in which the legislature is not superseded by group incorporation. However, the state must fulfil a crucial mediating role in terms of global macro-economic goals. This involves an active demand management role without extensive supply side intervention. The consequence of this will necessarily be a lack of need for the incorporation of key groups. Since the state is not pursuing any specific interventionist goals and leaving the market to follow its own logic, the threat of non-compliance by key social and economic groups does not arise. While the state may need to intervene to rescue inefficient or strategic firms in the national interest, the state's direct ownership role and supply side interventions are limited. Yet, at the same time, the state must adopt an extensive social welfare role of a social democratic and redistributive kind. This policy is in line with the increase in growth its demand management and deficit financing role may be able to engender. As a result of successful economic growth, this approach legitimises individual and group expectations and demands; leading directly to extensive interest group formation and bargaining over and around the state. This is a pluralistic form in which the state has to choose between a plethora of voluntaristic and autonomous groups and interests on a relatively *ad hoc*, pragmatic basis.

The neo-liberal state form and policy approach is significantly different, in that while the freedom for groups to organise and make demands on the state is recognised, the role of groups is not regarded as superior to the territorial basis of representation for individuals in the legislature. Individual preferences as expressed through the ballot-box are regarded as crucial in determining the government of the day and its policy mandate. Thus the government is seen as having no co-equal partners in policy-making (corporatism) or as having to balance the demands of individuals and the plethora of groups making demands in society (Keynesian pluralism). On the contrary, while interests are free to organise in the neo-liberal state, not all interests are regarded as equally legitimate when it comes to participation in policy-making. The neo-liberal state is directed towards the primacy of individual ownership and property rights and therefore can only regard as legitimate, once mandated by popular vote, those interests which accept the need to reduce the state's collective welfare and economic ownership role. Only those groups and individuals espousing these policy goals will have access to the policy process. It is a system predicated on the theoretical assumption of a pluralist state form but which must, in practice, deny this in operation and favour only some interests at the expense of others. Only those opposed to the collective bargaining and welfarist state can participate; those excluded are forced to rely on illegitimate forms of pressure (like strikes) until they can replace the neo-liberal state with a pluralistic or corporatist state form by the election of a social democratically inclined government. Therefore, the neo-liberal state is clearly different to the pluralist and corporatist state forms with their respective recognition of a plurality of interests and willingness to share state authority with functional interests. The neo-liberal state recognises no other interests as having the same authority as that of the democratically elected and mandated government. Nor does such a state form and government believe that it is any role of the government to redistribute or mediate the social and economic conflicts within society.

Ultimately the neo-liberal state is concerned only with the maintenance of internal and external order, the defence of individual and corporate property rights and the stability of the currency.

Having outlined the basic distinctions between these idealised forms of the state, it is not to argue that Britain has been characterised by any of them. It is our task now to analyse Britain since 1945 in order to discover whether any of these three forms of the state adequately summarise the British experience between 1945 and 1987. But before that, it is perhaps necessary to make two general statements about the state-society relationship in Britain. The first is that there has always been a historic lack of consensus about the proper role for the state in the economy and this has been a dominant theme of party political ideological debate.[1] Indeed this has led to an adversarial thesis of Britain's economic decline and of state policy-making – especially in the economic sphere.[2] However, the thrust of this chapter is different, in that it does not focus on what political parties say they will do. Rather this chapter concentrates on what the state has done, in practice, in terms of systems of representation and policy intervention in society. From this perspective, it is argued that changes in government are not a satisfactory guide to the form of the state. While changes in government at elections may result in a different state form, in the British context there has been a surprising consensus about the political form of the state and the policies it should pursue whatever the political composition of government in office. Only since 1979 can this conclusion be questioned when the neo-liberalism of Thatcher presaged a much more strident adversarial practice for the first time since 1945.

If this is so, then the adversary politics thesis is largely redundant as an explanation of the form of the pre-1979 state. What has to be explained is why there was a consensus in favour of Keynesianism[3] and corporatism,[4] and why it was that neither of these political forms could be sustained; and in the case of corporatism, why it could not be implemented successfully and was challenged by neo-Liberalism after 1979. To understand why, we have to explain how economic, electoral and political phenomena shape the form of the state in Britain. There are a number of salient features, one of which is the fact that none of the major political parties is in total accord about what form the state should take in Britain. The Labour Party is a coalition of social democrats, trade unionists and socialists.[5] The Conservative Party is a coalition of industrialists, financiers, property owners and commercial interests.[6] The Liberal Party was historically a coalition of landowners and industrialists, but today is primarily a middle-class party based on intellectuals and party activists committed to localism and regionalism.[7] The

Social Democratic Party (formed in 1981) is a party of disaffected social democrats from the Labour Party, and disgruntled industrialists and intellectuals reacting to the policies of a monetarist, neo-liberal Conservative Party, the Marxist left and role of the trade unions.[8] Since none of the parties speaks with a singular, distinctive voice, whatever a party does in office will result in a significant minority in each party ill at ease with the state role that is adopted.

Added to this of course is the defensive strength of the trade union movement committed to wage militancy and the protection of free collective bargaining in industrial relations.[9] But resistance to an expanding public sector role has also arisen because of the crucial role of the City of London and the financial sector. The financial sector has been historically committed to free trade to maintain Britain's invisible earnings and thereby to underwrite a growing historic balance of payments crisis.[10] This is supported by a desire for independence from state intervention among the leading sector of private industry and the lack of a well-developed interventionist approach among the British civil service.[11] The cultural commitment of British people to liberal social values and parliamentary forms of representation are also crucially important factors which constrain the state's role and make state intervention and a growing public sector illegitimate.[12] This perforce leads to an instability of electoral support for the political parties when they attempt to use the state and the public sector to resolve crises of economic affairs. Due to the fact that there have been recurrent balance-of-payment crises in Britain since the middle of the 1950s, and attempts to use the public sector to resolve these, it is hardly surprising that there has been a marked increase in voting volatility among the electorate.[13]

Because the state in Britain is regarded as illegitimate, electoral and public opinions has been unstable and governments have had to respond to this by offering alternative solutions to increased intervention. But this is often an electoral tactic which belies the relative continuity of approach adopted in Britain since the end of the Second World War. If there is any single explanation of Britain's economic decline and the shifts in the size and scope of the public sector, it is to be found not in adversary politics, but in the inability of the state to impose upon society and economy those policy solutions which it desired. This failure resides not in a lack of purpose, but mainly in the ability of trade union, financial and industrial interests and electoral opinion to block the state's role and the growth of the public sector in the economy.

The Postwar settlement and the Keynesian approach to the public sector (1945–59)

Between 1939 and 1945, Britain experienced a high degree of consensus over the role of the state. Britain came to the closest it has ever done to the creation of a corporate state, based upon public control of a mainly privately owned economy.[14] The state was used to control production, dividends, profits, rents, the supply of commodities and raw materials and wage rates. The mechanisms of control were not state ownership, but dirigiste, *ad hoc*, interventions by an expanded bureaucracy under the War Cabinet. Business and labour were incorporated into state decision-making and bargains were struck over wages, profits and savings nationally. These policy agreements were implemented through the creation of tripartite and bipartite institutions for war production and wage arbitration. The Ministries of Labour and Production being given compulsory powers to enforce national wage, production and profit agreements on employers and workers. While workers were able to question these national agreements occasionally, in general, the corporate state was sustained by the exigencies of national emergency and it was able to control inflation, massively increase military output, hold down wage rates, enforce national saving and enable Britain to fight the war to a successful conclusion.[15]

It would be wrong, however, to argue that this resulted in a postwar consensus on the role of the state. With the ending of the war, trade unionists, employers, financial interests and the public had no desire to maintain the state's role. True, the price of the war effort for the British people was a commitment to social welfarism. This was enshrined in the wartime creation of a Reconstruction Secretariat and the consequential commitments by the coalition government to extensions of social welfarism, educational services, a health service and full employment after the war. But while all shades of political opinion accepted that there would be no return to the mass unemployment and inadequate social services of the 1930s, there was little agreement about the extent of state intervention into the privately owned economy. There was in fact a fundamental disagreement in the political parties and among major social and economic interests about the role of the state and the public sector in the economy.[16]

The Labour Party returned to office in 1945 but there was confusion over the role that the state was to take. Left-wingers wanted Labour to create the Socialist Commonwealth by the continuous nationalisation of private property and industry. Staple, manufacturing industries would be nationalised first, to be followed by land and property, the financial

sector, and then the remaining privately owned and profitable industries. This view was opposed in the party by social democrats who
were committed only to nationalising inefficient staple industries (like
coal, steel and the railways) and massively extending social welfarism.
This might also mean an extension of state planning of the private
economy (along corporatist lines) but it fell short of full state planning
and ownership control.[17] The trade unions adopted a contradictory
approach. Some trade union political activists desired state control and
nationalisation, but these were in a minority. At this time, the dominant
goal of the trade union leadership was limited to nationalisation of
inefficient industries to protect jobs and a return to free collective
bargaining in industrial relations. The state would be influenced by
national negotiations and union participation; but this would fall short
of state compulsory arbitration of wage agreements or manpower
planning. This meant that the trade unions wanted a weak form of
corporatism which would allow union influence over state and employer
policies, without undermining the traditional freedom of workers and
unions to bargain unilaterally with employers over wages and conditions
on the factory floor.[18]

The Labour Party had to respond to these contradictory pressures
from within its own coalition between 1945 and 1951. There were,
however, alternative scenarios available for the state. The Liberal
Party, while still retaining some of its historic attachment to 'laissez-
fairism' and free trade, had been heavily influenced by the writings of
Keynes and Beveridge. As a result, they along with senior civil servants,
who had also come under the influence of Keynes during his sojourn in
the Treasury during the war, argued for a more indirect state role. Full
employment could be ensured, according to Keynes, by positive public
action of an indirect kind. While some inefficient industries might
require nationalisation (railways, coal, steel, etc.), the state need not
involve itself in detailed direct ownership control of industry, nor was it
necessary for the state to control directly the supply of goods and raw
materials in the economy. By indirect use of budgetary stimulus
(taxation, interest rates and public expenditure), Keynes argued that
growth could be maintained without inflation or high unemployment. In
a trade depression the state could increase public expenditure and lower
taxation and interest rates to stimulate demand. In an inflationary
period the state could cut public expenditure and increase taxation and
interest rates to take demand out of the economy. By this means, the
level of demand in the economy would be sustained, growth would be
exponential and the business cycle eradicated without direct state
ownership and control. It would also be possible then, out of increased

economic growth, to underwrite extensive social welfare provision.[19] This view was also likely to command support from manufacturers and financial interests because, if the state's role was to be increased after 1945, this was the least painful method available. However, many of these interests were mainly concerned with ensuring the dismantling of wartime corporatist controls and returning to a *laissez-faire* economic relationship.[20]

Finally, the Conservative Party was also offering alternative prescriptions for the postwar state. Since the 1930s there had been a number of young MPs and industrialists (Macmillan, Boothby, Stanley and Mond) who had argued for a corporate state. This desire had been influenced by the mass unemployment and economic inefficiency of the 1930s and had led also to a commitment to extensive social welfare provision. While this, and the acceptance of the ideas of Keynes by some Conservatives (in particular, R. A. Butler), was to have a marked impact on Conservative postwar policy, this was not the only approach to the state debated within the party. Churchill, in particular, while recognising the need for social welfarism, was a former Liberal free-trader and he and his supporters were concerned to ensure that the state's role was limited in economic affairs. Given the socio-economic base of the party among property owners, financial interests and industrialists, it was not surprising then that a commitment to neo-liberalism should remain as a continuing theme of postwar Conservative policy, particularly as the mass of the populous wanted an end to wartime regulations, controls and rationing.[21]

What, then, did the state do in economic and social affairs after the war as it responded to these contradictory pressures? Initially there was a degree of confusion. Labour was returned to office committed to a massive shift of ownership and control to the state, but they were faced with immediate short-term problems. A large proportion of the workforce was in the armed forces and staple industries were in need of fundamental modernisation and rationalisation. Britain's consumer industries were run down and foreign reserves had been eroded to pay for the war. International debts had risen astronomically and without American aid economic and social life would have been totally disrupted. Labour therefore faced the need to reconstruct the postwar economy, as well as shift ownership and control to the state, while having to repay massive foreign debts and expand export industries to pay for imported raw materials and consumer goods. Within these constraints it is not surprising that Labour could not create a socialist state. What is remarkable in fact is the degree to which Labour fulfilled its manifesto commitments. The major staple industries were nationalised, social services were expanded, the Bank of England was brought into public ownership and the extensive system of wartime controls over manpower, raw materials, production and rationing were maintained. But this approach, which also saw the state successfully direct resources into export industry between 1945 and 1947, could not last due to the counter-pressures in society and economy against such an extensive role.

Labour faced pressure from industry to limit its nationalisation programme. The City of London was active in countering proposals for further state control of the financial sector other than the public control of the Bank of England. Trade unionists demanded and achieved a return to free collective bargaining and continually campaigned against manpower planning of the state. Labour also faced public demands for an end to rationing and austerity. It was not these pressures alone, however, which led to Labour limiting the state's interventions into the economy in this period. The major factor was Britain's acute shortage of foreign currency – in particular, dollars to pay for imported raw materials and commodities. While progress was being made in export industries, it was insufficient to pay for imports and foreign debt payments. As a result, by 1947 Labour experienced a dollar shortage and balance-of-payments crisis necessitating an International Monetary Fund (IMF) loan, American financial assistance and a curtailment of Labour's plans for further public control of the economy. From 1947 the commitments to further nationalisation, manpower planning and dirigiste state controls were reduced as Britain adopted a Keynesian approach to state intervention. This meant that the state would provide social welfare benefits out of indirect state stimulation of economic growth. Nationalisation would be limited only to inefficient industries and rationing and controls on raw materials and output would be reduced. Only the steel and road haulage industries were nationalised against this broad philosophy because they were part of the original manifesto package adopted by Labour in 1945, and this policy was supported by key trade union groups in the Labour coalition. By 1947, then, Labour had shifted towards a Keynesian approach to the public sector in response to the financial crisis and the demands in economy and society for a reduced state role.[22]

This broad approach was sustained throughout the 1950s, and it is because of this that we talk of a postwar consensus in Britain. There are a number of reasons why this Keynesian approach was sustained, but perhaps the most important was that the 1950s witnessed a massive postwar economic boom which made it unnecessary for the state to intervene in the economy. Similarly, the desire by trade unionists and private economic interests to be allowed to pursue their own self-interests unfettered by the state undermined a more interventionist approach. In a period of sustained economic growth and rising material affluence workers were quite content to use free collective bargaining to secure higher wage rates without recourse to state economic intervention. Industrialists and the financial sector were happy to allow the state to provide social welfarism so long as the state's role did not extend into detailed economic control. Thus while Conservative governments after 1951 denationalised road haulage and steel (these had been more profitable than coal, railways and public utilities), and downgraded state aid for regions in decline and abolished most of the state's dirigiste instruments, this was not politically controversial because social welfare spending was increased and economic growth appeared exponential. These policy shifts did give the impression of an adversarial approach to the state's role, with the Conservatives apparently more prone to denationalise, but in reality these changes mask the central continuity of the Keynesian approach which had been accepted by the leadership of the Labour opposition and trade unions after 1947.[23]

Beneath the surface veneer, however, there were a number of factors which were likely to question this consensus about the public sector. First, a significant minority of trade unionists and Labour Party activists were appalled by the 1945–51 Labour record and the apparent shift, under the leadership of Gaitskell throughout the 1950s, away from nationalisation to an acceptance of the Keynesian consensus. In the Conservative Party there was also a significant minority of backbenchers and economic interests who wanted to reduce the public sector's role in the economy further and to adopt a more *laissez-faire* approach. Neither of these groups was able, however, to question the developing social democratic consensus until the 1970s when economic decline had undermined popular support for this approach. The realisation that Britain was a structurally weak economy was not apparent fully in the 1950s, and it only began to become common knowledge towards the end of the 1960s. The long postwar boom led to a massive increase in material living standards for most people and the fact that Britain's relative share of world trade and relative growth performance was in rapid decline was not evident. However, there was, by the end of the 1950s a growing realisation among informed political and economic élites that Britain's economic performance was in decline. This did not, however, lead to adversarial politics at the level of the state. Rather than Keynesianism being fundamentally questioned there was a metamorphosis towards corporatism by both the Conservative and Labour governments in the 1960s. The broad strategy of the 1960s was different to Keynesianism, but it was still consensually based as both parties used the public sector more directly to reconstruct British industry.[24] However, this corporatist strategy could not be sustained in the face of the contradictory counter-pressures against state intervention in British society and economy.

The failure of a Return to Corporatism (1960–70)

In the 1960s the British public sector/economy relationship is best characterised as failed corporatism. This is because, although there was a shift away from an indirect Keynesian demand management approach towards a more detailed state role in resolving supply side economic problems by extensive dirigiste and indicative planning experiments, a full-scale corporatist state was not created. Under a full-scale corporatist approach the state would be able to control investment decision-making in the industrial and financial sectors after bargains had been struck between employers and workers over wages, profits and output. In Britain this has rarely been achieved satisfactorily, even if attempts have been made to incorporate and 'buy-off' employer and worker opposition to the expanding role of the public sector in the economy. This failure of corporatism was to be experienced under both the 1960–4 Conservative and 1964–70 Labour governments.

The Conservative governments of the 1950s had adopted Keynesian policies with a neo-liberal face. By this, one means that social welfarism was maintained, and apart from some limited denationalisation, most industries brought into public ownership by Labour were retained. But Conservative governments continuously attempted to impose commercial criteria on nationalised industries in line with their market-orientated philosophy. Nationalised industries were not to be run as social services, and state aid for areas of regional decline was cut back, as government controls and regulations over the private economy were reduced. Thus, throughout the 1950s, the state maintained a 'backstop' role to prop up market inefficiency, while allowing the market to operate relatively freely. Broad economic policy defended sterling, the role of the City of London as a major money market and the financial sector as a source of invisible earnings to solve the problem of the balance of payments. This led to a 'stop-go' cycle of demand management in the 1950s as the underlying weakness of the economy in trade and manufacturing led to sterling crises and the use of Keynesian techniques by the government to restrict imports by curbs on consumer demands.[25] It was out of the realisation of this dilemma that some industrialists and the Conservative government, led by Harold Macmillan at the end of the 1950s, began to question the primacy of the defence of sterling and the City at the expense of consumer demand and the manufacturing base of the economy. Increasingly industrialists, looking to French indicative planning as an exemplar, called for state assistance for industry at the expense of the defence of sterling. It was due to this that the Macmillan government began to shift towards a corporatist approach after 1960.[26]

However, the strategy was not full corporatism because the Conservative government relied on *voluntary* participation by employers and trade unionists in state policy-making and implementation. There was little attempt to take control over the financial sector of the economy at all, and Macmillan merely created new administrative institutions – the National Economic Development Council, the Economic Development Councils and the National Incomes Commission – in an attempt to bring labour and employers together to discuss bottlenecks to industrial output, productivity and pay bargaining. This approach was not compulsory: the government merely encouraged participation but rarely demanded it or compulsorily imposed decisions on employers or workers. Only the six-months wage freeze in 1961 can be seen as part of a fully corporatist strategy by the state. This did not last, however, and the government did not try to force companies to accept the broad planning frameworks worked out in the National Economic Development Council (NEDC). Instead the government encouraged voluntary participation, increased financial assistance to regions in decline, promised increases in public expenditure and encouraged manpower retraining.[27]

The Labour government of 1964–70 which replaced the Conservatives adopted similar policies. Despite the ritualised adversarial, ideological battles conducted by the parties at British elections, what Labour was offering in 1964 was not socialism, but corporatism. However, what it achieved in office was not corporatism, but failed corporatism, and in this respect it was a mirror of the earlier Conservative administration. Labour re-nationalised steel and parts of the road-haulage industry after 1964, but the broad thrust of policy was a continuity of the Conservative approach. Labour's newness was in its apparent willingness to create even more extensive administrative reforms to ensure corporatism through indicative planning. To counter the dominance of policy by the City of London, Bank of England and Treasury, Labour set up a Department of Economic Affairs. The regional programme of the Conservatives was also extended, with a planning system created to parallel in the regions the national and sectoral planning approach being adopted by the NEDC and EDCs. All of this structure was to be based on the tripartite participation of employers, workers and civil servants/ politicians and was intended to lead to an indicative National Plan to foster higher economic growth. The National Plan was not, however, to lead to an increase in state ownership, but was to indicate the growth potential in the economy, which the government would support through dirigiste policies related to expenditure, taxation, financial aid and grants to industry. The National Plan would also set out the permissible levels of wages increases to guide a voluntary wage restraint approach by the trade unions.

Although more broadly based than the Conservative strategy, this package for the public sector was not full corporatism because the state had no mechanisms by which it could compulsorily ensure that its planning assumptions could be implemented effectively. There were no compulsory means of directing investment into growth sectors of the economy. The financial sector was left freely to decide its own priorities, and while the state did provide grants and other inducements for ind- ustrial location in regions suffering decline, these were not compulsory, but relied upon effective demand from relocating companies before they were taken up. Furthermore, although the National Plan did set out the basis for wage settlements, the government had, at first, no compulsory mechanisms to ensure that workers abided by these guidelines. Thus the National Plan was an edifice built on sand; while it tried to use the state to influence supply side economic problems and control a mainly pri- vately owned economy, it did not give the state the powers to do so effectively.[25]

This was revealed most emphatically in 1965 and 1966, when Britain experienced a further severe balance of payments and sterling crisis. Instead of the National Plan's strategy of ignoring the balance-of- payments constraint on economic growth, the Labour government was forced to cut public expenditure and reduce consumer demand in an attempt to bolster sterling and the role of the City of London. This meant that the National Plan was stillborn in the face of short-term financial problems and the influence of the financial sector and Treasury on government policy-making. Without state control over these sectors of the economy, it was impossible to implement the Plan. But this was not the only dilemma. The National Plan assumed lower wage settle- ments in an inflationary period, yet there were no effective mechanisms available to the state to ensure that unions accepted this. The govern- ment tried to win voluntary acceptance of wage restraint but, due to the strength of rank-and-file union opposition to this and the incidence of wildcat strikes in Britain against official leadership bargains with the state, the voluntary wage restraint strategy failed. Only then did Labour begin to shift towards a more fully corporatist approach on the wages front. In 1966 a National Board for Prices and Income was created and a six-month statutory wage freeze imposed. This was followed by severe wage restraint and a statutory policy until 1968.[29]

Labour faced similar problems with private industry. The National Plan tried to indicate the growth points in the economy, on the assumption that if government public expenditure commitments were maintained and consumer demand sustained, then industrialists would invest and stimulate employment and production. This did not happen because industrialists, left to their own devices, normally wait until effective demand rises before increasing investment and employment. Labour's financial strategy reduced effective demand and thereby undercut the confidence of industrialists to invest. Without government's positive inducement of investment or industrial rationalisation, there was no way that the National Plan could be implemented. It was as a result of this, and the failure of the Plan, that the government tried to provide itself with more positive instruments to control industry in the form of the 1966 Industrial Reorganisation Corporation and the 1968 Industrial Expansion Act. Both of these strategies, however, failed to overcome the inertia of British industry or to allow the Labour government to construct a fully corporatist state.[30]

It is clear, then, that the Conservative and Labour governments of the 1960s attempted to shift the role of the state into a far greater controlling role in the economy than had been thought necessary between 1947 and 1959. This was a change in political approach but it was not fundamentally driven by adversary politics. Rather the shift was in line with the logic of the Keynesian/social democratic consensus which had developed after 1947. The state did not try to create a fully corporatist arrangement, it tried to find a 'half-way house' between Keynesianism and corporatism. The reason for this is rooted in the dominance of liberal values in British society. Even as it becomes apparent to political élites that they must use the state to resolve economic difficulties, given the attachment to voluntarism by trade unions, the defence of free trade and *laissez-faire* by the financial and industrial sectors and the attachment to liberalism and anti-state values of the mass of the British populace, it was also evident that any attempt to create an extensive interventionist role creates acute problems of political legitimacy for the British state. Most attempts to move in this direction have been predicted on the voluntary incorporation of major economic and social interests. However, the problem with the strategy is that, given the strategic and defensive strength of trade unions on the shopfloor, the highly competitive and non-hierarchial structure of industry and the central role of the City of London in an international financial system based on free trade principles, any attempt to win voluntary acceptance of state-sponsored policies is bound to fail. The state may exhort compliance with its policies, but lacking the powers of compulsion, it cannot dictate and force through the implementation of the policies it desires. It might be thought that a corporatist structure based on compulsion would be more effective, but it is arguable whether this could be sustained in Britain given the defensive strength of socio-economic interests *vis-à-vis* the state and the illegitimacy of the state for popular public opinion. Every attempt to impose a corporatist incomes policy on workers in Britain has failed due to wildcat-strike activity or union pressure on the government to rescind the approach. This is but one example of the instability of corporatist structures in Britain.

This instability was glaringly apparent to the Labour government between 1966 and 1970. The economic decline associated with balance-of-payments crisis, and the need to devalue sterling in 1967 and impose expenditure cuts on the economy after 1966, made it difficult for Labour to provide the material inducements for workers and employers which were necessary in return for their voluntary acceptance of state-induced industrial and employment policies. Labour was forced therefore to take even more statutory powers to reorganise industry, encourage industrial investment and restructure labour relations. This could only be achieved by reducing social welfare expenditure (alienating the working-class vote) and raising taxation (alienating all classes of voters) to force resources out of consumption into investment. Thus, while Labour found itself moving towards a fully corporatist strategy after 1966, this led directly to the undermining of its own electoral support as it alienated many of its traditional allies as well as traditional foes. This was of course compounded by intra-party conflict in the labour coalition. The trade unions wanted no part of any attempt to limit the traditional freedoms of unions in favour of more disciplined labour relations, either through compulsory wages policies (1966–8) or legal restraint on union activities (1969).[31] The Labour left were alienated by the failure to extend nationalisation and the demise of the National Plan and social welfare spending. The result was that in 1970 traditional Labour supporters abstained from voting in much larger numbers than ever before. A Conservative government, appealing to the base liberal values of the British people and the anti-statism of the industrial and financial sectors, was returned to office.[32] The Heath government of 1970 was perhaps the first postwar government to formulate an electoral strategy and manifesto on the basis of a clearly adversarial philosophy.

Neo-liberalism (1970–2)

It would be fallacious, however, to argue that the 1970 Conservative
government was purely anti-state in its broad strategy. What the government desired was a shift of emphasis away from the state and public
sector to a far higher reliance on the private market. While neo-liberal
philosophy was then at the centre of the government's manifesto proposals, what Heath was offering was a return to Keynesianism with a far
more neo-liberal, *laissez-faire*, face. Social welfarism would be maintained but the burden of social services on the private economy would
be reduced through public expenditure cutbacks. Most of the major
industries which had been nationalised would remain, but they would be
exposed to more stringent commercial criteria and managerial reform.
A similar managerial innovation and slimming down was also envisaged
for central and local government. In line with this, a number of corporatist institutions – the NBPI, the Monopolies Commission and the
Land Commission – would be abolished. The number of EDCs and the
reliance on state indicative planning structures would also be reduced.
Finally, a number of profitable industries in public ownership would be
privatised and central government functions 'hived-off' to autonomous
independent agencies.

Economic growth would then be generated by private rather than
public action. In line with this philosophy, the government was resolved
that Britain should become a member of the EEC and that public
influence over the financial markets would be replaced by greater competition and less credit control. Furthermore, government aid to regions
and industries in distress would be reduced drastically in order that the
market could become the basis of industrial location and investment
decision-making. To facilitate the operation of the market government
wage controls would be replaced by free collective bargaining in the
private sector and an incomes policy would be maintained covertly in
the public sector. To assist management in wage bargaining the government, in 1971, introduced an Industrial Relations Act to control by law
the unofficial, wildcat action of trade unionists. Out of this broad
approach, it was expected that the state's role would be reduced.[33] This
meant that while the market rather than the state would be playing a
larger role, the commitment was still within the broad social democratic/
Keynesian approach of the postwar period. On the other hand, it
amounted to a new approach to the public sector when this strategy is
compared with the attempted metamorphosis of Keynesianism into
corporatism under the Conservative and Labour governments of the
1960s.

This strategy could not, however, be sustained. The assumption was that without state interference the market would regenerate industry and economic growth would occur to provide resources for state social welfarism. Unfortunately this approach was based on a number of misperceptions. The basic structural position of British industry was uncompetitive, and this meant that without state aid or direction the market was hardly likely to rush to invest in manufacturing industry, where profits were extremely low. As a result, investment funds, created by an increase in the supply of money and financial competition, flowed into property speculation rather than into industry. A property boom, with unfortunate consequences for inflation levels, was the net result of this policy. Contributing to this of course was the inflationary effect of the floating of the exchange rate after the collapse of the international financial system after 1970. The inflationary effect of a shortage, of, and speculation in, commodities and raw materials was a further destabilising factor.[34]

The effect of inflation and rising property prices was to stimulate wage militancy among the trade unions as the cost of living increased. This was further exacerbated by the rise in political militancy engendered by the government's attempt to legislate against the historic rights and privileges of the trade unions in 1971. Strike activity increased phenomenally and the government appeared to be questioning fundamentally the postwar consensus. The strategy might have worked but, with the ending of the long postwar economic boom, uncompetitive inflation-prone economies were to experience falling demand for their goods, a lack of investment and rising unemployment. This was Britain's fate under the Conservative administration, and by 1972 the government was faced with the collapse of a number of key strategic companies. When first Upper Clyde Shipbuilders and then Rolls-Royce, Alfred Herbert Engineering, Ferranti and British Leyland went bankrupt, the Heath government's anti-statist strategy came under severe strain.

In 1972–3, then, the Conservative government, despite opposition from ardent neo-liberals in the party, reneagued on its original strategy and returned to the postwar consensus.[35] This meant using the state to resolve economic crises and a return to corporatism. But like the similar experiments in the 1960s, this strategy also could not be sustained.

The Second Failure of Corporatism (1972–9)

The policy 'U-turn' by Heath in 1972 is further evidence of the broad continuity of party policy towards the state throughout most of the postwar period. It is also a shift which refutes the utility of the adversary politics thesis as a major explanation of the changes in the state and public sector's role. While there was an adversary relationship between 1970 and 1972, after this date both the Conservative and Labour governments which held office up to 1979 adopted neo-corporatist policies. Both these experiments were to face similar problems: initially they adopted a voluntarist approach to corporatism, and when this failed to work, they were then forced into compulsion. But even state compulsion could not successfully incorporate the main social and economic interests in British society.

The Heath government attempted to adopt a corporatist approach. The government made overtures to the unions and to employers and financial interests to bring them into state policy-making on a voluntary basis. Heath offered a package of pay, rents, dividend and price restraint, with expanded social spending, in an attempt to win union, employer and financial support to counter inflation and regenerate industry through the state. None of these three main economic actors was, however, prepared to accept this package fully. Employers wanted pay restraint but they railed against dividend and price restraint at a time of declining demand and falling profits. The financial sector wanted state help to solve a crisis in the City over property speculation, but freezes on rents and profits merely served to exacerbate the problem. The unions wanted price and profit restraint and increased social spending, but they have always been antipathetic to incomes policy and were further alienated from the government by its anti-trade union legislation. The result was that Heath was forced to impose his corporatist strategy on the nation without fundamental consensus from the major economic interests, and with opposition from his own neo-liberal backbenchers.

Heath's post-1972 policy 'U-turn' was, however, not fully corporatist. A statutory incomes policy was constructed and some controls were maintained over profits, rents and dividends. To assist the implementation of the prices and incomes policy, Heath re-introduced a Price Commission and Pay Board to provide guidance on policy implementation. While these new institutions may have had statutory backing, there was however, much less compulsion built into the government's policies for industrial regeneration through the state. This was a fundamental weakness of the strategy. While companies which had collapsed in the private sector were brought into public ownership, the main thrust of policy was built around the 1972 Industry Act. This Act was a major 'U-turn' for the Conservative government because it provided extensive state funding for industrial sectors and declining regions, much like the Labour Industrial Reorganisation Corporation and the 1968 Industrial Expansion Act. Like these, however, the approach was still neo-corporatist, in the sense that while funds were available, companies were not forced to take them up. Nor was government aid directed by an extensive state planning system. Rather funds were granted to companies when they asked for them and could make a case out of them. This meant that the government was not prepared to decide on growth sectors in the economy and then direct funds into these areas.[36] The strategy was therefore a failure. This conclusion is reinforced when one considers the state's action in relation to the financial sector. The government created a crisis in the City by imposing a freeze on business rents. This brought an end to property speculation and the collapse of a number of property companies and secondary banks. The government, however, did not then intervene directly to force through state control of investment decision-making. It chose instead to allow the City to find its own solution – a moratorium on property debts – and investment funds were no more readily forthcoming for industry than before.[37]

However, it was in the labour relations field that the corporatist strategy was to face its most severe test and fail. The unions were alienated from government by the Industrial Relations Act and the imposition of an incomes policy. This antipathy could not be allayed by either the increase in social expenditure or the controls on rents and dividends, or by the decision to ignore the 1971 Act and return to a more conciliatory approach in labour relations. Strike activity did fall in 1973 but, with the impact of the Yom Kippur War on oil prices and inflation, the government's incomes policy was bound to face a severe test. This came ultimately with the miners' work-to-rule and threatened national strike in the winter of 1973–4. The government was not fully prepared for this and cuts in power supply, resulting from a shortage of coal at power stations, led to a three-day week in industry and a national emergency being declared by the government. Eventually the government chose to fight an election on the issue of 'who runs the country' and lost office.[38]

The return of a Labour government, which had veered drastically to the left in policy formulation in opposition,[39] led many people to believe that the new government might move forcefully towards a more socialist state-economy relationship. This was, however, a media and party political fear and bore little relationship to what the government was to do between 1974 and 1979. Although manifesto commitments existed for a return to extensive nationalisation (aerospace, shipbuilding, major profitable manufacturing industries and sectors of the financial system) and state-directed industrial regeneration (through the National Enterprise Board, sectoral indicative planning and planning agreements), these were not to figure prominently as major planks of government policy after 1975. What the government did was to grant, initially, a number of major organisational and pay concessions to the trade unions, create new institutions for state intervention in industry and increase social expenditure. But after the severe financial crisis experienced by the country between 1975 and 1977, the government had to adopt a more pro-business approach.[40] By 1976 the government was embarked on a corporatist strategy, which it failed to sustain in the manner of all previous attempts.

Between 1974 and 1975 there was some confusion over what Labour was trying to do with the public sector. This arose because of the contradictory pressures within which the new government had to operate. In opposition, the party had become committed to extensive nationalisation, increased social spending, state industrial modernisation and organisational reforms and legal freedoms for trade unions. The problem was that Labour entered office with the worst balance-of-payments crisis on record, declining industrial competitiveness and investment and a widening public sector borrowing requirement.[41] This was also the period when the immediate stagflationary effects of the oil crisis were being felt, generating both recession and inflation. It was therefore impossible for Labour to do everything that it desired. If the government tried to increase public expenditure for social and industrial purposes, this would lead to a crisis of sterling, as international currency holders withdrew their money from Britain for fear of state control and ownership. If the government did not do these things, then it would lose trade union acquiescence to wage restraint and find it difficult to lower inflation and maintain Britain's competitive trading position in the international economy.

Until 1975 the new government tried manfully to fulfil its electoral pledges; in particular, those related to social spending and trade unions. Public expenditure on subsidies and pensions was increased, the National Enterprise Board (NEB) was created and legislation to nationalise aerospace and shipbuilding was introduced. Legislation to extend union rights at work and repeal the 1971 Act was also introduced between 1974 and 1976. The problem for Labour was that while they tried to fulfil their part of the bargain with the unions, the unions were not prepared, or able, to fulfil theirs. The unions had promised to show restraint in pay bargaining in return for the implementation of Labour's broad strategy. But the miners' strike had resulted in complete victory for the coal workers and other unions now demanded wage increases commensurate with their colleagues in the coal industry. This was understandable, given the lack of control exerted by the more politically and economically aware union leadership over their own rank-and-file and the rise in inflation in this period. The result was disastrous for Labour. Wage rates rose between 20 and 30 per cent in 1974–5 and the inflation rate rose into the 20 per cent bracket. This weakened Britain's competitive trading position and, with the increase in social expenditure and the implementation of pro-union legislation, led directly to a lack of international confidence in the government's economic strategy. Sterling began to decline against the currencies throughout 1975–6, forcing the government to rethink its public sector strategy.[42]

By 1975 it was clear to the government that unless they were prepared for mass austerity and economic and political dislocation in the face of the collapse of sterling, the government would have to adopt an alternative policy approach. Given the lack of societal and economic support for corporatism, Labour was forced to introduce yet another corporatist experiment. This strategy involved reducing public expenditure on social services in an attempt to direct resources into industrial investment. This would be assisted by the NEB, planning agreements and sector planning institutions. Controls over prices, dividends and rents would have to be reduced to win business confidence. This also meant that all of Labour's commitments to nationalisation of profitable manufacturing industry and the financial sector, as well as proposals for a wealth tax and industrial democracy and workers participation, would have to be shelved. This shift in emphasis came before, although it was encouraged by, the IMF loan granted to Britain in 1976.[43] The fact that Labour had a weak parliamentary majority, which led eventually to a temporary alliance with the Liberal Party in 1975, was a further contributory factor.

The major problem with this strategy was twofold. First, like all corporatist experiments before it, this policy approach suffered from a heavy reliance on private financial and industrial actors behaving in the manner that the government intended, even though the government lacked the direct financial and legal powers to impose its policies on them. The NEB might have been a focus for state-induced sectoral growth, but the NEB spent most of its time constrained by a lack of funds (due to public expenditure cutbacks) and the need to assist the ailing British Leyland car firm. Thus because the government could only insist on industrial reorganisation in those sectors which were publicly owned, the expansion of aid to industry in the 1975 Industry Act did not result in fundamental industrial change – most recipients of aid were ailing rather than growth industries.[44] The City of London was also still engaged in resolving the problems of the property market, and because of the world recession and rising unemployment, industrialists and financial institutions were unwilling to inject large amounts of investment capital into industry.[45]

The second major problem for the government's strategy was the trade union movement. Given that wage rates were increasing well above the level of industrial productivity and undermining Britain's international competitiveness, as well as contributing to a growing public sector borrowing requirement, the government needed to win acceptance for an incomes policy. But it had to do this while it was reneging on many of its public expenditure and pro-union policies to regain business confidence. The government also could not impose an income policy on the unions after its manifesto commitment not to do so. The government then tried to incorporate union leaders into state policy-making in order to convince them of the serious dilemma they faced. This approach worked initially, and between 1975 and 1977 the unions voluntarily accepted wage restraint. But after 1977, the unions were either unwilling or unable to maintain this commitment. There were a number of reasons for this. Inflation and unemployment were still high and public expenditure and the social wage had been reduced to cut public borrowing requirements. This directly affected low-paid workers. Unfortunately for Labour, the voluntary incomes policy had also eroded the differentials in wages between skilled and unskilled workers, which meant that all sectors of the workforce were alienated by the relative decline of their living standards. This, plus the fact that many of the government's radical policy proposals had been rescinded, and the fact that the British union movement is undisciplined and fragmented with high degree of rank-and-file wildcat strike action, ensured that the voluntary approach could not be sustained. This led directly to an increase in strike activity in 1977–8 and eventually to the 'Winter of Discontent' of 1978–9, when major unions went on strike for wage rates higher than the norm set by the government. There is little doubt that this, plus the economic decline of the mid-1970s, which generated higher unemployment and falling living standards, was the direct cause of Labour's loss of office in May 1979.[46] The result was the return of the most adversarily and ideologically based postwar Conservative government led by Margaret Thatcher and committed to a gradualist, anti-corporatist, neo-liberal approach.

Neo-liberalism (1979–87)

The policies of the Conservative government of Margaret Thatcher share some similarities with those adopted by Heath between 1970 and

1972, but they are far more adversarially based than that government. The Thatcher approach is much more stridently anti-state and anti-public sector, and is clearly directed fundamentally against the postwar Keynesian–corporatist consensus. The government does not accept that the state should be responsible for generating economic growth or maintaining full employment. Neo-liberals within the government also question the state's responsibility for extensive social welfare benefits. The commitment to privatise nationalised industries is far more firmly held than in the earlier period and the willingness to reduce public expenditure on social benefits has been clear since 1979. The government is also prepared to reduce the amount of redistributive justice in society. This has been revealed by the use of pay settlements to reward certain sectors of society – doctors, judges, the military and police force – while reducing the living standards of other public sector workers. This has been supported by a willingness also to reduce taxation for the wealthy, while increasing the tax burden on the poorer sectors of the community at a time of rising unemployment and falling living standards and cuts in the social wage. Finally, the government has shown a resolve to reduce the privileges and legal immunities available to trade unions.[47]

The strategy adopted by the government towards the unions is extremely instructive because it reveals the 'gradualist' neo-liberal approach which is being adopted. On first entering office and promising free collective bargaining for the private sector and a public sector incomes policy, the government has worked quietly and gradually to reduce union rights. After an Employment Act in 1980, which tried to limit workers' rights to picket and reduced some of the legal rights of workers in small firms, a second Act in 1982 has questioned the right of workers to have closed-shop agreements and has made unions legally responsible for the actions of their members. This was followed in December 1982 by a Green Paper which promises even greater reductions in union rights. This is clearly a 'step-by-step' approach to curbing workers' rights to fight for wages and conditions, and it is the approach which the government is adopting towards the public sector as a whole.

The trends are already apparent in the government's action to date. The selling off of the publicly owned Cable and Wireless, Amersham International, Britoil companies, BP, British Gas and British Telecom among others, are clear examples of the desire to erode the state's role of economic ownership and control. The downgrading of regional financial aid and the decision to reduce trade union membership of tripartite institutions – many of which are now being considered for closure – is yet further evidence of the anti-corporatist strategy of the government.[48] The fact that the government has not gone further than this is not out of lack of commitment, but due to the economic crisis that Britain has faced since 1979 and the opposition of interest groups to the government's strategy. This explains why it is that public expenditure as a share of GNP has not fallen rapidly since 1979. The government has severely reduced social expenditure (on housing provision, social services and education), but this has been counterbalanced by increases in defence and law and order expenditure, and the rise in state spending on unemployment and other social security benefits as a result of the massive rise in unemployment – the latter caused largely by the government's deflationary monetary strategy and the world recession. This maintenance of a high share of public expenditure in the GNP does not mean, however, that the government is not prepared to cut social expenditure further, it merely means that the government has experienced difficulty in moving as quickly in this direction as it would wish.

Thus while the government has not followed through the full logic of its adversarially based, anti-state approach, it has made significant inroads into the postwar consensus over the public sector's role. What is surprising is, perhaps, that this has been achieved without generating intense political opposition or social conflict. London and Liverpool may have experienced urban social conflict in the inner city areas of Brixton and Toxteth, but such manifestations of decline have not reappeared, despite the unwillingness and inability of the government to do anything fundamental to help these areas. Why has this come about even though there has been, as we saw, a fairly continuous consensus about the need for an extensive public sector role since 1945?

To answer this question, one has to understand what has been a continuous underlying theme of this chapter. I have argued that despite the relatively consensual approach to the state in postwar Britain, Keynesian and corporatist policies have failed in implementation. This failure has been due largely to the anti-state, liberal values of the mass of the populace and the ability of trade union, industrial and financial interests to ignore government policies. By implication, these economic interests are as a result unwittingly committed to liberalism because their desire to pursue their own self-interest, unfettered by the state, is in reality a defence of 'laissez-fairism'. The Thatcher approach, while facing some opposition, has been sustained because it appeals to the liberal values of the populace and these major economic actors. If the neo-liberal strategy has not been fully implemented yet, this says more about the economic crisis that Britain faces than the willingness of the government or economic interests to support an interventionist state role. The unions may desire state-induced industrial regeneration but they are not prepared to pay the price of this: manpower planning, indicative planning and incomes policies. Industry which is in decline requires state subsidies, but it is not prepared to pay the price of state-induced modernisation – a high degree of state control over investment and output decision-making. Finally, the financial sector, committed as it is to 'laissez-fairism' and an international role, is also unprepared to allow state control over investment decision-making because this might lead to state controls on imports and trade and a closure of profitable overseas investment areas in an attempt to direct capital into the domestic industrial base. This means that the Thatcher government, which rejects the post-1945 social democratic consensus over the state and public sector's role, finds that its policies tap a deep root of liberal support (both conscious and unconscious) in 'British society and economy.

Thus while there may be alternatives to monetarism and neo-liberalism for some countries, corporatism has been discredited for Britain because it presided over a relatively continuous postwar economic decline. This has meant that the historic illegitimacy of state interventionism in Britain has been reinforced by postwar decline. The growth of the public sector is now therefore perceived as *the cause*, rather than *the consequence*, of economic collapse. But if the analysis presented here is correct, the true cause of decline has been the failure of liberalism, not statism. The state has never used the public sector to control or direct the market effectively. Keynesianism was a strategy based primarily on social welfarism and *indirect* state assistance for the private sector. If it failed, it was due to the failure of the private sector to compete, innovate and modernise. The state took no responsibility for controlling the supply side of the economy, but left this to the private sector. The increase in social spending may well have become a burden on the private economy, but this followed, rather than precipitated, the decline of trade competitiveness.[49]

Nor can corporatism be seen as the main cause of decline. Full corporatism may involve the state in controlling and directing the demand and supply sides of the economy, but as we have seen, in Britain this has rarely been achieved and state exhortation of industrial reorganisation without effective controls has been the result. In Britain whenever this approach has been adopted, it has normally been in response to decline in the private market rather than a cause of it. Furthermore, corporatist policies have failed due to the unwillingness of the major private economic interests to accept the price of state-induced modernisation. This shows clearly that corporatism is fundamentally constrained politically and economically in Britain. It also shows that while Pahl and Winkler may be forgiven for assuming in 1974 that corporatism would be institutionalised in Britain, it is very difficult to exonerate anyone who argued from this perspective in 1988. While there may be even today pockets of tripartite bargaining and intermediation in specific policy areas in Britain, this is hardly sufficient evidence to warrant the use of the term corporatist for a state form which systematically denies key functional groups participation in decision-making and appears to know no bounds to its desire to reduce the state's role in society. While the fully neo-liberal state may not be with us yet, it appears likely that if there is ever a reversal of this trend, it will be towards pluralistic Keynesianism rather than the discredited and derided corporatism of the 1960s and 1970s.

Notes

1. Andrew Cox, 'The political instability of liberal and social democratic state forms in British society', *Parliamentary Affairs*, XXXV (4) (Autumn 1982), 381–95.
2. S. E. Finer, *Adversary Politics and Electoral Reform* (London, Anthony Wigram, 1975).
3. Michael Stewart *Keynes and After* (Harmondsworth, Penguin, 1972), pp. 185–258. But see also the debate between J. Tomlinson, 'Why was there never a Keynesian Revolution?', *Economy and Society*, 10 (1) (February 1981), 72–87, and Kerry Schott, 'The rise of Keynesian economics: Britain, 1940–64', *Economy and Society*, 11 (3) (August 1982), 292–315.
4. Andrew Cox, 'Corporatism as reductionism: the analytic limits of the corporatist thesis', *Government and Opposition*, 16 (1) (Winter 1981), 78–95.
5. David Coates, *The Labour Party and the Struggle for Socialism* (Cambridge, Cambridge University Press, 1975), 177–230.
6. Nigel Harris, *Competition and the Corporate Society* (London, Meuthen, 1972), 23–76.
7. Michael Steed, 'The Liberal Party' in H. M. Drucker (ed.), *Multi-Party Britain* (London, Macmillan, 1979), pt III.
8. Ian Bradley, *Breaking the Mould* (London, Martin Robertson, 1981).
9. For an extended discussion of this role, see: Andrew Cox, 'Le mouvement syndical brittannique et la recession économique des années 70' in Georges Couffignal (ed.), *Les Syndicats européens et la crise* (Grenoble, University of Grenoble Press, 1981), 61–99.
10. Hamish McRae and Frances Cairncross, *Capital City* (London, Meuthen, 1977), 1–20.
11. Jack Hayward, 'Institutional inertia and political impetus in France and Britain' *European Journal of Political Research*, 4 (1976), 341–59.
12. Ken Dyson, *The State Tradition in Western Europe* (London, Martin Robertson, 1980), 186–204.
13. Ivor Crewe *et al.*, 'Partisan dealignment in Britain 1964–1970', *British Journal of Political Science*, 7 (1977), 120–90.
14. Cox, 'Corporatism as reductionism', *op. cit.*
15. Keith Middlemas, *Politics in Industrial Society* (London, Deutsch, 1980), 266–306.
16. On the prewar debate within the parties, see: Jacques Leruez, *Economic Planning and Politics in Britain* (London, Martin Robertson, 1975), 3–13. On the postwar consensus, see the Tomlinson–Schott debate, n.3, above.
17. Coates, *op. cit.*, 44–74.

18. Leo Panitch, *Social Democracy and Industrial Militancy* (Cambridge, Cambridge University Press, 1976), 7–40; and Samuel Beer, *Modern British Politics* (London, Faber, 1969), 160–2, 206–8.
19. Stewart, *op. cit.*
20. Stephen Blank, *Industry and Government in Britain* (Farnborough, Saxon House, 1973).
21. Harris, *op. cit.*, 77–148.
22. David Howells, *British Social Democracy* (London, Croom Helm 1976), 9–46.
23. Harris, *op. cit.*, 149–248.
24. R. E. Pahl and J. T. Winker, 'The coming corporatism', *New Society*, 10 October 1974, 72–76.
25. Samuel Brittan, *Steering the Economy* (Harmondsworth, Penguin, 1971), 179–226.
26. *Ibid.*, 227–69.
27. Michael Shanks, *Planning and Politics* (London, Allen and Unwin, 1981), chapter 1.
28. On the problems facing the Labour strategy, see: Stephen Young with Anne Lowe, *Intervention in the Mixed Economy* (London, Croom Helm, 1974), 15–38.
29. Colin Crouch, *The Politics of Industrial Relations* (London, Fontana, 1979), 45–65.
30. Young and Lowe, *op. cit.*, 31–7, 166–210.
31. Crouch, *op. cit.*, 66–72.
32. Crewe, *et al.*, *op. cit.*
33. Robin Blackburn, 'The Heath government: a new course for British capitalism' *New Left Review*, 70 (November–December 1971), 276–82.
34. Young and Lowe, *op. cit.*, 131–64.
35. *Ibid.*
36. *Ibid.*
37. 'The city and industry', *The Banker*, 123 (January 1973), pp. 9–10.
38. Martin Holmes, *Political Pressure and Economic Policy: British Government, 1970–1974* (London, Butterworths, 1982), 55–126.
39. Michael Hatfield, *The House the Left Built* (London, Gollancz, 1978).
40. David Coates, *Labour in Power* (London, Longman, 1980), 2–147.
41. Robbie Guttmann, 'State intervention and the economic crisis: the Labour government's economic policy', *Kapitalistate*, 4–5 (Summer 1976) 225–70.
42. Coates, *op. cit.*, 148–201.
43. *Ibid.*, 38–43.
44. Wyn Grant, *The Political Economy of Industrial Policy* (London, Butterworths, 1982), 62–73, 101–24.
45. 'The New Leviathan: property and financial institutions' *The Economist*, 267, 10 June 1978, 3.
46. Cox, 'Le mouvement syndical brittannique . . .', *op. cit.*
47. K. Coutts, R. Tarling *et al.*, 'The economic consequences of Mrs Thatcher', *Cambridge Journal of Economics*, 5 (1981), 81–93.
48. 'Changing the mixed economy's mix', *The Economist*, 28 November 1981, 102–3.
49. Robert Bacon and Walter Eltis, in *Britain's Economic Problem: Too Few Producers* (London, Macmillan, 1976), take the view that public expenditure on social welfare has become a burden; it is also assumed to be a cause, rather than a consequence, of economic decline.

Index